Saturn's Return

A Boomer's Memoir

Peter LeVine

ISBN-10: 0615448607
ISBN-13: 9780615448602

Author's Note:
Some names of persons and locales have been changed.

Saturn's Return- once around the sun from birth, taking nearly twenty-nine years, is the psychological end of youth, the beginning of real adulthood. Standing in the way is the confrontation with one's fears, a struggle that if resolved results in claiming the mantle of Self that sets the course for the rest of the journey.

This book would not have been completed without Allison's love and encouragement. It might never have been started if not for Rebecca.

In Memory of my Mother

PART I

Chapter I

TEMPLATE

Lake Hopatcong, New Jersey, a Saturday in September of 1963

My father pulled over to the side of the road when I complained that my face felt numb. My upper body tingled. Pull over and stop the car, old man. I'd been receiving another installment in the episodic litany regarding the current course of my life—my misguided interest in folk singing and my desire to learn the guitar, how vital instead it was for me to consider the importance of entering the military, specifically the Naval Reserve as an officer, in my planning for the future. A few people milled around the beach as he came to a stop. I exited the car, walking closer towards them staring at the water, trying to take some comfort in their presence as an unknowing buffer between my father and myself. *I'm going to sit by this tree and you are going to leave me alone.* I sat down figuring that he was a few feet behind me, at about *seven o'clock*, nautically speaking. *I'm not strong enough to get away from him.* Let me live my life the way I choose, please- Among this small group of people lingering on the beach, I could see he didn't know what the hell to do. For a moment I reveled in the relief over his loss of control. Let the presence of others immobilize him, I thought, while it gave me time to regroup. Axiom number one of self-defense: whenever possible, try to ensure the presence of others.

"Get up, son," he finally said, blunting his anger. His only son who had none of his engineering aptitude, his only helper who had slogged through the mud and marsh with him earlier that day dredging a minute portion of Lake Wasigan. Standing next to an infernal piece of pump machinery it dawned on me that I could spend the rest of my natural life on this impossible project and it wouldn't even be ten percent completed when I would take my last breath. What could possess him to give up this early autumn weekend afternoon to pursue such an endeavor, and why was it necessary that I participate in his folly? As a scion of Wasigan, and the aforementioned only son, I would accompany Herman during the off season on some maintenance project where inevitably I would be reminded of my general inadequacy as a helper.

I gazed from the pump's ceaseless drone to observe the changing colors of the leaves. My heart ached for the recently ended summer of Camp Wasigan, and I fervently wished I were home with my compatriots Hal, Artie, and Aaron, any and all of them experiencing a more recognizably normal Saturday than me. That's right, *be here then or be there now*, a variation on Ram Dass' mantra only a few years from becoming an anthem for my generation. Standing in the mud on the perimeter of Lake Wasigan, I realized that my present state rivaled the feelings of emptiness that consumed my sisters and me each year when camp vacated in late August, when the family (we being the youngest generation) closed the facility down for the season. Waving to our friends aboard the buses that would take them home from their summer hiatus, Miri, Marta and I would sink into the bleak silence of the deserted landscape for three long days before we ourselves could return home.

* * *

During the nineteen thirties, in the midst of the Great Depression, my maternal grandparents, Anna and Morris, had purchased land in the pastoral region of northwestern New Jersey. They established a children's summer camp, Camp Wasigan, whose existence spanned thirty years. I never truly knew my maternal grandfather who died before I was three. He was by all accounts a gentle man. He had augmented his law school funds as an extra baritone in the New York Metropolitan Opera, and he reached the rank of colonel in the army during the Second World War. Having bought out the partners early on my grandparents ran Wasigan until Murray's death in 1951, after which Anna continued as director until the mid-sixties. Possessed of great joie de vie combined with a strong protective presence, Anna was an ideal individual to own and operate an eight-week children's summer camp, with the result that many campers and counselors would return for several summers. My mother, Clara, served as the head girls' counselor and her brother-in-law, my uncle Doug, had the same role with the boys. Doug was a highly competitive sports-minded person who had coached the three major sports at the high school where he later became principal. His wife my mother's sister, Paula, helped Anna run the office and supervised Wasigan's canteen, repository of Nehi orange sodas and such exotic candies as Black Crows, Dots and Chuckles. I was born not far from camp, spent the first year of my life there and nearly all my summers until I was eighteen.

In the presence of all this family, I found myself in the strange position of immensely enjoying my summers but also wishing that like my peers, I too, could get away from my parents for those eight weeks of July and August. Then, too, there were also those awkward and uncomfortable moments when a counselor would drop some uncomplimentary comment regarding my mother that either I couldn't help but overhear or was stated with my ears in mind. On these occasions, I had needed to inhibit my reaction with feigned coolness, a tactic at which I was not very adept, i.e., when during Friday nite services a chorus of male counselors had modified the lyrics from "Swing Low, Sweet Chariot" to "Swing High, Old Evil Eye." Directed towards Clara, my mother promptly exited the amphitheatre. The camp was stunned, but snickers could be heard among the campers. I hoped against hope that the redness of my face would be short-lived and unnoticed. Regardless, while others expressed bewilderment or silent acclaim, I alone felt acute embarrassment. My mother had a strong personality that at times may have rubbed some of the counselors the wrong way, she was a woman with high standards and expectations of others, but it felt to me they were merely showing off for their female counterparts at her (and my) expense.

My father Herman's role at Wasigan was not as staff. A mechanical engineer and a brilliant handyman, he and the harmonica-playing camp caretaker had often involved themselves in maintenance projects together. This was all to the good because these opportunities provided my father a fellow traveler, as neither my fanatically athletic and competition-obsessed Uncle Doug nor the younger intellectually pre-disposed generation of counselors, were people with whom he felt much affinity. My father was a brilliant mechanical engineer and a consistently excellent provider; however, he also was an impatient teacher whose anxiety often rose to an anger that nearly almost froze me. From early on I had shown little aptitude and less interest for any skill involving mechanical reasoning, a fact that had frustrated both of us throughout my childhood and adolescence. During my school years Herman had spent a good deal of our weekends adding a den and sitting room to our home where my presence was often required for many hours, not so much for helping him or learning any skill, but merely to watch him work and keep him company. Depending on his mood these could be inordinately unpleasant occasions. Once when I was maybe nine or ten he became so exasperated and incensed with my inability to unbend a pocket ruler, he left me alone in the garage, ordering me not to come in the house until I figured out how to do so. His return, no doubt at my mother's behest, had lasted an eternity in my young mind. If his mercurial and authoritarian nature were not apparent at Wasigan, it was all too well known by his family.

This family stuff aside I loved Wasigan. I couldn't wait for camp to begin so I could play ball every day, swim, dance and flirt with the girls at rec hall, and to breathe in the hills, woods, and water. My closest camp buddy Marvin and I shared a love of baseball. This swarthy Sephardic and I spent hours consumed in playing APBA, the era's fantasy baseball game. When the Major League All Star game was played in early July, Marvin and I constructed a makeshift stadium in the back room of the bunk, assembling the boots and galoshes into a grandstand and bleachers. We divided our baseball cards into American and National league players and using a ping -pong ball have the pitcher roll to a batter who would try to *hit 'em where they ain't.*

Anna had done an amazing thing with Wasigan. The proof of it was visible during the two visiting days when I could see in what esteem the parents of the campers held her. For our part, my sisters and I had to slog through those days awaiting the resumption of camp routine, which for me meant getting back to my bunkmates' rituals, like *Mad Libs*, where we honed our skills in the vocabulary of profanity, or an after dinner surprise canoe fight. Running to the lake exuberant in the early evening sunlight on the water, we would paddle out past the stone "lighthouse", banging paddles on the aluminum in preparation to splash, douse, tip over, and hoist ourselves back into our vessels. There wasn't a summer I wasn't bummed when the season was over.

Of course, I told no one about the strange incident at Lake Hopatcong, at least not until years later and only then to a university shrink. Back home I behaved as if nothing unusual had transpired in the hopes that Herman might demonstrate enough in the way of gratitude for my silence to cut me some major slack. It was his custom whenever he was angry with any of us to protractedly seethe, and when the anger was directed at Clara the tension between them often continued for weeks. My mother would hold her ground, much to the admiration and consternation of her children who eagerly waited for the next truce. Having paid my penance, I went off to visit my compatriots, Hal, Artie and Aaron. Bound for med and law school, respectively, on that evening they were primed for our customary game of Hearts. Three six packs of Dad's Root Beer awaited, as we sat down for what was likely to be a drubbing for me at the hands of my three left-brained compadres who, if they actually couldn't count cards, at least understood the laws of probability far better than I.

* * *

The town of Boonton was a hilly hamlet of seventy-five hundred souls located in north-central New Jersey. Clara and Herman had purchased a fine stucco house back in 1949 where my sisters and I were raised. Boonton sat between two restricted communities, towns that until the mid 1960's had forbidden Jews and African-Americans to own property within their town limits. While Waspish Mountain Lakes embodied a kind of country club discriminatory pattern, overt Wagnerian overtones were more evident in the other neighboring suburban enclave's name of Lake Valhalla.

In addition to our large yards there were woods off to the east where we played until they were sold off around 1960 to create a subdivision. Directly south of our property stood a carriage house, part of an estate owned by an elderly Prussian who became an object of fascination to Herman. He had asked my sisters and me to refer to him as "Uncle Duke," a term of endearment that I loathed and which made Clara look as if she were about to vomit, and never more so than on that unfortunate afternoon when a fire had erupted in the Duke's kitchen. Herman and the girls happened to be paying the Junker a post-Christmas visit. Because I was with friends enjoying an afternoon of bowling I was unavailable to see the spectacle that Clara witnessed through the kitchen window, aghast as her husband carried their two daughters past the carriage house into our back yard, through the snow, the smoke rising from the house on the hill. Because of the damage, the Duke stayed at our home over the holidays, consuming a significant amount of Herman's liquor, driving Clara to apoplexy, and reminding me that my breaking 150 in bowling for the first time was not all that impressive in the face of his misfortune.

Boonton occupied the headwaters of provincial America, lying just outside the great suburban perimeter of New York City. Two miles south of its boundary sat the junction of two old federal highways 46 and 202. On the sign in the northerly direction of 202 some iconoclastic soul had scrawled the word *is* between Boonton and Suffern (the latter a border town in New York State). The fact that this small piece of conceptual artistry was not immediately removed proved more compelling than its existence, causing me to wonder whether the powers that be were themselves colluding in its creator's assessment. Near the same junction flowed the reservoir that provided the drinking water to Jersey City. Known as that city's waterworks, it too had provided entertainment in the form of the removal of two mayoral names from its marquis, one because he was discovered not to be an American citizen, and the second for, what else, corruption.

My parents' decision to settle in Boonton was inspired by a desire to live far enough from the New York metropolitan area but close enough to Clara's family ties-her mother, two sisters, their husbands, and children. During the late forties, however, settling as far west in New Jersey as Boonton was uncommon for my tribe and more or less akin to plunking down stakes in Indiana or Colorado. My parents were strong assimilationists. My sisters and I attended Hebrew School, but the circle of my parents' friends included more people from outside the tribe then was likely the case with their co-religionists. Assimilation may have been the underlying connection between Herman and Clara, who differed significantly on so many issues. For Herman, to assimilate meant that he was an American who happened to be Jewish. While he admired the Israeli toughness and tenacity in the face of its enemies, he was hardly what could be called a Zionist.

Clara's roots were urban, having grown up in that very Jersey City whose tap water came from just down the road. She'd spent a year at the University of Wisconsin during the thirties, pursuing her interest in journalism, and beoming an accomplished tennis player. During the war years, she secured a job writing for a military newspaper aimed at increasing civilian morale. Through connections with the tennis pro, Alice Marble, she received the opportunity to interview Eleanor Roosevelt in the White House. At the conclusion of their meeting the First Lady surprised her by leading her through the executive mansion to its swimming pool, where my mother was introduced to its two relaxing occupants, the president and Mr. Churchill.

My mother's assimilation translated to her being a person of the world who happened to be Jewish. Clara's best friend, known to my sisters and me as Aunt Rae, her family Methodist, lived at the end of our street in a home surrounded by woods. Her husband was a man with whom my father also found ease. One benefit of assimilation was that it made for a more palatable holiday season. We actually celebrated Christmas, the only missing element being the tree, as that would have been over the top. Nevertheless, Clara would retrieve branches from the enormous pine tree that loomed over our driveway to place on the mantle in our living room, embracing the pagan celebration of the return of the light. We would light the Hanukah candles faithfully, but unlike many other Jewish homes, ours would be as green and warm as the Gentiles' come Advent, and, we received gifts on the Yule as well.

Herman took holiday pictures of the family that he had developed and printed in the home dark room that was our kitchen. Beneath the photo read the caption *Season's Greetings: From Our House to Your House*. This activity constituted the most satisfying memory I have of quality time with my father, outside of our having attended a few ball games. The pastime itself was fun; it took place in our home; there was little pressure, and the father/son interaction demand was minimal.

As the eastern sentinel of American small town life, Boonton was a predominantly Republican town, but most of my co-religionists were of the Democratic persuasion. Clara was among them, a partisan of the twice-defeated Adlai Stevenson. In 1960, her ambivalence toward John Kennedy's Catholicism (the role of the Church during World War II being a fresh memory), was exceeded by her apprehension over the prospect of Richard Nixon becoming president, a politician she had loathed for having built his career through red baiting and a subsequent embrace of McCarthyism. The subject of Nixon as a lightning rod in our household had its origin during that historic campaign. In moments of particular tension between my parents it was easy to think that Clara perceived Herman and Nixon to be nearly one and the same person. Herman's Republican sympathies were undeniable.

If Nixon had been my parents' lightning rod, then Franklin Roosevelt was their fault line. Herman had nothing but contempt for the country's four time-elected, thirty-second president. Though having grown up not far from New York, the Tappan Zee area was virtually rural during his childhood, the heartland, and as such the repository of bedrock conservative values. He loathed the New Deal, but it was the GI Bill for which he had reserved his real contempt, a puzzling attitude as more than one of my friends' dads, returning from fighting in Europe, were helped considerably by it. But that was precisely the point, if not stated, then as subtext. *If the government didn't put me through school during the Depression why should they do it now for these guys?* Never mind that Hal's dad had sustained a wound fighting in the European theatre, while my father had built bridges in the Canal Zone as an officer in the Seabees thousands of miles away from either theatre of war. Even as a twelve-year-old, I had some questions about that, although with little desire to inflict that much pain on myself I avoided raising that point with him. The navy had given him a lease on life, no question, as opposed to the fate of his younger brother, Gerald, who died fighting in the Pacific during the Second World War, and who, according to Clara, had been a man of artistic temperament and was also his mother's favorite. After graduating from Penn State with a degree in mechanical engineering, Herman had a tough time finding a professional position during the Depression, a task made all the more difficult by his ethnicity. With war approaching the navy needed engineers and the opportunity to become a commissioned officer through an officer candidate program freed him from this struggle.

Fast forward to Election Day, 1960, not to the national drama where the winner wasn't determined until the next morning, but to the one that began in my father's Corvette after he had picked Hal and me up from school that first Tuesday after the first Monday in November. Dropping me off that morning Herman had surprised me by telling me he intended to vote for Kennedy. So excited I must have been that I had failed to hear also his injunction that I not disclose this to anyone. A tight fit in that vehicle suddenly had become that much more uncomfortable when Hal let my father know how pleased he was to hear about his vote. My wish to postpone my friend's exit to his house an impossibility, I now readied myself for the first of several waves of anger that emanated from my outraged father, now that he knew I had committed the unpardonable betrayal of his instruction.

Upon arriving home I was ordered to rake and bag the leaves until dark and don't bother coming in the house until then, etc. Within moments Clara emerged, a rake in hand, in an inspired show of solidarity, upbraiding my still angry father for his 'lesson in democracy'. In whatever version of *you go, girl* I had at my disposal, I silently cheered her on and experienced much gratitude for the validation. *It's ok, I'm not the one with the problem,* I breathed to myself.

As the time of my bar mitzvah drew closer six months later, I witnessed the weirdness of my father's family of origin. Up to now I'd only known that he and my paternal grandmother did not get along, and that Clara had felt nothing but contempt for her. The poor man had now been placed in a most untenable position by the woman who for her own peculiar reasons had given him an ultimatum—that my as yet unknown about half sister be invited to my special day or my family would face being shunned. Rather than inform my grandmother where she might get off, Herman decided instead to call a family conference where he dropped the bombshell to my sisters and me, that he had been married before and had fathered a daughter, who it so happened would be attending my rite of passage. Upset, my mother had left the room, determining that this was her husband's kettle of fish. During his senior year in college Herman had fathered a daughter who couldn't have been more than five years old when he entered the navy. His absence from them eventually resulted in divorce. The two facts may not have been all that at odds. He had married out of obligation.

Clara disclosed years later that she had tried early on to form a supportive relationship with her stepdaughter. She had been thwarted by the relentless and insidious efforts of her mother-in-law whose alliance with Herman's first wife appeared to be something akin to the Axis Pact of Steel.

Looking out the classroom window at the blooming maple tree the next afternoon, I experienced a first insight into the origins of my father's weirdness, now knowing that he came from a strange family and had lived a secret life. This information also explained why he had customarily wanted one of us, usually one of my sisters, to sit next to him when he dialed his mother's phone number, often through use of his middle finger and always out of Clara's sight and earshot. Even so, I wondered, why hadn't either of my parents told us about our half-sister? I could only conclude that my father had to be more scared of his mother than I was of him. What was that all about? It was hard to imagine Herman afraid of anyone. He was usually the one doing the scaring. An older sister who I never had seen- had he seen her all this time? Did my mother know whether or not he had seen her? Now I knew why she despised her mother-in-law, and also why Herman revered my maternal grandmother. Anna had become his real mom.

There wasn't time for reflection, because the day was fast approaching when I would stand before the congregation and be called to read my Haftorah portion, even if at four-foot-ten inches I would require a platform in order to be seen by the assembled guests. We were no slouches, the bar mitzvah class of 1961. Our thirteenth birthdays coincided with that of the state of Israel, of whom all Jews were understandably proud and no more so than recently for that nation's bold apprehension of Adolf Eichmann from his Argentinian sanctuary, to try him on Israeli soil for organizing the murder of European Jewry. Moreover, that year had seen a spike in the number of Boonton bar mitzvah boys. I was to be the fifth since January in our small congregation, following in the recently trod footsteps of Artie, Aaron, and Hal. In the case of Hal and me, our rabbi had instructed us to conduct the entire service, not just the traditional bar mitzvah Torah reading. Thus was there opportunity to experience an undeniable bliss in the form of a radiant smile from my love object of the seventh grade, the diminutive Marcia Nangourney, when I hit the high note on the "Alaenu" nearing the home stretch of the morning's prayers. The realization that she would be seated next to me at the afternoon's reception provided the impetus to bring it on home with the "Adon Olom."

I basked in the attention from family and friends. The day's only sour note (and then not undeserved) came from my second cousin, Erasmus, who had felt it necessary to call me out for my having invited, then ignored, and thus humiliated my also invited Wasigan girlfriend. I couldn't disagree. Clearly, I had behaved badly, an adolescent prototype of Charles Grodin's *The Heartbreak Kid,* who on his honeymoon had abandoned his wife to pursue the ultimate *shiksa*, played by Cybil Shepherd. Here I was caught up in the crosscurrent of my disparate environments, Boonton and Wasigan, with the former unquestionably winning out. I'd engaged in showing off for someone I already knew showed little more than amused disinterest, while my distressed love interest from the summer before was left to lean on the shoulder of my second cousin, who in all probability was attending only reluctantly in the first place. As for my half –sister, her presence was essentially irrelevant for me and probably for her too, although she got far more information about my family than I ever got about hers.

Six months older than me and oddly my mother's first cousin, a fact that had never quite registered with me in my youth, Erasmus, from Upper Manhattan, embodied a nervous energy that would grow into an unconventional charisma—his shuffle, infectious laugh, and within a couple of years his cigarette smoking. His orange and black sailor hat would earn him the nickname "Tiger" from the Wasigan counselors. He moved with a kind of shadowboxing, loping finesse, and could be both endearing and vulnerable as he doled out selective friendship. Other campers, the offspring of suburbia, would come to look upon him as a guide through the murky waters of impending sexual development to the safe and distant shore of "cool." It was evident to me that he had some awareness of his status, milking it pretty well, but why the hell shouldn't he? I wanted his acceptance; he was rebellion by proxy.

Outside of camp I'd usually only see him at Thanksgiving when the extended family would engage in a one-day westward migration from New York City and eastern Jersey to my family's home on the frontier. The cousins enjoyed our large side and backyards, but eventually the girls would split off and Erasmus and I would remain tossing a football. My mother's family was a boisterous bunch, a fact unpleasant to my father, who had to balance his obligations as host with his instinctive revulsion for their chatter, what he came to call their "idiot streak". Despite his reverence for Anna (their Pinochle games being periods of ease and calm), his two sisters-in-law as well as Anna's own sisters regularly drove him to the brink. I evaluated his mood fluctuation throughout those afternoons, observing the increased swelling of the veins on the back of his neck. Before he reached what I judged to be critical mass, I would nudge Erasmus outside to the large side yard that also served as a domain for wiffleball. Our exit from the white stucco house had served the dual purpose of having what would pass for quality time between the two of us as well as removing Erasmus from the scene of Herman's escalating frustration. Erasmus himself was a lightning rod for the old man's contempt, who saw in my cousin what I might become if I were to digress from the rigid path he had been planning for me. Our recreational interval kept my cousin and me far enough apart that I could avoid any questions or comments from him about my father, or any perception he had regarding my suburban life. As the distance between our throws increased, so too did the gulf imposed upon our relationship by his gangly urbanity versus my *white bucks* way of life. I sadly realized there was nothing I could offer him.

When my cousin and I were in the senior bunk with ten other fourteen-year-olds, at the apex of Wasigan's census, he received the news that his mother had died. If he had known how sick she was—it was leukemia—he hadn't shared it. During rest hour after lunch that afternoon, when the boys' campus took their blankets outside and spread on the *Coppertone* (a primordial sun tanning agent whose value at preventing sunburn and skin cancer was indubitably less than zero), I noticed him being guided down the hill by our counselor, the latter's arm around my cousin's shoulder as he left camp for the city. I stood still and watched him leave. My bunkmates and I could only watch and wonder: *Would he come back? What will he be like and what will it be like for us with what he will be like?* Our respective silent contemplations preoccuping us, I sought to banish my thoughts as quickly as they arose.

Wasigan went on. After Erasmus and his sister had returned a week later the subject was closed among campers. I had to suck up the visceral sense that my cousin and I would drift further apart, knowing that despite my grandmother's injunction, one not unusual for the times, the passing of her sister-in-law would remain an elephant in the middle of many rooms. By default it was left to the counselors to provide most of the support and friendship to him in the years to come.

* * *

A month and a half into high school The Cuban Missile Crisis threatened to destroy civilization. That

Friday afternoon's dismissal might be, I sensed, the final time I would see my classmates, that there would be no Monday morning. Earlier that week, President Kennedy had informed the nation in a televised address of the existence of offensive missiles in Cuba deployed by the Soviet Union with the capability to destroy American cities. In his speech, the president had stipulated that any attack launched against our country from Cuba would be regarded as an attack by the Soviet Union and would result in a full retaliation on that country. By Friday it wasn't looking good. When the Berlin Wall had gone up some fifteen months before, there had been strong nuclear war alarm, but this situation was far more dire, such that even the most clueless among us had a sense of imminent doom.

The look on our homeroom teacher did little to assuage our dread. He tried not to make eye contact with his youthful pupils, whose only common characteristic was that the first letter of their last names ranged from J to P. Sitting next to me was Mike Mansito, a cleat-wearing, high roller-in-training whose older brother performed in a doo-wop quartet with whom he sometimes sang. The two of us had displayed the minimal necessary tolerance necessary between greaser and preppie during the previous six weeks of school, but there was an instant just as the bell sounded, ending school for the day and week, when we looked into each other. When the crisis had passed the next week we resumed our mutual avoidance. He and I, along with the rest of civilization, had just dodged the biggest bullet aimed our way, and could now resume our respective positions in high school society.

Several years later, Mike Mansito would die in Vietnam.

* * *

A change had taken place in the attitude, appearance, and demeanor of Wasigan's counselors by the next summer. Attired in cut-off shorts and sandals, some were playing guitars to accompany the folk and civil rights songs that had sprung forth on their college campuses. Dylan, Baez, Peter, Paul and Mary and others had emerged over the last year, and I now heard their music for the first time. The lyrics from the spiritual "We Shall Overcome," from Bob Dylan's "Blowin' in the Wind" and from his "A Hard Rain's A-Gonna Fall", spoke to the terror of living in the nuclear age and to the injustice that existed in what was supposedly the most free nation in the world. Watching the counselors, and one of my Beat-inclined bunkmates play their guitars, and observing their fingers forming the few basic chords, I thought I could learn this instrument. As for the songs themselves, not only did their topical lyrics address real issues, but also the depth of longing in the love ballads provided a welcome antidote to the pap saturating the airwaves. Folk music went deeper and was more emotionally compelling with its focus on lost love, freedom and death.

Since fourth grade I'd played the clarinet in school bands and orchestras. Hal and I had started at the same time, taking lessons in the musty old office of our elementary school instrumental teacher, Mr. Ransky. His workspace located above the combined gymnasium / auditorium at the end of an upstairs bleacher section was about as far away as one could get from any normal school activity, suggesting just how important school officials regarded their musical program. Hal and I had alternated first chair. We stuck with it for as long as we did because of our bemusement at the Walter Mitty-esque demeanor of Mr. Ransky. An outcast from the faculty, as far as we could tell, he embodied our own version of Bob Newhart, whose comedy monologues had become a national phenomenon by the time we entered what was then known as junior high school.

It would be left to another music teacher, however, to facilitate the decline of my clarinet playing and transition to the guitar—the puffy and beleaguered pedagogue who conducted the Boonton High School Orchestra—and not through anything he did. His contribution was as the town crier that would end one era in our nation's history, when on yet another apocalyptic Friday afternoon, the one before Thanksgiving during my sophomore year, he was abruptly called to the office, gone for a longer time than usual for a teacher. Upon re-entering our rehearsal area, he gingerly mounted the small podium and announced to his ensemble that, "President Kennedy has been shot and they don't know whether he will live or die." Staring in disbelief, I remembered nothing else afterwards until I returned home. When my father arrived from work he and my mother shared a look of concern I'd never seen between them before, more frightened even than thirteen months before when the husband of my mother's middle sister, Lina, had dropped dead of a heart attack at the age forty-five. Kennedy's murder didn't seem possible, even as the crushing reality inched then lurched forward, as the old men took back the government, the era's awful beginning. Then the Kafkaesque murder of the accused assassin on live national television as a Dallas detective escorted him towards a paddy wagon in the basement of the Dallas Police Headquarters added yet a more bizarre dimension. I heard my father shout from the living room,

"*They've shot Oswald! They've shot Oswald!*" The sound of his voice—panic-stricken and vulnerable- conveyed to me, in fact confirmed to me that my life and world had unalterably changed, ushering in Absurdity's reign.

Chapter 2
CENTRIFUGE

Three weeks after the assassination I received my first guitar. Clara had the $15 Kay out of its case, parroting a strum as she walked into the kitchen that first night of Hanukah. I was delighted and surprised, because it hadn't occurred to me that she would take my interest in learning the instrument all that seriously. I didn't think I'd helped my case all that much when earlier in the week I'd abandoned my attempt to make the Junior Varsity basketball team. This was my first and only effort at high school athletics and in the early going I actually had a good shot at making the team, but my enthusiasm plunged after Dallas. I didn't see the point of anything.

Hal and I had spent our time commiserating, becoming less competitive with each other and drawing closer out of our shared pain. I had always felt a little behind him academically and athletically, and most importantly in the timing of our respective puberties, but these concerns had largely left the building in the wake of the president's murder. Now we bonded as if we had both lost a favorite uncle, jointly surmising that JFK had been done in by elements of the military-industrial complex while most of Boonton was either blaming Castro or subscribing to the "lone nut" Oswald theory, if they wondered about it at all. Having read *Seven Days in May*, the political thriller published earlier in the year describing a planned military coup against a US president, Hal and I held similar suspicions.

That first guitar helped ground me. Once I got the hang of proper wrist placement, having been so instructed by a visiting Wasigan counselor, I soon mastered the basic chords, allowing me to learn the hundred songs I would know within my first year with the instrument. I sang and played for hours, pausing only enough to do homework and to put in the required face time with the family. First, I learned the songs from the first three Peter, Paul and Mary albums, carefully lifting and lowering the phonograph needle while I copied the lyrics of each song and figured out the chords. This process was certainly more absorbing than when at age eight and nine I had taken a bat into the side yard where faithfully following the schedule of the real New York Yankees I had improvised my own baseball games.

My repertore included Bob Dylan's early tunes and works by other prominent folkies- Joan Baez, Judy Collins, Phil Ochs, and Tom Paxton. My room, located at the end of a hall, away from the rest of the family's bedrooms, afforded privacy, at least until Herman decided to convert the adjacent guest room that occupied the hall's terminus into his office. For me the consequence was that whenever I heard his footsteps I hoped he would be heading there instead of on his way to pay me a visit. Though he chose the office far more frequently, I could never be sure until that pivotal step at the junction. My privacy thus adversely affected, spiked my anxiety, but also helped hone my singing chops, giving me the edge of urgency that I needed in order to develop my interpretation of the suburban blues.

During that same December, Hal and I took a bus into Manhattan, our first foray into the city on our own. En route, he asked me if I'd heard about the four rock-n-rollers from England whose mop hairstyles and rock and roll harmonies were taking Europe by storm. Confessing that I hadn't, I was intrigued and a little embarrassed, unsure how he'd derived this knowledge. I thought we'd read the same papers and listened to the same news. We took the subway downtown and wandered around the Village for the first time and then hung around 14th Street, the Village's northern boundary. It was too cold to walk around for long, but the impression that I took from this inaugural solo trip was the east of Eden nature of the world- all a matter of degree. From the bums to the garbage workers to the harried office workers, there seemed to be no way to escape the sheer drudgery of existence. The Beatles helped. Within six weeks they had arrived in America and appeared on the Ed Sullivan Show. They electrified the nation, filling the void created by the loss of its youthful and vibrant leader (at least the void felt among the young). That Mersey beat was provocative and their lyrics and harmonies approved of a male vulnerability not nearly so present in American pop or rock. True, they were electric, which had bothered some of the purer folkies I was coming to know, but it didn't matter to me. Neither did it motivate me to want to become a rock-n-roller. Their songs worked on acoustic guitar, validated, when John Lennon played his very cool Epiphone. I played their tunes at parties. Since my cohort was more familiar with the Beatles than with folk music, I increased my confidence, singing in front of people I hadn't known that well or felt I'd had much in common with, but with whom I could develop connection through playing music.

Dylan was another matter entirely. My close friends initially balked, ridiculing his voice and taking me to task for being so enamored of it, even if they admired the songs themselves. Although their criticism caused me discomfort I was not about to abandon my admiration for his style. It had something to do with the alternating harshness and vulnerability in his voice, along with the wisdom that made him sound like a much older man. He cut through pretension and in doing so spoke to the inevitability of that east of Eden thing. If my buddies couldn't see that, then so be it. I was up against more than they were. My father was grinding his ax. Since I'd started playing guitar and identifying with progressive causes, he had begun to lean on me more heavily, insisting that I needed the discipline of the United States Navy. As it appeared a lock that I would not turn out to be Annapolis material, he had started angling for me to apply to colleges that offered NROTC through college. He never hesitated to make the point, at least when he spoke with me outside of Clara's presence, that since he would be paying for my education, then he should have some major say in where and how I would eventually matriculate.

If I was having none of it, I didn't exactly say so. The thought of outright conflict made little sense to me, as there might be consequences I didn't need. His increased pressure had also coincided with his decision to leave his chief engineer job at a pipe factory forty miles away. He was going into business as an iron foundry owner because, as he put it, if he continued working for other people then he deserved to "take all the shit they gave him," a large quantity apparently, as this was not the first time he had made this complaint regarding working for others. So he made the leap, bought into an iron foundry, one that was not close to home, but located in upstate New York near Albany, four hours away from Boonton. His absence during the week served as respite, but weekends were often rife with tension. He left that foundry after a year during which time he'd had to deal with, among other things, a labor strike. I hoped he'd go back to work for somebody else. Instead, within months of the collapse of his first foundry, he chose to buy another ironworks, this time in the Amishland of southeastern Pennsylvania, but just as equidistant from Boonton as the previous location.

* * *

I arrived at Wasigan for the camp's last two weeks of the summer of '64 at sixteen, too old to be a camper, too young to be a counselor. I had spent the first part of that summer at a YMCA camp, long attended by Artie and Aaron, where the three of us were junior counselors. My thrill upon returning to Wasigan could not be understated as the Y camp experience, while fun at times, lacked one essential ingredient—the presence of girls. My return to camp coincided with the end of Wasigan's spirited and competitive *color war*, where for three weeks both campuses (boys and girls) had been divided into two teams engaged in athletic combat culminating in the annual *Sing* on the second parents visiting day. Mercifully, this year I could be a spectator at that event, where the teams performed tunes called "the march," "fight," "cheer," "alma mater", and "optional" for the assembled guests. With lyrics written by counselors to to the melodies of popular tunes their quality would be judged by the *high command*—that group consisting of my uncle Doug (not generally known for his musical appreciation), and one or two chief counselors not assigned to teams. I was invited to join them as they retired to the porch of Anna's cottage, where by their deliberations they would determine the winner of both the afternoon's event and of *color war* itself. This was an offer I couldn't refuse, as the deliberations of the *high command* had historically been an object of intense fascination and speculation for most, if not all, campers over the course of Wasigan's history. As with many idealized person and events, however, the reality of this legendary ensemble turned out to be far more mundane. We met for a banal few moments of lemonade and escape from the heat. When the tallies were reported, half the camp exploded in glee, the other half sulked, and by evening the post color war phase— its most harmonious—was happily underway.

Wasigan's nearly fifty percent drop in census, though had become a cause for concern, its alarming suddenness having yielded a general sense that Wasigan's halcyon days had passed. Perhaps the new "luxury" camps were drawing away prospective campers, or maybe there were fewer children from which to draw, but the long held predictability of happy summers had lessened. The decline coming the summer after the assasination added emotional truth to the beginning of uncertain times. Speculation was that we had one year left, two at most. Anna might retire earlier than expected. All I knew was that between summer 1963, which had culminated in the March on Washington and Dr. King's *I Have a Dream* speech, and this season, immediately having begun with the murders of three civil rights workers in Mississippi, a major change had happened to the country in which I was growing up. In the aftermath of Kennedy's assassination an era of hope had been replaced by an edginess about which my teenage consciousness was quite ambivalent. Something had been shaken loose and nobody seemed to know what it meant, but the process had also involved something darkly liberating, not unlike coming of age generally, but with far more drama. I was sixteen, so this all fit perfectly, continuing as I returned home to begin my junior year of high school.

If not for Clara, I would have been completely lost-not that she couldn't go over the top from time to time. An avid radio listener who still intermittently wished she had continued her career in journalism, my mother had become so enamored with a pioneer of sports talk radio that she had contacted his New York station with a request that he would speak to an assembly at my high school, with no apparent regard for my feelings about such an intrusion. Unlike my father who loathed most of what television offered, my mother was a media aficionado. On Wednesday evenings during my elementary and middle school years, with Herman off at his navy meeting, she had conspired with me to watch a program he had expressly forbidden me to view, *The Many Loves of Dobie Gillis,* a show he felt both ridiculed hard working American fathers and idealized the beatnik lifestyle.

Mom had long had pull with the schools, having spearheaded the bond issue that led to the building of the new high school, been president of the PTA, and had close relationships with many of my teachers and principals from elementary through high school. To my chagrin she had even invited a few of my middle school teachers to my bar mitzvah, an embarrassing irritant for me. She, of course would now be on hand to introduce the radio celebrity at the just approved assembly, a personage whose obscurity rating among my peers had to be at close to ninety five percent. Anxious for weeks beforehand, my dread only slightly exceeded my embarrassment at the assembly. I could find no way not to attend.

Generally though Clara's sensibility was far more in tune with the parents of my friends than with her nineteenth century-inclined husband and she gamely straddled the no-man's-land between these domains. Having to repeatedly bear Herman's accusations that she favored her son over him she responded in kind by insisting that she would not agree to move the family to Amishland, that I graduate high school with my class, that there was no way she would ever move that far away from her mother and sisters. Herman had to acquiesce, if not to the first point, then to the second.

During the workweek we were a single parent family. He'd leave on Sunday nights and return either Friday evening or Saturday afternoon and start the routine over the next day. Eventually, I came to realize that it wasn't just the lower corporate tax rate that had attracted him to Amishland, but that its more provincial setting was even more reminiscent of his childhood than Boonton's, which now seemingly was not sufficiently distant from the New York mentality that he so loathed. That the accompanying reality of living above his office, across the street from the foundry one hundred fifty miles away from his family was preferable to living with his wife and children was a strange and confusing thing. How was I supposed to process this new situation, aside from ignoring it when possible and resisting it when necessary?

On most Sunday mornings after breakfast, my father's accountant would drive the twenty-five miles from his home for their weekly business meeting in our kitchen, its Formica counter serving as the locus of their review of accounts, a tete-a tete my family routinely hoped would proceed in a calm and collected manner. As it fell to me to walk the half mile to purchase the Sunday *New York Times*, I timed the errand to coincide with the two men settling down to business so as to minimize the probability of bearing auditory witness to some accounting inconsistency that would result in a probable verbal thrashing of this poor man. "Uncle Eddie," known to us out of his earshot, was a meek soul, who unfortunately for me, also had a son who aspired to and eventually entered the United States Naval Academy. Herman himself had provided a recommendation for the lad, but it must have galled my father no end to think that from this genetic pool had emerged the son he himself had wished for. Poor "Uncle Eddie," parking his big brown car in our back driveway, plaintively asking my father as he sat at the counter, "Herman, can I please have one of those crullers?" awaiting my father's strident retort, "That's what they're there for, Ed."

Once I achieved sufficient competence on the guitar to play in public, my father got nervous. There was a local inn, the Puddingstone, offering open mic Wednesdays. Clara had told me about it and encouraged me to try it out. Herman opining that my Wednesday nights might be more constructively spent at naval reserve meetings, having seen the writing on the wall that I was unlikely to aspire to officerhood, now wanted me to enlist while still in high school.

I was determined to put this off for as long as possible. Figuring I might foil his plan if I could score an American Field Service placement abroad for my senior year, I applied and was selected by the school but wasn't placed overseas, Europe apparently wanting girls that year.

* * *

Lyndon Johnson had campaigned as the peace candidate in the '64 presidential election, which, in comparison to his Republican counterpart, Barry Goldwater, wasn't saying much. Most Americans had been downright scared that the Arizona senator would be quick on the nuclear trigger. A paid political tv ad exploited this fear: a little girl picking petals off a flower while a countdown is in progress, culminating in a nuclear explosion, thus admonishing the country to vote for LBJ. The fact that Johnson pledged to carry on the work of his martyred predecessor also insured him a huge sympathy vote. Within two weeks of his inauguration, however, LBJ ordered the bombing of Vietnam and within six months had increased the number of US ground troops to over one hundred thousand, with many increases of cannon fodder to come. Most of the country had supported him at least in '65 and early '66 when the belief that more firepower would prevail remained strong. The draft, though, steadily unnerved all men over eighteen, and while student deferments remained in play one couldn't predict how long this would continue. This unfortunate contingency had buttressed Herman's rationale that I should apply to NROTC, as he remarked frequently, so that I wouldn't wind up in the army as a "piece of meat." While appreciating the sentiment and understanding the reasoning, (It carried some weight.) I refused to forsake my desire to go to college in Boston or to another area of progressive thinking. Herman's pressure on me to apply to a college near his Amishland ironworks, a good school with an NROTC program, only served to reinforce my conviction that his concern for my welfare was inextricable from his need to control my life.

At the end of my junior year I was selected by the school to attend New Jersey Boys' State, an American Legion sponsored weeklong leadership workshop held at Rutgers. I was not all that excited. Designed to immerse its attendees into the workings of our state governmental institutions, it had the flavor of what today John Stewart has referred to as 'democracy inaction'. Between the seminars I frequented the college bookstore, perusing its psychology section where I purchased Freud's 'Interpretation of Dreams.'

Along with my clarinet that I would play in the orchestra's two slated performances, I had brought my recently purchased gut string Favilla guitar, a replica of one belonging to one of Wasigan's more prominent folky counselors who had strongly influenced me musically and politically over the past two summers. Selection for the orchestra had been ironic as I planned to hang up the clarinet at school year's end, so what was another week? Only Dvorak's Largo from the New World Symphony had been worth playing anymore. I sang and picked in the dorm room the first couple of nights and was subsequently asked to perform at the first of the orchestra's two scheduled concerts by the Legionnaire who was our floor supervisor, an extremely kind gesture and not a little scary invitation. The almost exclusively male audience's response to my rendition of 'Blowing in the Wind' was incredible, their cathartic ovation emanating from our concerns of the times. There was no doubt that just as Dylan had tapped the zeitgeist, the assembled 'leaders of tomorrow' were now ready to see it brought into the mainstream. I achieved celebrity status for the remainder of the week, surprised also to be asked to sing again for the much larger crowd on Friday evening, thinking that the Legion might nix a repeat especially in front of a wider audience.

They didn't though. Three months after Selma, the Voting Rights Act about to be passed at the zenith of the Great Society, the Legion may have been either indulging or actually supporting the period's idealism. That alone, however, couldn't account for the level of the emotional release the song had engendered, what with Vietnam and the draft on everyone's radar. When I stood to sing this time I introduced it saying, 'This week we have learned about how our democracy works, and that's fine, but what we really need to do is search for peace.' My peers' rising ovation carried me into the reprise of Dylan's first masterpiece that had, along with 'We Shall Overcome' become our generation's signature song- again an eruption among the attendees accompanied by decent enough applause from the families (including my parents) in attendance. Unbelievable- of all the lousy gin joints – quite unexpectedly I was sad for the week to end.

* * *

For the summer of '65, in part as a money-saving move, and partly to re-involve Erasmus, Marvin and me, Anna hired the three of us to be camp waiters. For nearly thirty years, Anna had employed a chef from one of the college houses at Princeton University to run the camp's kitchen, and he had routinely brought his own wait and kitchen staff, young African-American males to camp. Along with Ishmael and his wife, his cadre had not socialized with counselors and campers aside from an occasional pick up basketball game, or on the rare but very fortunate occasion when some combination of them performed as an entertaining accapella quartet. During the summers of '63 and '64, the waiters had come from Tuskegee, Alabama. More interaction now occurred between the waiters and counselors, a chipping away of the de facto segregation that had existed at Wasigan as at so many other Northern institutions and establishments. Well before desegregation, however, Anna and Ishmael had enjoyed a long and mutually respectful relationship.

After the ordeal of serving and cleaning up from that first breakfast, a task that had taken an inordinately lengthy two hours, I gradually settled in. Erasmus and Marvin, on the other hand, had taken to their duties like fish to water, and as with athletic competition I found myself behind them in both natural ability and stamina. I remained the slowest to finish my tasks, but still enjoyed sufficient time to participate in a more adult role at Wasigan, socializing with the counselors and having free time. The changes in Erasmus had startled me. Now taller, thinner, smoking at least a pack of Marlboros a day, he embodied the Wasigan version of *Mr. Tambourine Man.* I envied how comfortable he and the counselors were with each other in comparison to my own insecurity with some of them, the scion, living in the sticks of Boonton, so far removed from the centers of their otherwise erudite worlds. It didn't matter that I could play Dylan (one counselor's back-handed compliment: "I didn't know you had it in you"), when Erasmus was Dylan-like.

He had taught me to smoke, a rough go because it took me several days to grasp the mechanics of how to draw in on the cigarette, with the result that I would breathe in without inhaling any tobacco and would exhale without any smoke emerging from either my mouth or nostrils. It was of some small consolation that my embarrassment was limited to the snickering of only the guys, since I had not yet demonstrated my newly learned sophistication in mixed company. Within a few weeks Erasmus had fallen hard for one of the camp's few non-Jewish counselors who would break his heart before summer's end. Their romance catapulted him to center stage that season: *Tiger*, the charismatic city boy trodding Wasigan's ground in the summer of *Like a Rolling Stone*. I hadn't had all that much luck with girls up to that point. My burgeoning sexuality had been characterized by the Cartesian mind / body split. Those girls with whom I could talk I had little desire to engage with physically and vice versa, but with one notable exception. It had begun in Boonton the winter before, in the form of a yearlong phone relationship initiated by the girlfriend of a prominent and intimidating football player. When she had indicated that she had broken it off with him and was now free to be with me, I never quite believed her. I chose a path of non-pursuit: a whole lot of nothing, I judged, would be less nasty than having to deal with the supposedly jilted athlete, had I followed up hormonally. Later, I would understand the wisdom expressed by the not-yet created science officer, *Mr. Spock of the USS Enterprise,* when in an utterance to his rival after a failed pursuit of a prospective mate on his home planet of Vulcan: "Sometimes wanting is better than having".

This paralysis of will, associated as it was with the avoidance of the school's higher-status jocks, was sublimated in the guise of a series of mischievous theatrics by my friends and me as we sought to represent our disaffection with the social order. Hal and I were now joined by the ebullient presence of Artie who had spent his middle school years at a prep school. He had a knack for the intellectual practical joke, a sorely needed commodity in the halls of Boonton High. Chief among his accomplishments had been the smuggling of D.H. Lawrence's *Lady Chatterley's Lover* into, and then, as his book selection, out from the City for Decent Literature's bookmobile when it made Boonton High one of its ports of call. The target for this operation had been the head of the high school's English department, a charter member of the CDL. Artie fervently desired to see the expression on her face when she asked him what book he had chosen. He had pulled off the stunt with the help of a cooperative classmate and her handbag. Upon disclosing his selection said teacher, a.k.a. the'Ruptured Duck' was subsequently seen waddling down the high school's main hallway, muttering in dazed incantation, "filth in the bookmobile, filth in the bookmobile…."

Artie's triumph soon launched the creation of what we termed "the central cheering section" for Boonton High's football games, a group armed with slide whistles and kazoos in homage to our WOR *voice in the night* role model, Jean Shepherd, whose romp -through -the –absurd monologues had provided hours of inspired entertainment for the young and intellectually disaffected denizens of the New York Metropolitan area. We would arrive en masse at Boonton High's Saturday afternoon football games soon providing our own inane cheers to the bewilderment, amusement, and eventual indifference of the more traditional boosters. Artie would stand up and conduct his minions in any number of chants such as the "how how" and the "short yea," incantations he'd learned from his many summers at the Y camp. Years later, he informed me that he had employed this same drill once as an exercise in crowd control at a rowdy Dublin pub where he had taught its disgruntled patrons the words and music for "Hail to the Redskins," their subsequent rendition having resulted in a significant improvement from a general surliness that had preceded his intervention. We didn't quite realize at the time because it hadn't yet occurred, that we were staging our very own mini be-in.

Our 'piece de resistance' had been a fundraising to bring an elephant to the Thanksgiving Day game. The members of the "central cheering section" metamorphosed into the "Elephant Committee." Cardboard badges with the words "Elephant Booster" were given to students who contributed funds to the enterprise. When the local media mistook our project as a demonstration of school spirit rather than for the enlightened guerilla theatre that it more accurately represented, the generous outpouring of funds from local businesses put us over the top. On the day of the game, to our delight and consternation, not one but two elephants arrived from a New York animal agency. Placed near one end zone, the only personnel allowed within immediate proximity were the animals' trainer and the members of the "elephant committee," We had at last put our footprint—more accurately, those of the pachyderms—on our high school scene, as we milled around taking questions, acknowledging curiosity as well as the occasional kudos, in short looking "official," which had all along been our primary objective because the satire of absurd bureaucracy and adult pomposity was what we were about during those days. The fact that one of the creatures came too close to trampling a bleacher section on our side of the field didn't diminish our sense of accomplishment.

As our next mission we helped quash the idea floating among the powers-that-be of placing a model of an Air Force Bomber on the football field to commemorate our school's nickname, the Bombers. Having caught wind of this scheme before it got off the ground, so to speak, our vanguard had circulated a petition demanding that only a model of a *defensive* weapon be authorized for public display. We gathered enough signatures that the Establishment abandoned the idea altogether. Inspired by this success, we took our bravado on the road to the opening of the second year of the New York World's Fair, bringing signs that read, *Peace Through Restrained Bombing,* a creation of Hal's, in the hopes that we banal iconoclasts would be the first to be kicked out of the Fair. Alas, all that happened: the admitting officials confiscated our creations and wished us an enjoyable experience, advising us we could retrieve our signs upon departure.

* * *

There weren't many topical folk songs that pleased my father's sensibilities for the reason that they were largely of leftist persuasion. Given his memories one could understand his bewilderment at the younger generation's idealization of the Great Depression. One song, however, appealed to him: "Little Boxes," written by Malvina Reynolds, a clever polemic that eschewed the conformity of postwar American suburbia, education, and status. (In recent years it has been used as the theme song for the TV show *Weeds.*) Herman had delighted in the song's lampooning of contemporary society's conformity, specifically in reference to its professional and intellectual classes, but less concerned with the song's barb toward entepreneurial elements. My father embraced a non-conformity of his own, a rejection of the modern world with a refuge to be found in the world of *iron men and wooden ships.* While the content of his non-conformity left me bewildered, the fact of his own rebellion had the unintended effect of drawing me even closer to that of the emerging *zeitgeist.*

Herman soon met and went into business with a like-minded ex-Navy salty dog, the fellow traveler becoming his business partner at the Amishland ironworks. No "Uncle Eddie", he was comfortable with the idea of working far away from his family and appeared equally enthused with the concept of *bunkhouse* über *office*. Their association pleased my father to such an extent that on his weekends in Boonton he took such pains to extol his partner's virtues that Clara wondered aloud why didn't he just didn't divorce her and marry the man. On some level I must have prayed for the new associate's continuing good health, so that my father might take his eye off the ball long enough for me to slip away and pursue my own destiny. Moreover, the ironworks was now successful and our family acquired a greater measure of financial security.

If my mother's frustration had involved any thoughts or worries that Herman's relationship with his apparent *doppelgänger* was of a romantic nature, it wasn't evident. Chalking it up to her oft-repeated characterization of my father as "a man's man," she resigned herself to the fact that in spite of his romantic charisma in their early years, their marriage was grinding down. Divorce, though, was never a consideration. Or at least *I* didn't perceive divorce to be even a remote possibility, but now, when she recounted the story of their first years together, their honeymoon in New Orleans and Herman's plan to outfit a tramp steamer and sail to India, my mother focused more on the ship's having run aground near Cuba and the consequent aborting of this adventure than on the exotic places they'd hope to visit.

* * *

My first choice for college was Boston University. The school had wanted an interview as part of the application process, and Clara relished the prospect of a leisurely afternoon in the city with her husband and son. Her vision also ran aground though, because Herman was determined to drive the five hundred fifty mile round trip in one day, on the very Saturday of my interview, a demonstration of both displeasure at my interest and the burden of sacrifice on his part. In a shared sullenness, we backed out of our driveway two hours before dawn in order to insure our arrival for my 11:00 a.m. meeting, after which we would take our lunch and begin the journey home. The four hours en route had been characterized by little more than silence, my father and mother offering the occasional yawn, although Clara tried to make conversation with me in an attempt to keep me relaxed. While I appreciated her effort, I thought better than to engage in too much talk, as I wondered at what point Herman might choose to offer an observation regarding the pointlessness of the day's purpose. It didn't help that the perfunctory interview lasted less than half an hour.

During the mid-afternoon, on the way home, fatigued, my father pulled over to the side of the Merritt Parkway near one of those affluent towns that housed those denizens of medicine, law, advertising, and public relations with whom he felt so alientated, in order to catch some sleep. As he nodded off, Clara's sagging shoulders appeared before me, an expression of weariness and sorrow, a gesture of the unlived life. I exited the car and sat on the trunk on what was an increasingly cold, if still sunny, late autumn afternoon. What were the stories of the lives in those cars whizzing by our resting sedan? Could any of them be as peculiar? An hour passed before we resumed the drive home.

* * *

Miri had started singing and playing guitar during the past year and we now performed a few times during the winter of her freshman year at Boonton High. She was playing my old Favilla as I had graduated to a Yamaha 12 string, and the girl could sing. The fact that my sister and I shared this embrace of the folk genre provided me some misguided hope that the old man's disapproval of my own musical aspiration might be lessened. He and my sister had, of course, a much different dynamic in their relationship. He did get angry with her, but Miri also experienced a much more dependent side of him.

* * *

In February, BU accepted me (glory be!). Quickly following suit were two other choices as well as Herman's Amishland-area pick. His lobbying would not prevail; I would not be denied. Fortified by Clara's full determination that her son's heart's desire constituted his best option

I committed to Beantown. The Compromise soon unfolded: I would go to Boston and not train to be "an officer and a gentleman." Instead, I would enlist in the naval reserve, so I wouldn't be drafted into the cannon fodder army. Yes, and enlist so I could attain the illusory peace of mind that my father would be sufficiently satisfied.

Of course, none of my friends had rushed to enlist in the reserves, the possibility of student deferments being yanked away by the government notwithstanding. This was 1966. Few seemed concerned. Just finishing high school exerted greater preoccupation. Compounding my recent enlistment, enthusiasm for my own graduation slipped down another notch when, to my consternation, I had observed the photo of my father administering the oath of serive to me splashed on the front page of our local rag, no doubt courtesy of Clara, whose contact at the paper must have hustled someone over to catch the moment.

Wasigan's last summer then followed on the heels of graduation. Marvin and I were now counselors. Erasmus had elected not to return. I had learned more Beatles songs singing them with my thirteen and fourteen-year-old charges. Starkly disruptive, however, was the two–week interruption for my basic training requirement in Illinois. While boot camp was shorter than its army or air force counterparts, one's active-duty obligation would nevertheless be four times longer, two years, to be exact. I would be allowed to defer for four years while earning my degree, but during the interim be required to attend weekly reserve meetings and give two weeks every year for active duty. Immediately, this obligation became burdensome, and I was already filled with regret for having made this deal. The disruption of my summer constituted only the first of many practical and symbolic slings and arrows I would absorb in my efforts to integrate the navy into my life. The two weeks of boot camp were nothing short of bizarre. Standing the midwatch eyes ahead, gazing across to the adjacent barracks taking note of its own midwatchman... On the second Monday, I received an incomprehensibly large quantity of mail from what seemed like everyone at Wasigan, much to the bewilderment of my fellow seaman recruits. Five days later, I flew home and received a strange hero-like welcome upon my return to camp. My buzz cut still fresh I basked in the unexpected spike in female attention. Now I was really confused. How cool could a currently butch-cut seaman apprentice whose hair would need to meet a strict military code over the next four years be, and how would he fare in a world where guys' hair was getting steadily *longer*? What was with these Wasigan girls?

Camp's last night saw the ceremonial "burning out," a traditional season-ending event. Across the lake, counselors dug out the words *Camp Wasigan, 1966,* laid charcoal in the inscribed logo, and, after sunset lit the letters aflame, the fires a shimmering reflection in the dark lake. Customarily, hugs were exchanged and tears shed in prelude to the following morning's ritual, when in full catharsis my sisters and I watched our fellow campers board buses to leave Wasigan. On what was to turn out to be camp's last nite, however, after Taps, the older kids from each campus descended on each other's campuses in what was undoubtedly the only permitted co-ed gathering en masse after-hours in the camp's history. Even Marta, five years younger than me, was out there revving it up with her bunkmates and their respective male counterparts. Although there had been no official word regarding Wasigan's future—or lack thereof—everyone sensed the end.

Chapter 3
REVOLVER

Upon arriving in Boston I was presented with a peculiar opportunity for early discomfort and a tablespoon of humiliation when instead of being housed with other freshmen, I was shoehorned into a suite with four snobbish upperclassmen in the converted Kenmore Square hotel that served as our dormitory. In the space of a week my roommates had placed a diagram on the main door denoting that the four of them resided therein while the newcomer's lodgings were off to the left. Add to this the weekly navy meeting regimen, and alienation had reared its head before I even opened a textbook. Still reeling from my father's latest round of irritability at having to leave me at this school he detested, I set about orienting myself to my living situation, where in order to use the bathroom I either had to walk through my suitemates' bedroom or exit the suite re-entering through the front door. I had registered for five classes, including some eight o'clock offerings, but these hardly worried me, except perhaps for Geology, and its fiendish lab, selected to fulfill a science requirement in lieu of the more fearsome Math. Alas, it soon became evident that even my English course, which I had mistakenly assumed to be a lesser challenge, would be no lock for an *A*.

Classes were nonetheless child's play when compared with psychologically managing the transition from student to reservist that I now had to face with respect to my new weekly navy meeting. Changing into dress blues in my room for the first meeting while other students were going about their normal routines made for difficulty in remaining unobtrusive as I left the dorm, hurrying to the subway. How would I continue to do this every week once I got to know other students? This could only get worse, I reasoned, as I wound my way downtown on the T, Boston's venerable subway system, to Park Street, where I would change for South Station, awaiting a bus that would bring me to the Harbor in South Boston depositing me in front of the Navy Building. The reservist demographic was blue-collar, with an occasional college student, one a melancholy BU junior who had decided to forsake his senior year for imminent two years active duty. To say that I had no affinity with my fellow enlistees would be an understatement. Nevertheless, new to Boston and essentially friendless during the first few weeks of the term, these contacts afforded me some opportunity, however circumscribed, for superficial interaction. For three hours each Wednesday evening I memorized abbreviations for names of various naval ships, bureaus and procedures, stand for inspections, shined shoes (only my own, I should add), and probably the most challenging for my limited mechanical reasoning skills, almost always unsuccessfuly tried my hand at knot tying, the calling card of every sailor, whether or not his job classification called for it. The overall experience was characterized by an anxious sense of wasting the precious time that would have been more constructively spent absorbing the nuances of geosynclines, drumlins and other fun facts pertinent to the Geology course that was already kicking my ass. That there were lockers in the facility, so that in the future I could change my clothes there, instead of traipsing through the dorm in my sailor suit was the only early encouragement (admittedly a significant one), that and the free pea coat I would be issued with the approach of winter.

I had the guitar, though, and played coffeehouses from the Why Not near my BU dorm to the Army and Navy YMCA in gritty Charlestown. I came to appreciate having active duty sailors enjoy my performances since it looked like I would be one in four years. Down the hall a mustachioed, stoutish New Yorker named Karlinsky and I struck up a friendship, and I moved into his suite at semester break, a huge improvement. Karlinsky's company proved stimulating, hilarious, and understanding. When walking back to the dorm down Commonwealth Avenue from the local hamburger stand where we had discussed arrangements for my moving in, he indicated his tolerance for general slovenliness with the notable exception of the importance he had attached to maintaining a clean floor. He then reached inside his pocket for the ashtray he had lifted from the eatery only moments before and without breaking stride flicked the ashes from his recently lit Newport filter into the heisted receptacle.

Herman would hate him, of course, and Clara would never forgive him for putting his feet on the couch in our Boonton living room, but without Karlinsky I might have dropped out and done my two years active right then and there. Since I had been issued a top- secret clearance, dropping out could have meant a posting on the *USS Liberty*, a spy ship which the Israelis would 'mistakenly'bomb during the Six Day War the following June. Perhaps with a little more experience deployment instead could have been aboard the

USS Pueblo seized by the North Koreans in January, 1968, its captain and crew's ass subsequently in a sling for nearly a year. The selling point of Naval Intelligence—its presumption of greater personal safety—was losing its sheen.

The grimness of the period's political reality had been drawn into focus when, in October of 1967 (early in my sophomore year), two army soldiers went AWOL from Ft. Devens before their deployment to Vietnam, taking sanctuary in BU's Marsh Chapel. Word spread fast. Immediately after Economics class, I hurried over to sit with them in a show of support. The initially small gathering of students and faculty swelled throughout the hour, increasing with each day. One soldier smoked Camels and I left to replenish him. Their sanctuary lasted five days, and the chapel became the focus of university life, portions of which were featured in a recent documentary on the late Howard Zinn, the brilliant BU history professor who had authored "A People's History of the United States." Entitled *You Can't Be Neutral*, the film shows his speech at the event. I stopped by every day, and on Saturday night I returned with my guitar and sang "We Shall Overcome," half-hoping that among all the pictures the Navy would notice my enthusiastic presence among deserters and anti-war activists and use the occasion to bounce me out. (Since I was reserve status I didn't think that I risked the brig.) One of the soldiers had turned himself in and then, in the early hours of Sunday, as the assemblage slept, the FBI raided the chapel hauling off the Camel-smoking soldier to a fate about which I never learned. If any photos had reached my commanding officer, I heard nothing about it, but I found myself thinking about the arrested soldier over the next several weeks, wondering whether in a few years I might not be contemplating a similar action. Or what if, by some unlikely fluke, this war would end and with it also the draft? I'd be stuck with a two-year active duty obligation. Every scenario was miserable to contemplate, so I plodded on, putting the future out of my mind as much as possible.

None of my close friends had protested against the war in Vietnam. None had shown any interest in political activism even as (unlike me) their hair had grown longer. Still, I hung out with these guys, not only because I liked them, but also because through my association with them I hoped to avoid having to establish meaningful relationships with other peers who might challenge me to do something more drastic about my present circumstances, a state of affairs about which I felt immobilized. When Karlinsky chose to pledge a fraternity at the end of freshman year, I knew I would probably follow suit the next fall. Although doing so hadn't excited me, at least it would keep me from having to find another social scene where I would need to explain anew the incongruence between my social and political attitudes and my participation in the military.

* * *

I decidedly was not looking forward to my first summer without Wasigan. After a brief vacation in June, it meant ten weeks at the ironworks alongside Herman and hard men doing hard labor, along with more navy meetings and shorter weekends at home—and to top it off, no privacy, as I would be bunking in with the old man upstairs in the office building across the street from the foundry. When his beloved associate was present it could get right crowded in those quarters, but real men being real men, one didn't complain, even if sharing space with two middle-aged men felt a bit peculiar. Two and a half months of this: leaving Sunday night and coming home Saturday afternoon. Eventually, I knew Herman would lose his temper over something and I'd have to deal alone and undefended.

It arrived on schedule the second week. After one of his second-shift employees had called in sick, a job involving the shaking out of castings from their molds, a particularly unpleasant row ensued. Returning from a navy meeting, I encountered my father shaking out the castings by himself. As I had thought my day complete and not wishing to dirty my summer navy whites, I absented myself to the bunkhouse, not grasping he had expected my quick return to aid him in a job I'd not previously undertaken. How foolish to think that my working a full day combined with my service obligation had not been sufficient. I had evidently failed to comprehend his mindset, and had only to wait a short interval before he went off on me for being a "clock-watcher." Three days of placement on his least favored person list ensued that ended only beyond the northeastern border of Amishland on our way back to Boonton that weekend. Inevitably there was a point when he would give it up, but that moment could never be accurately anticipated. When peace came it was as if the previous blows had never been administered, *except of course that they had.* A tentative normalcy took hold as I made out the "all clear" signal.

I had no place to run or hide when he was in that zone. I had no social life in Amishland, nor much any interest in forming one since by the end of the workday I had no energy except for guitar or reading. During the bad times, my only practical means of escape involved walking the small town watching people go about their normal lives, couples holding hands, parents playing with their children, and families sitting on their porches enjoying the summer evenings. Driving to the ironworks from Boonton on Sunday nights, when I gazed out the car window to behold the hamlets of southeastern Pennsylvania, the blue of their television sets gleaming through the windows, I tried to hold on to the notion that this was temporary, that in a couple of months I'd be back at school, and that come hell or high water I wouldn't agree to this again next year.

A cruel irony, though, that this season had become known as the *Summer of Love,* this first after Wasigan's closing, as my grandmother was moving towards full-blown dementia, my life now a kind of indentured servitude far from my home and friends. I did experience some relief during the workday when I could be in the presence of other people, even if they were only my father's employees. The day's monotony was eased somewhat by the songs on the molders' radios, although the hourly interval of "If You're Going to San Francisco, Be Sure to Wear Some Flowers in Your Hair", repeatedly evoked the life I wasn't living. Newark and Detroit were burning in the worst race riots in the country's history. The moorings of LBJ's Great Society had come untethered with the escalation of troops to Vietnam. All of this provided support for Herman's position that liberalism had failed and that the navy would keep me out of inevitable conscription.

But I wanted in on some of that *summer of love.* One Saturday I met Artie's cousin visiting from Brooklyn, and we arranged to meet the following Saturday in Manhattan.

I would need to tell my father, so as to ensure that we could return from Amishland the next Friday, a risk as I had no idea whether he would assent. I intended to bring it up as quickly as possible, but it would have been a minefield to do so in front of Clara. Any support she provided would have been construed by Herman as a manipulation likely resulting in trouble for me on the journey back to Pennsylvania, but my nerve also failed me on the ride back to Amishland. I avoided the subject until late in the week, my anxiety building with each passing day. Any request of him carried so much vulnerability, all the more so now because of our proximity. Finally, I broached it watching him as he calculated his own cost-benefit analysis, eventually agreeing that we could go home on Friday afternoon. While curious about his thought process, I made sure I was not verbally so. I tried not to show any more gratitude than was minimally necessary for how could a nineteen-year-old be grateful for so little of a life in his control?

The date's most notable moment, and beforehand at that, was having been issued a summons for a jaywalking infraction in front of the old Madison Square Garden.

* * *

As a kind of consolation prize for the closing of Wasigan, Herman had arranged for our family's three women to vacation, for most of July, at one of Amishland's older, more established resorts located approximately forty miles north of the ironworks. Its belle-epoque glory long faded, Clara, Miri, and Marta had been the resort's only guests for days at a time. A middle-aged male social director with too much time on his hands showed some interest in Clara, much to the amusement of my sisters. They would often mimic his conversational gambit with our mother—"*Clara*, let's talk…."

Meanwhile, Herman's plan had called for he and I to stay there a few times a week, but the distance from the ironworks made that prohibitive—even my Calvinistically inclined father eschewed arising at 4:00 a.m. He also envisioned spending weekends there. To his surprise, his wife and daughters mustered little enthusiasm, having experienced just about enough of that understimulating environment, and of each other as they could take by Friday evening. Nevertheless, Herman had insisted the family stay there for one weekend, a decision I rejected, as I perceived this as my time to do with as I chose. Grabbing my guitar, I hitched into Reading, central Amishland's main city, where I planned to continue thumbing my way back to Boonton. With each successive step and a couple of short rides my confidence strengthened until the unfortunate moment when the handle on my guitar case broke, causing me a sudden and unanticipated inconvenience. I trudged along higway 222 pathetically hugging the guitar case. The ludicrous nature of this now doomed effort at footlosseness apparent, I turned around and made my way back to Calvin Hill Resort where several hours later I licked my wounds at its shaded Hadrian Villa-like swimming pool.

* * *

As the summer wore on I was evermore aware of my status as an *observer with no place to hide.* When Labor Day weekend approached and with it my final day at the ironworks, I asked the old man to let me make a mold of hammerheads. Throughout the summer I'd performed nothing but unskilled labor, but I'd watched the molders at their work. They prepared their creations for the pouring of the iron while I'd kept them supplied with their *facing sand* (the treated sand that covered the patterns in the molds) in wheelbarrow loads throughout the morning and early afternoons. With one worker's assistance I made a mold and placed it on the floor. It felt good to actually produce something, but I could tell the old man was merely indulging me on my last day. Just as I'd had no choice in being with him at the ironworks this summer, my prescribed role was to *watch and learn*, which in my case translated into *watch and keep him company.* Didn't he have his associate for that? With the man present, which was not every day for reasons about which I knew nothing and never asked, Herman seemed more jovial, and I felt safer. Couldn't my father see that I had no interest or aptitude for ironworks life? No matter, as his son I served as an extension of him, and with no one around to tell him otherwise, what would alter his perspective?

My Amishland experience I summarize thusly: I worked hard and thought about weekends in Boonton. After work I'd sing and play my heart out to no one even if no one or Herman was present (but I repeat myself). Safe opportunities for masturbation did not easily present themselves. Adapting to my intellectual environment reading Ayn Rand's *The Fountainhead* and *Atlas Shrugged* provided opportunities for father-son discussions on relatively safe territory, since our interaction proved the least damaging to me when they involved ideas he already found worthwhile. September would arrive, and next summer I would dare to do something /anything different. That's what I learned at the ironworks during the nation's *Summer of Love.* Thoughtfully, upon my departure Uncle Eddie gave me a carton of Parliament cigarettes.

Clara sympathized, but she had bigger fish to fry. Anna could no longer live independently. She was less and less coherent, and, of even greater concern, she wandered. The nursing home where she would spend the final three years of her life presented itself as the only solution. Lost in all this was Herman's relationship with his mother-in-law. Her warmth and wisdom no longer available to him, my father struggled with the knowledge that the benevolent mother he'd acquired in adulthood was slipping away. Lost too to my sisters and I was her protective presence and sense of humor. I wondered whether my parents' marriage would survive her passing.

* * *

Karlinsky's father had died, bringing about a sad set of circumstances that required my roommate to move home and transfer to Stony Brook University (also known as the 'pharmaceutical capital' of Long Island). This had marked the second consecutive summer in which a friend of mine had lost his dad. Artie's father had died the previous summer. In the midst of my sadness for the roommate so instrumental in preserving my sanity, I realized that not having him back in the Hub wouldn't make life any easier there, especially with my decision to pledge Alphus Enos Pontius in the fall.

Whether because of my friendship with some of the brothers through Karlinsky's introductions, or simply due to charisma (all relative), I assumed the presidency of my pledge class, a role with somewhat less to this title than met the eye. My principal task had entailed acting as negotiator between the brothers and pledges while keeping the spirits of my minions to a minimally acceptable level. The greatest challenge had involved our dealing with the brothers' blackball of a pledge for no other reason than his social ineptness, a cruel but not uncommon tool of fratenity-related image protection. Our attempts to dissuade them having failed, it was left to my trusted aides and myself to console the unfortunate fellow. We could have, I suppose, have all turned in our pledge pins in protest but we didn't, because all of us were too invested in getting in. It sucked, but we collectively rationalized it was all for the best-so much for any practical demonstration of the era's idealism. The final drama of Hell Weekend had required pairs of pledges to crawl through a gauntlet of brothers, at the end of which one of the dyad was informed by the virtual grand inquisitor that he hadn't made it. When my partner was so informed and in the midst of exhaustion, I stood and placed my hands around the aspiring Torquemada's neck. Promptly restrained by his colleagues, my new brothers explained that their last minute blackball had been a ruse to test the loyalty of the non-insulted pledge, the secondary victim, me. I then relinquished my executive role, and have never been president of anything since.

The Alphus cohort embodied a more or less similar cohort to the Wasigan males. One notable exception was Mal, a redheaded, introverted psychology major whose devotion to British rock and blues, not infrequently aided by marijuana opened new doors for me. I identified with his alienation, a person of few words who experienced periods of depression comparable to- even exceeding my own. I moved into the House in January along with two pledge brothers, Sol and Barry.

* * *

That Christmas Clara told both Miri and me about the Java Lobe coffeehouse recently opened in Morristown, just five miles away. Miri and I soon scored a gig there. Just off Morristown's main square, the Lobe, run by a local couple, the Granvilles, became a focal hangout through my college years where I also gigged as a solo. The club held around fifty though on busy nights when standing room only was available another twenty could be squeezed into the storefront. Behind the kitchen a backroom served as a warm up and backstage area, allowing for pleasant mingling and schmoozing between the wait help and the performers. Mostly the players were local folkies like Miri and me, but from time to time some Greenwich Village troubadours (of no great fame) would appear.

The timing of my involvement there was fortuitous. With Hal becoming more involved with his girlfriend Beth, Artie and I were often at loose ends. Beth had become friends with us early on but on occasion we lamented Hal's lack of availability with the refrain, *He's in the ages*, a parody of Edwin Stanton, Abraham Lincoln's pugnacious Secretary of War, who had eulogized the slain president with the words, "*Now, he belongs to the Ages*." Artie and I had marveled at the idea that not many of our peers would arrive at such metaphorical brilliance. The three of them were often in the audience as was Aaron, whose recent acquisition of a beautiful new Martin twelve-string Dreadnought certainly raised my eyebrow. He had not yet developed the performing interest that he later would as a talented bluegrass singer and picker.

* * *

Now ensconced in Alphus House, I had to admit its digs and vibe provided more comfort than had the dorm. The general camaraderie considerably lightened daily life. A water balloon fight between two adjoining addresses of the House, its thrill factor harkening back to canoe fights on Lake Wasigan, provided needed catharsis from the stress of school and dealing with my ongoing weekly military obligation. I had to acknowledge that it had been a good move to join Alphus, because as fraternities went, ours was not so much *going Greek* as it was *going Hebrew.*

Customarily, I would call my parents from the phone booth located off the dining room once a week, almost always on Sunday evenings and always, *always,* after six o'clock when the rates went down. So I was surprised when the chapter's housemother, (Now there was a career choice.) informed me that my father had phoned one weeknight, and that I should return his call at the ironworks. I nervously dialed and heard him breaking down as he told me his associate had been diagnosed with lung cancer. *Jesus Christ,* could there be no break for either of us? I imagined him sitting in the ironworks office, wondering if he'd even shared the news with my mother before calling me, thinking probably not. If his doppelgänger were to die, how much more expectation would he then have of me? I even wondered if he expected me to drop out of school and come to him, although he must have known that if I did so I'd immediately be eligible for active duty, an ironic fact under the circumstances.

* * *

The Tet offensive in Vietnam showed America that we were failing to win the hearts and minds of the Vietnamese. In March, Senator Eugene McCarthy, campaigning against the war, essentially won the New Hampshire primary in losing to LBJ by only a few percentage points. Immediately thereafter, Robert Kennedy entered the race, pitting himself against the Minnesota senator. This initially angered many of the young, having perceived RFK as an opportunist reaping what Mr. McCarthy had sown. I agreed, but didn't doubt the fact that Bobby could better face down the teetering LBJ and also be a stronger standard-bearer for the party to win the general election. Two weeks later, Johnson shocked the nation by announcing that he would decline to seek another term. After his speech that Sunday night, the students of Boston took to the streets as if the Red Sox had won its first World Series in fifty years. The euphoria carried on far into the night, but the hope engendered by this development lasted only four days until Dr. Martin Luther King, Jr. was murdered in Memphis, bringing about a state of social unrest in the form of riots in cities across the country, along with anguish and dread almost everywhere else. Good news had a short life span.

Throughout the spring RFK and McCarthy fought in the primaries. Bobby won Indiana, Nebraska, and South Dakota, but had lost to McCarthy in Oregon. McCarthy had earlier won Pennsylvania, Massachusetts, and Illinois, so a victory in California was essential for Kennedy's continued candidacy. Meanwhile, Hubert Humphrey, erstwhile progressive senator also from Minnesota, and for the last four years, LBJ's emasculated Vice President, had thrown his hat into the ring as the defender of the administration. The California primary coincided with my two weeks active duty, this year unfolding in the environs of Bainbridge, Md. Having demonstrated a talent for Morse code during the previous year's active duty, (my mental acuity no doubt augmented by the newly released *Sgt. Pepper's Lonely Hearts Club Band*), I now resumed the honing of my skills in this area of unexpected expertise. Waking early that Wednesday morning in June in the barracks, I quietly turned on the television in anticipation of learning the results of the all-important California race, and thus became the bearer of the news of Robert Kennedy's shooting to the still slumbering reservists. A second Kennedy shot, seconds after claiming victory in the primary that would have established him as the front-runner for the party's nomination in Chicago. Any hope now for reconciliation between the generations evaporated. Bobby's death was the end. There was no way now to believe there was any good remaining in the country- two beacons two months apart- a mean-spirited lawless and villianous nation.

* * *

This recently declared US History major returned from his two weeks active duty service determined to not give up the entire summer to Herman, much to the latter's irritation. My father hadn't helped his cause, when, driving me from Boonton to the base to begin my fortnight of code tapping, he responded with considerable contempt after I asked if he thought the navy lockers would be secure enough for the guitar I insisted on bringing. Within the next week he composed and sent me a disparaging twentieth birthday greeting. Upset with me for not having signed on for another summer in the ironworks he chose to castigate me instead in longhand.

Clara had supported my staying in Boonton for at least part of the summer, a process paralleling her attitude towards what her husband had to say or think about anything. My mother had genuine and growing sympathy for the emerging plight of my generation in the wake of Bobby's murder. I secured a job as a carpenter's helper until early July, when, worn down by my father's incessant sulking, I joined him at the ironworks for the remainder of the summer. I felt I'd made my statement. His beloved partner's illness notwithstanding, I had no qualms about wanting to spend my time doing something, anything, different from what he preferred. I showed some initiative by arising before him to prepare the facing sand for the molders, and hoped that my diligence would keep him off my back. I knew he was aching about his partner but I had resolved not to take any more nonsense, and for the most part we reached an uneasy truce. I played a great date in mid-August at the *Lobe*. He and Clara had attended along with many friends from both college and high school—Karlinsky, Sol and his girlfriend, Barry, Artie, Aaron, Hal and Beth. Clara told me later that when I sang Dylan's "Dear Landlord," my father tightly gripped her hand, asking if I'd written the song.

Then came Chicago. As our family viewed the spectacle of that city's finest beat the living crap out of the protesters assembled in Grant Park, my mother's apologias for the *ancien regime* took another noticeable dive. By contrast Herman uttered that perhaps Mayor Daley's constabulary hadn't gone far enough. The bloodied protesters were victims of what would subsequently be termed a *police riot* by the Walker Commission, which subsequently investigated the violence of those momentous and terrible days in the

Windy City. Humphrey had won not a single primary but nonetheless secured the nomination. Mercifully, the end of summer and my need to return to university cut short the opportunity for further familial discourse.

* * *

Mal and I lived together junior year in Alphus. The ledge off our room looked toward a girls' dorm across the street so on occasion he and I sat serenading the young women, me on the Yamaha 12 string while he tapped on his set of bongos. Introverted as he was our interaction often resembled a monologue, but that didn't matter too much of the time. Most of all, his love for and knowledge of the blues cemented our affinity and considerably broadened my repertoire. After Nixon's election in November, I joined him in partaking of the weed. Mostly it proved beneficial to my mood and anxiety levels, and I loved the enhanced quality of listening to music, never more so than when I first heard the Beatles' *White Album* and especially George Harrison's "While My Guitar Gently Weeps." Mal also had family issues to which he seldom referred, but that served to strengthen our friendship. We would regenerate ourselves through the music we loved as the year wore on.

I had learned from a fraternity brother who held a position on the BU social council that Joni Mitchell would be appearing in concert at Sargent Gymnasium and that the council would hear me audition as an opening act. I didn't require coaxing. Ecstatic to get the gig, slated for a thirty-minute set, I was sky high for the several days before the show. Along with Dylan Joni Mitchell was now acknowledged as the most talented and popular singer-songwriter of the period. Appearing on that same stage was about the most unexpectedly cool thing that could happen for any aspiring singer; however, concert day machinations caught me off guard. First, the show's preliminary act, Jamie Brockett, had insisted on opening, bumping me to second, not a helpful development for an unknown. Then, Ms. Mitchell herself requested that Livingston Taylor be put on the bill immediately before her own appearance. All of that could have scratched me and, in fact, my set was cut to ten minutes. Fifty dollars for ten minutes, I felt like a hooker, but nervous now that something else might go haywire, and it did after a fashion but not in any way I would have anticipated.

Backstage with Livingston Taylor: he was seventeen and this was one of his first big shows. He was nervous but friendly, and asked me to accompany him to 'say hello to Joni.' I hesitated for fear that something else could still go wrong, that if I weren't ready to play the moment my number was called I might lose my opportunity. So I stayed put. I sat, bummed, and noodled on the Yamaha, forcing myself to acknowledge that not meeting Joni Mitchell would be less difficult to justify than losing those now recently reduced ten minutes of fame.

The whimsical Jamie Brockett had meanwhile worked the crowd in an interesting way. In a genuine demonstration of the times, the singer-songwriter had requested that the audience of some three thousand manifest their approval of his efforts neither by clapping or hooting, but instead by yelling the word *shit*! Unaware of this fun fact soon after I took the stage and began Dylan and Rick Danko's "Wheel's on Fire". I heard Brockett's injunction coming from the crowd, a phenomenon not a little unnerving, puzzling, and disturbing. Looking for Karlinsky, Sol and company in the front row I couldn't help but notice gesticulations designed to assuage my mortification, but what could they mean? Weirdness galore! I couldn't be that bad, could I? Oh, *shit.*

Then it was over. I was well received despite the barrage of unpleasant epithets. Preparing to go on stage himself Livingston offered kudos. That felt good. What the fuck? Karlinsky and Sol then enlightened me as to the meaning of the message. My template for the music business had clearly been established.

* * *

Soon afterward I learned that my father had been diagnosed with prostate cancer. He had arranged for his surgery at a VA hospital near the ironworks, showing no inclination to be near Boonton, providing further evidence where his real home lay. During his post-operative recovery, Clara clearly but inadvertently revealed the extent of her own alienation. Unable to understand and follow his driving directions to his hospital at some point she turned around. Finishing my junior year, I was spared the day-to-day drama. His hospital stay lasted several weeks. Eventually my mother and sisters successfully navigated their way to his bedside, just before visitors from the ironworks came to inform him that in his absence his ironworks had burned down.

Chapter 4

MORATORIUM

My father initially thought that one of his employees had set the fire, a vendetta, the circumstances of which I knew nothing about, but more than likely its cause was accidental. His beloved associate was losing his battle with cancer and would soon succumb. Herman's foundry now lay in ruins, and his own health was terrible. I could understand his possibly paranoid belief that one of his workers had sabotaged him, for all I knew it was true, although there had been no evidence of arson.

The cobalt treatments that followed his surgery had halted the malignancy's metastasis, but also resulted in significant weight gain and a decline in virility. Over time the latter unhappy fact only compounded his ire at the increasing length of the long hair of the males, but that fallout was not apparent in the immediate aftermath of his surgery. The fire had reoriented him towards Boonton as home. Thus after my junior year, I learned with relief that he and I would spend only a week in Amishland while he dealt with insurance adjusters and liquidated the business. The recent events had ushered in greater calm in our family than any in recent memory. Clara had even consented to spending time with him on the sloop he'd purchased the previous year, a vessel she once had suggested he christen *The Seabitch.* When the Granvilles threw a 21st birthday party for me my parents showed up with a chocolate cake to the delight of us all. This summer I didn't miss Wasigan, because of this unanticipated harmony. Miri had now graduated from high school. She would be attending college in Colorado, not far from where her boyfriend would be matriculating. Our parents felt sadness and anxiety over how far away she would be, but the customary tension was absent. That would leave only Marta at home, and she didn't readily reveal how she felt about both of her sibs being away at school. She would have the folks to herself, a mixed and belated blessing. My younger sister had given the impression to Miri and me that she believed she may have been a parental afterthought.

Just before leaving home for summer school, to get a head start on my senior year before student teaching in my final semester, Herman and I had viewed a news report on the upcoming moon landing. We were lunching at one of his favorite watering holes where I concurred with his observation that Apollo 11 had to be the greatest engineering achievement of his lifetime and probably in all of history. I added that I thought it involved more, something of a psychological and spiritual quality, silently reflecting on Stanley Kubrick's masterpiece *2001* I'd seen over a year ago. My father looked puzzled, regarded me curiously, but didn't dismiss the sentiment, and I took his silence as some attempt to reconcile his world with mine.

I headed back to the Hub to meet up with Mal. We hitchhiked to Newport for the jazz festival over Fourth of July weekend. The Newport Jazz Festival was being touted as *the* biggest festival of 1969. We made it, albeit from a hill overlooking the festival grounds, having not bought tickets. The '69 festival was a departure for Newport jazz, showcasing a fusion between jazz and rock, thus attracting a much wider audience. On Friday night, Mal and I saw Blood, Sweat & Tears, Jeff Beck, and Jethro Tull. As a harbinger of Woodstock, only five weeks away, the crowd outside the gate below us broke the fencing at the concert's perimeter, a prototype of the *it*'s a free concert from now on. Rock had arrived at the hallowed grounds of Newport.

Woodstock weekend in the Hub, Mal and I dipped into eternity courtesy of mescaline, experiencing *God in a Hurry.* Winding through the munchkin-like Brookline Streets in a welling of ecstatic rapture, occasional flickers of anxiety morphed into a transcendent state that I never knew existed. We encountered a fellow student ambling towards us on Strathmore. In his hand he held a scroll, the *Desiderata*, upon which my eyes set for the first time. Its carrier, assumed the appearance of Joseph in his coat of many colors. He unfurled the parchment sharing its message of self-acceptance and compassion with my buddy and me. I was truly lifted. In the coming weeks I would take long walks in the vain hope of recreating the atmosphere that would trigger that expansion of consciousness.

* * *

Visiting home before fall term, I learned that my father had found a job as a president of a brewery located just over the border in Pennsylvania, a long but not impossible daily commute. I spent a day with him at his new job relieved that he was no longer under the duress of owning a business. Restless after a not uninteresting tour of the facility, I left him a note to tell him I'd be walking the neighborhood. My nerves tightened, and I judged the cause as a yearning for freedom that I could barely contain after having had a glimpse of the higher realm. On our way home he seriously surprised me by telling me I should pick out a Martin guitar, a D-28, for which I'd been pining for years. It was an act of generosity that I couldn't quite absorb. Of course I found a way to sabotage the purity of the gift by failing to get the best deal on the purchase. I made the psychologically overdetermined, but nevertheless boneheaded move, of then disclosing this to him needing some way to fuck up his generosity based on our axiomatic history that no good deed goes unpunished. Still, he got over his irritation more quickly than was customary. He told me to enjoy my music, but "don't be an asshole with it," an injunction that I understood to mean that I should maintain my hair at an acceptable length and eschew the hysterical, unwashed masses that had recently descended on Woodstock.

* * *

Sol, Barry, and I had rented an apartment for our senior year over a bar in Brighton. Mal intended to live at home for his final year and we couldn't talk him out of it, but he frequently came around to crash on our ratty couch. These were good times, although I couldn't help looking ahead to next year's active duty in the navy, a reality that was becoming harder to accept. Nixon's secret plan to end the Vietnam War increasingly appeared to be neither, with only rising casualties and no end in sight. Rumors regarding a draft lottery alarmed my fellows and also provided me with the only rationale, thin as it felt, for remaining in the reserves, another spin of the wheel of imminent conscription.

All of this weighed on me that night I met Meris. At a party thrown by friends I had stared across the room at her for far too long. We took a walk and embraced. Three years younger, a freshman at a junior college, a young woman older than me, Meris and I soon got it on. She asked why it had taken me so long to acknowledge her. The little I could manage in way of reply spoke to how painfully shy I was in the presence of someone so spellbinding. Our circumstances of introduction involved smoking a not insignificant quantity of opiated hash, but even if I'd been straight she would have held my attention. She had an enveloping smile, a relaxed manner, and a speech cadence that could only be characterized as anomalous Long Island drawl. Meris was a true citizen of the newly recognized Woodstock Nation. Although of the Tribe, she was blonde, and could almost be taken for a *shiksa,* and as I possessed the sensibilities of a Boonton assimilationist, I naturally found these attributes quite appealing. We cuddled in my Brighton nook, a three- bedroom dump with a rickety and dilapidated back porch, and an aerie from which to view Sol's extremely red Alpha Romeo. Within this dive and to our mutual delight, Meris and I would fortify ourselves with a modest, if steady, quantity of weed along with our favorite dessert delicacies: *Susie Q* Devil's Food cupcakes and the aptly named Cool and Creamy chocolate pudding.

The shortness of my hair-how to explain that and all it stood for, my servitude in the military-this I avoided but on some level intuited that if I didn't soon take meaningful action this romance would wither. A confluence of events occurred, something that a few years later would be readily understood as synchronicity. Within days after Meris and I knew we'd be seeing a lot of each other came the Moratorium against the War in Vietnam (October 15, 1969), a national day of rallies. That this date fell on a Wednesday, the evening of my weekly navy meeting, had proved fateful because it allowed me no time to compartmentalize the disconnect between my life as a student and my military obligation.

That afternoon I walked to Boston Common, home to the largest of the day's rallies. Senator George McGovern, who had taken up the mantle of the late Robert Kennedy, spoke solemnly and was received with an outpouring of emotion, both for the content of his criticism of the war as well as for the evocation of RFK. The sun had moved behind Beacon Hill, the capitol dome of the state house glistened in the late afternoon light and the crowd dispersed. On Commonwealth Avenue amidst those walking the Back Bay I neared Meris' dorm. I couldn't bring myself to see her, afraid I would scare her off if she saw me so preoccupied and vulnerable this early on —*God, how good it would feel to be held by her, but no, not now, too risky—keep walking up past Bedford, past Clarendon and Dartmouth, past Exeter and Fairfield and Gloucester—why can't I see her, hold her, be comforted by her? Keep walking—get to Mass Ave—to Kenmore—take the T—keep going, damn it!—it must be getting late don't take this sweet life from me—how will I get my uniform and get back down to Southie on time?—it's too much—it's all too much—George Harrison—yellow submarine—it's all too much for me to take—Sol, Barry, I need help—the T rising above ground past the university and the armory—through the junction at Commonwealth and Brighton Ave—past the billboard sign bearing a picture of The Band advertising their second classic album—the one with the Night They Drove Old Dixie Down —then Brighton Center —cross the street—watch for the cars-the T—get upstairs—Teeth chattering—Sol holds my shoulder- lays me on my bed—blankets——I'm freaked!—, I haven't taken anything——I can't do this anymore- Get me out...Help me get out...*

As I lay on my bed, my body shivered and my face became as numb as that day at Hopatcong. Sol dialed a phone and while Barry threw another blanket over me I could make out Sol talking with what sounded like Student Health setting up an emergency psychiatric visit for the next morning. My roommates hovered over me, one suggesting I pop a Seconal, while I still in possession of some small mental functioning wondered from where that pill might come. It didn't do much, though, as I answered two questions from them: should they call Meris and should they call my parents? I shook my head with as much vigor as I could summon-*No on both counts.*

The next morning's meeting with a university shrink made me realize that I had needed help for a long time. Restating my conflict with my father, I recounted my family history, the incident at Hopatcong, and the present prospect of a seriously desired primary relationship. He understood, but wanted me to come in a second time before he would write me a letter for the navy. He diagnosed a dissociative episode. The diagnosis didn't bother me. So many peers were using shrinks to evade the draft that I worried not at all, having experienced a genuine emotional crisis. Agreeing to meet again the following Tuesday, I had several days to mull over my new situation knowing I'd have to get through at least one phone call home without letting on to what had happened. I had no trust in my capacity to handle my parents' reaction, nor did I wish to disclose anything that would set them against each other. Not that I believed that Clara would celebrate my decision, but she would nevertheless defend me at considerable cost. As for my father, I anticipated a hard time when I didn't need it, so I chose to fight another day. Here I stood, twenty-one years old, a college senior, and only now engaging in an act of major concealment.

I cherry-picked the situation with Meris, relating family history but minimizing the actual emotional crash I'd experienced on Moratorium day. This felt disjointed, but her easy manner and affection boosted my confidence such that I knew I could move ahead. I had a girlfriend and anticipated the happy fact that the length of my hair would soon mask my modestly large ears and allow my appearance to become decade-appropriate. Whatever anxiety I struggled with over the imminent end of peace with my father would have to assume less importance. After my second session the doc provided a letter recommending that I be discharged from the service for psychiatric reasons, I took this to my commanding officer, who then suspended my attendance pending an interview with a navy psychiatrist. I left the building. Although the navy's evaluation wouldn't occur for nearly a month, I could barely contain my relief as I boarded the bus to South Station en route to my apartment, confident this prolonged ordeal was coming to an end.

The following Wednesday I didn't have to attend a meeting. I felt the deflation of separateness that had followed me through all the years of Wasigan and through the first three years of university. Being in love, playing music, enjoying school, I felt good getting in touch with life's possibilities. In November, my newfound sense of self underwent a major test though when Meris informed me that she had sometime ago made plans to attend the Mobilization in DC with her old boyfriend, along with a suggestion that I shouldn't worry, but it set me back. I decided against moping in Boston and instead found a way down to DC to march anyway, relishing the opportunity to travel to Washington to participate in a demonstration without the burden of my navy service hanging around my neck. I made my way to Harvard Square—renamed *Freedom Square* for the occasion. Dylan's strident "Masters of War" blared and my blues started lifting. I found two Harvard med students looking for fellow travelers to help pay expenses down to DC. Heading down the Mass Pike I felt a bit unmoored, but consoled myself with the recognition that sulking among strangers was preferable to doing so with friends.

Half a million people marched down Pennsylvania Avenue from the Capitol that sub-freezing Saturday, gathering on the grounds of the Washington Monument while Richard Nixon sat barricaded in the White House, reportedly watching a football game. Pete Seeger, among others, sang to the huddled throng trying to keep warm that November 15th. Between verses of "Waste Deep in the Big Muddy," Pete yelled, *"Are you listening, Nixon, are you listening Agnew?"* Pumped at the start of this incredible march, embodied in the limitless solidarity now here in the afternoon I must have nodded off from time to time, on the cold ground near the Washington Monument, waking with the awareness of the proximity of Meris and her old beau. I acknowledged the unpleasant fact that I wouldn't be sleeping with her tonight and for all I knew maybe not again. I hadn't counted on being abandoned so soon. *Steady on, old boy, she told you not to worry- maybe it is just unfinished business.*

The long drive back north that began early the next morning gave me plenty of time to think and not only about Meris, but also about the upcoming Thanksgiving break and what strategy I would employ in dealing with my parents. I needn't have concerned myself, because once the navy had completed their evaluation, they sent me a letter at my Boonton address, informing me that their psychiatrist had recommended that I should be discharged from the service due to what they hubristically referred to as an *adjustment reaction to adult life.* Of course my father had opened and read it.

As my parents had decided to stay mum regarding their knowledge of said events, I had no idea I was about to be blindsided, my mental preparation for naught, but good news also arrived: I had Meris back.

Before I left for Boonton with Sol that Wednesday before Thanksgiving, on an errand to return a library book, I saw what I could not believe. The radical and militant Students for a Democratic Society had convened a meeting in the university union building when, without provocation, the Boston Tactical Police stormed the building, and having randomly employed their nightsticks, manhandled the SDS attendees, dragging them off into waiting paddy wagons. Chicago had now arrived in Boston. In a window above the scene, I saw the white hair and tanned face of Dean Mackel, the head of the College of Liberal Arts, hands folded, observing the events with a look of smug satisfaction. The school's administration had manipulated the timing of the police intervention, as over half the students had already departed for the holiday weekend. By the following Monday, it would be old news.

Sol dropped me off in Boonton and wished me luck, a sentiment that would soon contain some irony. On that very Wednesday evening at his parents' home he received a phone call from my father requesting to meet with him on Friday in order to ask questions about me. I would only learn of their encounter when I returned to school and Sol disclosed. So on Wednesday into the house I went and immediately felt the vibe.

Crocodile tears, I surmised, concerning the parental disappointment in my failing to keep them abreast of my plans, of which I now knew they were already aware. Folding the laundry Clara halfheartedly observed that, "every man should serve his country," I thought my mother's demeanor reflected more concern about the prospect of my being drafted now that I had bailed from the reserves. After giving my hellos to Marta who now regarded me with bewilderment and admiration (Miri wouldn't be coming home until Christmas), I made arrangements to crash with Artie and his family until Saturday, at which time father and son would spend the afternoon letting it all out in the same kitchen where Herman had developed those Christmas family pictures and where Clara had brought me my first guitar.

That Friday night I went with Artie, and Karlinsky, along with his long term and my more recent friend Sid, to see Jefferson Airplane at the Fillmore East. I couldn't think of a better warm-up to dealing with Herman. The Airplane didn't go on until nearly two a.m.—not that they weren't worth waiting for—preceded by The Youngbloods and Hot Tuna. A great show, but it was nearly dawn when we emerged from the legendary concert hall. I was eight hours away from my own rendezvous with destiny with some need for sleep in between. More than a long time coming this day was to be a long drag to get through.

My father now adopted what my sisters had called his 'dry voice', a wounded and sullen speaking style. He wondered aloud why I hadn't come to him first, a thought that predictably had never entered my mind. He expressed concern for what I would do with my life, as if avoiding the service during an unpopular war constituted the worst thing anyone could contemplate. Round and round we went for a good part of the afternoon. He had trouble not taking my stance personally. I found a distraction with the knowledge that only a few blocks away Hal was also involved in a marathon of *sturm und drang* with his parents over his decision not to break up with Beth who was Roman Catholic. His parents had long suspected the unacceptable likelihood that their son might marry outside the faith. Myself, I felt that whatever rift developed in Hal's family would be of shorter duration than my impending introduction to pariahood but was nonetheless fascinated by the Joycean revelation, that here in Boonton on one afternoon between my friend and me the bastions of state and church were under siege. Watching my father I remained unusually calm, steadfastly knowing that I had correctly decided for me and that the worst was over, so I thought, even if he decided to throw me out and/or refuse to pay tuition for my final semester. There seemed to be no middle ground. He demonstrated no interest in the more upbeat aspects of my life and that pissed me off. He didn't ask me a thing about school, and about Meris he asked nothing. The fact that he gave me his father's watch at the end of the day, signifying some release on his part, confused me and weighed me down.

On Sunday, Clara suggested I ask him to drive me to Barry's, for the trip back to Boston, in her by now long established, well-intentioned and misguided belief that my initiating contact with him would patch things up. Reluctantly, I agreed, but the tension during the ride lifted only minimally. When we pulled up to Barry's I contemplated inviting him to meet my roommate's dad, a decorated WWII fighter pilot, an individual as against the Vietnam War as anyone could be, who had absolutely no interest in seeing his son in a military uniform, and even enjoyed sharing a joint with Barry and friends from time to time. But I decided against it, knowing too well that he had lost his brief interest in my world. Our moratorium, our era of good feeling had ended. The dust would have to settle.

I went to see Meris on Monday. She noticed the watch and said, "So your dad gave you a present." I got the subtext. I self-consciously nodded, registering her statement as well intentioned but low on empathy. "Come to Boonton over Christmas, Meris, will you?"

She smiled.

Marta wrote me in early December informing me she'd started smoking dope in her room and that the parents were clueless. My youngest sister now relished taking big risks that my parents still refused to notice. As for my mother it was not clear with whom she was more irritated-her husband both for his relentless expectations for their son and for his elevation of spartanhood as a core value; or with me, whose timing of exiting the service, something she understood far more than she cared to admit, had destroyed the peace she'd been enjoying with her husband since he liquidated the ironworks in Amishland.

Chapter 5

NEW MOURNING

...And ye shall know the years of your matriculation as follows: Revolver (freshman), Sgt. Pepper's Lonely Hearts Club Band (sophomore), White Album (junior), Abbey Road (senior), and Let It Be (the end)...

Thanks to Nixon's anxiously awaited nationally televised draft lottery in early December, the lay of the land got roughter. Fate had dealt me not just any low number, but the provocative # 69. Sixty-nine in'69-I gnashed my teeth, unamused by the sexual connotation. A low number meant not only guaranteed conscription but also having to absorb the *I told you so* across the two hundred forty miles separating the Hub and Boonton. I had six to eight months to figure out a way to avoid going to Vietnam, my father's protective efforts having simultaneously been validated and made moot. Still I harbored no second thoughts. If I'd have to slip away to Canada, I guessed I'd find a way to get there. I'd heard about American musicians getting cabaret cards and finding work in Toronto and Montreal. Of course, once there they couldn't return home without facing prison, and I was emotionally unprepared to go into exile, permanently leaving behind my mother and sisters, even at that point, my tenaciously incorrigible father. Only Barry had also drawn an impossibly low number, and miraculously avoided induction when, in what more closely approximated an act of God than anything I'd ever heard, was stung by a bee on the way to his physical. His allergic reaction meant rejection for conscription. As for the rest of my compatriots my sentiments consisted of *a hearty congratulations to you all and don't ever complain to me about anything in your lives.*

A situation had transpired within a week after the draft lottery providing confirmation that my new course was certainly no more flawed than the navy charade. Clara informed me that my father had made a sudden trip to the Hub set on a dual mission. First, as a retired Naval Reserve Seabee Captain, he pulled rank to assure I was not dishonorably discharged. Noble enough, he had assumed responsibility for the doomed compromise, but he also had a bone to pick with Dean Mackel over the university's unwillingness to release my psychiatric records to him as tuition paying parent. According to Clara, my father had scheduled no appointment, but after having been kept waiting for a prolonged period, instead gained access to the Dean's office through removing a window, the stuff of legend. Not surprisingly he hadn't seen or contacted me during his brief time in the Hub. Curious, too, though, because on the Thanksgiving Sunday, as we had prepared to leave for Barry's and apparently in some intended gesture of good will, he had offered me a strange peace offering in the form of a plaque that resembled those placed on barroom walls, inscribed: *There are a Thousand Excuses for Why Things Can't Be Improved.*

The outright strangeness of this episode had now cast his clandestine meeting over Thanksgiving weekend with Sol tame by comparison. Back in the Hub Sol had sheepishly acknowledged he'd been caught in a bind not knowing how to refuse my father's request, afraid even to give me a head's up. My friend's behavior validated my long-held belief that Herman could pretty easily intimidate anybody he chose. I let that go, but found myself too embarrassed to tell Sol or anyone else, including Meris, about my father's episode with the Dean. For the first time I questioned the old man's sanity, that maybe he was not just a man with a temper who held grudges. From that point on, whenever I would hear from friends or from their parents that things would eventually work out between us, I thought differently.

* * *

Anna died in January. I flew home after my first day of student teaching, met by my unhappy father at the airport, neither he nor I prepared for another encounter so soon. He remained silent on the trip home. Few Wasigan alumni had gathered at the funeral home, a source of recurring disappointment for Clara. Wasigan had been closed for three consecutive summers, but it still seemed that more people should have paid their respects. Word had certainly spread, hadn't it? There in the casket lay my grandmother's body. Some months back, Clara had related to me that when she and Herman were visiting at the nursing home, Anna raised her finger, pointed it at my father, and in a loud voice admonished him, "Leave him alone," advice that Herman did not of course follow, in a departure from his usual consideration of most of her counsel. Her death could now only advance and accelerate the polarization now establishing indefinite residence in our family. Hardheaded, but light-hearted, my maternal grandmother had been the benevolent matriarch.

Her passing—coming now at the moment of my rupture with Herman—starkly fortified the end of such beneficence.

I looked up from the casket to see Erasmus. Now a senior in college on Long Island, he expressed uncertainty about his plans for the future. I thought of asking him about his draft lottery status but decided against it, preferring to avoid going through my long and still unresolved tale. Our encounter was not uncomfortable. Having recently asserted myself with my father, I felt more secure in my cousin's presence now. As I stood there with him, though, I felt less need for the closeness I'd wanted years before. We shared a few minutes, went to the cemetery, and then said our good-byes with no sense of when or even whether we would meet again. Holding my mother's arm as we walked from the gravesite, I felt the sadness beneath the façade of her stoic demeanor. Unable to calculate the enormity of her loss, a loss mitigated only by Anna's protracted mental decline, I gripped her hand tightly in an effort to reassure her that I was ok.

* * *

In March, Hal and Beth tied the knot in Lewisburg, PA, home to two venerable institutions, a federal minimum-security prison in whose digs some of the later Watergate convicts would find themselves, and also Bucknell University, where Hal was now a senior. He and Beth had dated for over four years, back and forth between his campus and Beth's Greenwich Village teaching hospital. During his own college interview there when unexpectedly asked if he had any questions about the school, he had desperately come up with an inquiry regarding the status of town/gown relations. Later, during his junior year of college he had written me an amusing letter illustrated with extensive diagrams, about how he had managed to tie up traffic in lower Manhattan by driving the wrong way up a one-way street near Beth's building. In this adventure my oldest friend had demonstrated behavior consistent with our driver education teacher's observation that 'Hal does exciting things with a car.' I flew to Syracuse to meet up with Artie, now a senior at that city's university. The two of us motored to the event in his maroon Citroen, a vehicle that resembled an overgrown toad and possessed the unique and remarkable capacity of raising its chassis a few inches above the ground whenever the ignition was turned off.

Hal and Beth had at last discovered the one foolproof antidote to his parents' opposition to their marriage. Their ceremony was attended by only by the few guests who could be counted on for their discretion, the wedding announcement diplomatically delayed. Now Artie and I celebrated Hal's permanent place *in the ages*. He would begin medical school in the fall. On our return trip to Syracuse Artie revealed his own plans, that of a door –to- door encyclopedia salesman in the southern states after his graduation. Looking at him with restrained incredulity, I wondered both how long that venture might last and what had possessed him to undertake such an endeavor. The South, after all, still being the South made it difficult to visualize him engaged in that endeavor in that environment. Of my own plans, I said little, insofar as I had none.

* * *

I completed my student teaching at a boy's technical school off Harvard Square. Again, I experienced the peculiar state of misapprehension, wondering why I couldn't have scored a placement at a co-ed public high school? What was with my karma? The eight weeks had gone well enough once I'd adjusted to the school, but teaching US History to a group of teenage boys, many of them likely Indochina-bound before even having an opportunity to learn a trade, disconcerted me. Most showed little interest in the subject matter, and when discussing current events they could be counted on to parrot their parents' contempt for war protesters and longhaired hippies. They were good kids. Their goodbye letters to me emphasized the curliness and length of my hair, captioned with my words imploring them to evaluate our country's history from a more critical standpoint. I hoped that the few with intellectual curiosity would go on to college and that every last one of them would somehow avoid conscription.

In six weeks I would graduate, but little did I think about it, making up for lost time in the full thrall of a passionate life. I tried to put off worrying about what effect Meris' plan to transfer to school in Ohio next year would have on our relationship. With the arrival of spring, I started playing music in the parks, where among sizeable groups of people routinely up for singing and jamming, I noted how much my new- found self-confidence was facilitating greater ease in meeting women. I plowed through my last semester preparing for finals and commencement, a ceremony I felt I could safely avoid, as I was sure my father was unlikely to attend, and my mother probably unwilling to make other arrangements to attend alone. Then Nixon invaded Cambodia and all hell broke loose on virtually every college campus, except perhaps for places like Texas A & M.

The history unfolding in the streets shoved aside any concern about a now meaningless graduation ceremony or any plans thereafter. Striking students from the university's staid School of Education, mostly young women from Long Island and Westchester County, were among the first protesters I saw that May Day morning as I sensed the imminent possibility of a major student uprising. The Cambodian incursion unleashed the previous day had stirred up the nation's universities like nothing else yet. Rallies and marches sprung up throughout the weekend. Finals were cancelled. Then, on Monday afternoon May 4th, the news spread that National Guard troops deployed to Kent State in Ohio in the wake of protests had shot and killed four unarmed students. In all, National Guard troops had fired sixty-seven rounds of live ammunition in a thirteen second period that, ended the lives of four, and paralyzed nine others, all participants of an angry but unarmed crowd of protesters. Kent State thus became the powder keg that everybody had feared, resulting in mass strikes at more than four hundred fifty colleges and universities, including (unsurprisingly) my own. Ten days later, another overreaction by police resulted in the deaths of two students at Jackson State in Mississippi. My college graduation, along with those ceremonies at many other schools, the sacred rite of every American parent, was cancelled.

Graduation cancelled. Now his son's generation had deprived my father of the *option* to attend an event he had likely had no interest in coming to anyway. Leaving the Hub to return home made even less psychological sense now, but our lease had expired. I had graduated minus pomp and circumstance and about to engage the world in the midst of an ever-burgeoning national trauma now morphing into the nation's most divisive phenomenon since the Civil War. This failed to matter a hill of beans, however, relative to the undeniable fact that I had no job.

Once home the clash followed swiftly. The wailing of Tim Buckley's *Goodbye and Hello* from the Stromberg Carlson stereo in the living room accelerated the process in much the same manner that inflation had grown the Big Bang. Production values notwithstanding, Mr. Buckley's razor-like tenor raving against the *ancien regime* had exhausted what remained of Herman's sensibilities. Charging down the stairs, he demanded that I get out. Unadvisedly choosing to mumble a remark about the sudden spike in the household's current misery index, I came dangerously close to being assaulted. Clara moved into crisis mode, her behavior suggesting she'd long seen this coming. She accompanied me to the house of a trusted friend, another educator, a retired superintendent of schools, a decent and enlightened man who asked me two questions: did I think my dad had been drinking and was I afraid for my mother and sisters? Intrigued, I considered this. How much had Clara disclosed to him about our family drama up to now? I assured him that I thought things would be calm with me out of sight.

We had walked together to the superintendent's home and I thought how fitting that Clara should accompany me as I took my first steps on the road, a knapsack now slung behind my back, encased guitar in hand. For two nights I slept at the Granville's, moved on to stay with Meris at her family's home, then followed up on a tip from Artie's younger brother about *Abhain,* a free school based on the educational philosophy of A.S. Neill's Summerhill School. A group of high school teachers were intent on creating a summer educational alternative incorporating the radical notions of learning without coercion, optional courses, and a voice for every student in the educational community's activities and direction. Forty students had signed on. A recently disaffected college-graduated troubadour might find welcome and succor in this fold, located on the sloping hills of the Delaware River in northeastern Pennsylvania.

How fitting, I thought, after I met with the teachers, that at long last *I* would have the opportunity to go away to camp.

Chapter 6

DEAD BECKONING

Well I'll be sure to come back someday when I'm more fucked up, but I can't stay now-, an imminent draft physical, being away from Meris— but, hell, leaving so soon?

In the true spirit of dialectic, *Abhain* simultaneously represented an oasis and a maelstrom during the summer of 1970. There was no salary, just room and board. A version of George Leonard's Esalen Institute but for the youthful progeny of well-heeled Essex County families, *Abhain* was a perfect place for a minstrel. With a head count of some forty high school students and a faculty of five couples, three of whom had taught most of these students in high school, the facility functioned as a kind of retreat with art, dance, photography, and ceramics among its expressive activities. Having arranged for Meris to join me, and oblivious, or not, to the mutual attraction between a student and me, we both knew we had a shitstorm on our hands. It was partly just changes, but also I belatedly realized I had wanted to broaden my sexual horizons. A number of the underage women in this pastoral setting, thirty miles and one year on from Woodstock, would have been willing to oblige. In the spirit of the day, the wife of a faculty member undertook her own extramarital liason her deceived partner having subsequently suggested a tryst with Meris, an invitation that with some degree of difficulty she turned down. I fretted mightily at the summer's spiking drama.

And then, of course, there was music. Among the *Abhain* community music emerged at any time. Daily encounters had involved such intense conversation in both large and small groups that the relief provided by music would often roll forth for hours, fortifying my belief in the transcendence of the sharing the songs of the times. On occasion I would lead my youthful denizens in renditions of 'Tommy', having learned to play the iconic rock opera in the days following my first date with Meris, a concert by the Who.

Down the road from *Abhain* was a candle- making commune filled with lefty twenty-somethings. These quasi-Marxists exuded a humorless air, but a couple of them found acceptance in the *Abhain* community, and with some ambivalence I felt my superstar sheen wear off. The candle makers perceived Meris and me as petit bourgeois while they themselves constituted the *vanguard* living the Marxist dream. Never mind that the other adults of *Abhain* had long been ensconced as bourgeoise; these older, more established professionals were ripe for ideological plucking. The candle makers had it right about me not being a Marxist. How long they held their own separate identifications with communist ideology, I couldn't say.

Meris and I slogged through our changes. Our situation was best described by her decision to turn me in for having shared a joint with one of the students who had procured a small quantity of hooch during a brief visit home. The program had billed itself as an alternative to drugs, so my behavior had constituted a huge no-no, but her solution only bespoke her frustration with our relationship. The faculty showed displeasure with my judgment and let me know about it, but they also gave her little support for having squealed. Meris subsequently hatched the idea that at season's end we accompany her brother Spence and his girlfriend, Helene, to California. We could depart from them in Los Angeles and hitchhike up the coast together. She could leave me in San Francisco, where I might possibly sort out my life and determine what place she might/might not have in it. She lobbied hard for this plan, and I eventually came around. No other alternative sounded more interesting, and her idea had the advantage of being fun without forcing a commitment towards any single direction.

Truth told, Meris might have been thinking more seriously about my future than I was. I'd embraced *Abhain* as home. Remembering my first day there full of doubt and before her arrival, a teacher had twisted her ankle getting up from the lunch table, and in rushing to help her my fear suddenly evaporated. That evening I played for the first time, singing "Bob Dylan's Dream," in the kitchen for the staff and the first few students who had arrived. I felt immediately and totally accepted. In that moment I generalized this feeling, thinking that the music's affinity and my capacity to deliver it, would ease my way into many future scenes. The acceptance at *Abhain* only grew stronger even as Meris and I struggled. The students and I related well, in part because I was younger than most of the teachers. I easily adopted to the role of freewheeling mentor. Had I been so inclined, I might have sought to use some of the contacts at the program to find a high school teaching position in history or social studies, but if this thought ever occurred to me its presence had all the permanence of a passing neutrino. As with my reluctance to pursue anything practical, I didn't visualize myself in a band or pursuing music as a career, or for that matter pursuing anything as a career. The subject seldom arose because the teachers themselves were envious of my freedom and hardly looked forward to returning to their fall classes themselves.

Walking towards the car where Spence and Meris waited, I realized I didn't want to leave these people or this place. I recognized that not unlike when I'd sung at Boy's State, I'd made an impact. Their faces showed nothing but love. One of the teachers said to me, peering through the car window, "In ten minutes you'll know the meaning of *Abhain*." As we wound our way back to the city, and revealing questionable judgment. I wistfully concluded aloud that *Abhain* did embody love, but Meris responded only with a snort.

During the week before our westward odyssey, I met with Clara at a local diner, unaware that such a venue would provide the setting for many of our future interactions. She staked me several hundred dollars in the hope that I would use it to get started in California. Like Meris, she also thought the Bay Area suitable for me. My gratitude was accompanied by an unexpected sadness. Things were getting ahead of themselves with my mother thinking I was actually moving across the country.

Our entourage stopped in Boonton on the first day of our journey with the small hope that I could manage a short and civil goodbye with Herman, a gesture that I thought might make my leavetaking feel more real, but he and my mother were not home, so Meris and I hung out with my sisters for half an hour, sitting in the late afternoon sunshine of our front yard. Miri would soon return to Greality for her sophomore year of college, and we spoke of a possible visit, what with both of us out west. Then it was time to go.

* * *

In the early dark hours of Sunday morning, the four of us, tentless, plunked down our sleeping bags at an eastern Ohio rest stop. At daylight we traversed the Buckeye state, drove through the endless expanse of the near-harvest of the Indiana corn crop, and ended the day in Springfield, Illinois, where we visited Lincoln's home and grave. The next day we passed through the St. Louis arch and rumbled through the eastern front of the Great Plains. Meris and I had become irritable, in part from sharing the compressed quarters with her brother and his girlfriend, but also from the visual impact of the land itself—ever more flat and monotonous once we left eastern Kansas at Lawrence. The sheer emptiness of the prairie grated. For diversion Spence and I traded lines from the acid comedy troupe, The Firesign Theatre, driving Helene to distraction. Unknown to us, over the next several hundred miles, the land climbed inches per hectare to the mile high front -range in Colorado. Seeing the mountains for the first time from a rise twenty-five miles east of Denver thrilled us all. Beyond was the true west. We marveled as we traversed the Sangre de Christo and San Juan Mountains of southern Colorado, stopping for an eerie nighttime view and tour of the ruins at Mesa Verde and arriving at the Painted Desert in Arizona the following afternoon. Twenty years later I would travel hundreds of miles just to linger in such places in contemplation of their natural beauty and mysteries, but on this maiden voyage I needed to be in motion; constant movement was the only real salve for my anxiety as I obsessed over my intentions.

"What's your problem?" Meris asked. Maybe she had regretted asking me along.

Staring off into the desert I wondered if I hadn't in fact taken on more than I could handle, profoundly unsure if I was prepared to deal with separating from her and with living three thousand miles away from everyone I knew. We parted from Spence and Helene in L.A.

After busing to Santa Barbara, we hitched the coast road north. Meris wanted to visit the Hearst Castle and, reluctantly, I went along to view the gaudy spectacle. She and I were the only jeans-wearing tourists, seriously outnumbered by men in red or green slacks with wives in pastel or khaki. My discomfort with regard to being with such *straights* exasperated her. My girlfriend deemed my attitude immature, having found this monument to crass grandiosity far more fascinating than did I. *If I should marry this woman, we will be experiencing this chasm for the rest of our lives.* We were petit bourgeois, but evidently I was more petit and she more bourgeois. I couldn't bear the thought that she would meet someone more to her liking, someone with greater facility for experiencing life in a mellow tone. It failed to occur to me that I might do the same, having ignored her observation that once I got to California "you'll wonder what you're still doing with me."

This melancholy was interrupted by the arrival of a vehicle that slowed down to pick us up at Route 1. Getting in, we instantly recognized our anticipated California. A joint was forthcoming, and we exchanged tales with the simpatico couple heading to visit friends up north. Droppping us at Big

Sur's Pfeiffer Beach we explored its sea caves by the light of the full moon over the Pacific where we then met additional like-minded souls who drove us to their apartment in Monterey where we enjoyed a first listening to the *White Bird* album by the Bay Area band It's a Beautiful Day. Romance had re-entered our lives in those few days as we reached San Francisco.

"Take as much time as you need," Meris said at the airport.

* * *

Rhode Island Eric should be here any minute, I thought, as I ordered a burger. He'd been right about Dark-Haired Gina. I sighed, knowing that I had one, two nights at the outside of sleeping on his couch before his expected company would require me to either find somewhere else to crash or to leave town. I'd just gotton off the phone with Clara who had told me the Selective Service had dropped me a line with a date for my physical. I had related this news to Eric with some trepidation, but any worry that I held about him trying to persuade me of a specific course of action proved unnecessary. His presence calmed me after that phone call. When Clara had put my father on the phone, his first and only question to me, as became his pattern over the next decade was, "Where are you?"

Where I am now is Sproul Plaza, Berkeley, darting towards Dark-Haired Gina, who I spotted walking in the plaza, accompanied by a couple of her also attractive roommates who, as if on cue, exited the scene as Gina and I clasped hands and continued walking down Telegraph, up Dwight Way and then into the hills to watch the bay shimmer in the September sun and gaze at the Golden Gate Bridge between kisses.

The night before, Gina was already sitting on the steps leading up to Sproul Hall when I ambled onto the scene of some twenty odd people listening to guitar and conga. I walked up the steps where, six years earlier, Mario Savio had made his Free Speech Movement splash against UCal's regents. I launched into Tim Buckley's "Morning Glory", a ballad lamenting our generation's alienation not only from our bourgeoise parents but also from the hobos of yesteryear with whom we had so strongly identified. At the song's conclusion over a hundred people have congregated, a larger and more diverse communion than that of *Abhain.* The assemblage had attracted the attention of the campus police who, with a nastier reputation than the city cops then formed a perimeter around the swelling crowd. They eventually abandoned their vigil once they determined that our gathering was not an unauthorized political demonstration.

Gina moved closer. What kind of future might she be? My heart raced. There's another girl playing a recorder, Judy from Mills College, and then a beaming Eric who has sidled up with a mouth harp, each with a small cadre of their own. Together, we comprised *the thing itself* winding our way through the joy of song. The night sustained its rapture. Our cosmic decet drifted across the plaza to sit in the light of the university bookstore to meet and talk with each other for the first time, as finally the music gave itself up, the larger crowd having dispersed. Rhode Island Eric produced a flask filled with Mateuse that passed among us in a ritual of shared gratitude. I sang Dylan's "Chimes of Freedom," a celebration of the intimacy of sudden friendship among people unexpectedly thrown together in the midst of magic, a giving thanks for this night. Gina and her cadre slowly rose and peeled away and I looked at her, transmitting the thought, *Tomorrow-Here.* Eventually, Eric and I walk Judy and her companions to meet the all-night bus that will take them back to Mills. Returning through near-deserted streets to Eric's digs, he remarks that I would be better matched with Judy. He opined that I was no more than a transient object of fascination for Gina. "Watch out," he cautioned, "a moving target, that one." We enter his small rental house, tiptoe to his room where he beckons me to hear Bert Jansch's "Running Running from Home." I crash on the sofa in his living room.

Throughout Monday I knew I risked the brink. *It's all hanging by a thread. If I stay, then I need to find a place to live and deal with the army here.* Sipping my coffee at the Med, while gazing at the red headed Tarot reader at her station down the street, I knew I didn't trust what could happen to me here, at least as far as the army was concerned. Visions of induction at the Oakland processing center immediately followed by eight weeks of boot camp and then off to Vietnam like the piece of meat Herman had feared. I won't last a week in Southeast Asia.

Arriving was one thing. Staying would mean quite another. Staying involved cutting ties, letting Meris go, something that might be the best for both of us, but hardly simple. In the swirl of the weekend events I had almost forgotten her face, a fact that now brought me up short. Gina was an unknown quantity, but I was interested. I bargained now, the very nature of growth bearing down on me. I persuaded myself that I could meet its challenge if it weren't for the draft, wondering, though, if that weren't just an excuse. Maybe I also wasn't ready to leave Meris, or live somewhere so far from anyone I really knew. I left the Med and strolled the small square block of People's Park. Sixteen months ago, California governor, Ronald Reagan, had ordered two hundred state police to seize it from the University of California for having permitted political demonstrations to occur there, thus having fulfilled his campaign promise to rid the university of what he had called "communist sympathizers, protesters, and sex deviants."

It's all coming down right now. Damn! I thought I would have more time, wanting adventure and predictability all at once, not asking for too much, was I? Monday in Berkeley seemed like Monday everywhere else, only more so.

There, Gina's now walking towards the apartment, carrying two grocery bags that she lets me help bring inside. She motions to the courtyard, where she confronts me, "You love someone else somewhere." *There's no room at the inn.* Stunned, I am speechless. Of my fears of the draft, I said nothing yesterday. Now, I don't have it in me to do so. This thing is ending before it begins. I decide for the sake of my ego to turn it into a prophecy. Fate has intervened, that's right. Instead of dealing with the hard fact that she won't make life easy for me, I seize her rejection as the reason I should return east, where among the familiar I will find a way to beat conscription.

* * *

Not forty-eight hours later, those freedom chimes had disintegrated into a bottomless Monday malaise. "Come back when you can," Eric said. I nodded appreciatively.

I saw Judy before leaving. Over dinner with friends she extolled the happening of the previous Saturday evening to her assembled friends. We walked the campus where I summarized my dilemma. "We could meet in Boston next June," she suggested. I agreed, feeling the curtain coming down. She and Gina, respective oracles of light and dark were pointing me home. *You love somebody else somewhere.* I perused the bulletin board in the UCal student union building for a ride east. One was departing the next day for Boulder, the first stop eastward on the trail of the so-called "liberated zones" of Lawrence, Madison, Ann Arbor, and Cambridge, notable cities where higher consciousness allegedly reigned. I signed on.

Waking up somewhere beyond Reno among my fellow travelers, hurtling inland, a bitterness now filled me, the perceived sin of self-transgression, the malady of existential guilt, its primary symptom an acute regret for decisions that involve the abandonment of the path of authenticity. *Something has gone out of me...*

Chapter 7

THE 4F HIGHWAY

I looked at Boulder's Flatirons. Wasn't I just here? Thumbing my way to Greality for a visit with Miri I arrive within a couple of hours having first observed the mountains in distant silhouette, a reminder that I was now in the Great Plains. One could imagine the early settlers on their westward odyssey coming to a sudden halt as they gazed at the two-mile plus high barrier before them.

How Miri would react to my earlier than expected arrival had preoccupied me as I entered this town named for the nineteenth century newspaperman who had exhorted his countrymen *Go West, young man...* The quiet unsettled me. I reached her apartment that she shares with three other young women, and after a heartfelt hug my sister offered her expected surprise. Taking this in, I realized that what I could minimally justify to myself I would find even more difficult to explain to her, that my compliance with Uncle Sam required my being near people I knew in the event of induction, and this meant returning to New Jersey. The words faltered, but if Miri understood my reasoning, she made no reply. I took her silence to mean that she might be disappointed, having hoped I would stay in California. Having just come from Berkeley, the hotbed of radicalism, why couldn't I have found the help to resist conscription there? My answer made internal sense but saying it aloud did not. I had lacked the bravura to walk into a draft resistance group or committee and explain my situation in the hope that I could find a place to stay and work out a plan, including, if necessary, an exit strategy from the country. After Gina I gave no serious consideration to that plan, feeling as if I might be in the early stages of bad luck. The truth was that I was just plain scared to let go of so much that was familiar while under such duress.

In the evening Miri fronted a trio at a local watering hole, where I joined her onstage for a couple of well-received songs. The next day I caught a Greyhound heading north to Cheyenne, Wyoming, a locale that made Greality resemble a liberated zone. I transferred to an interstate bus headed to Chicago, planning to get to Ohio to visit Meris. On the long journey across the plains, I expected to be accompanied only by R.D. Laing's, *The Politics of Experience*, and was thus startled by the vivacious brunette who sat next to me. By the time we had crossed into Nebraska, I fervently wished for the vehicle's transformation into an overnight sleeper train. My new companion too was bound for the Windy City, on her last leg of a westward jaunt that had included the Pacific Northwest. In the midst of our fooling around she invited me to come with her to Chicago. Such an adventure was not without appeal, but as the bus approached Des Moines at dawn, my left-brain had assumed control. I bailed and flew to Ohio. Catching a bus to the city's airport, I sat next to a high school kid on his way to school, who asked me where I was going, telling myself I will always remember this conversation knowing that over the ensuing years I will think about him. By noon I had arrived in Ohio, realizing that my lust for experience was turning out to be much tamer than I had imagined it to be. The bus encounter I construed as another message from the universe imploring me to be careful about what I wished for. Anyway, I'd let Meris know I was coming. If California was out, Chicago was only more so.

Managing to hitchhike successfully out of Ohio's capital city, its defiant governer still justifiying the Kent State shootings, constituted no small achievement, as Columbus was well known for its hostility to hitchhikers. Halfway to Athens, nearing the western foothills of the Appalachians, I had anticipated our reunion might be tense; hence my lack of impatience with the length of time it took to find another ride. One eventually came, and I arrived in town early Friday evening, joining some students sitting at a monument on the east end of the campus, where I hoped to gain my bearings before meeting Meris at her dorm. I took out my guitar, played a couple of songs that broke the ice, and struck up a conversation with a poli sci senior who subsequently invited me to crash at his apartment. Intrigued by the brief summary of my hejira, Benson and I soon established an easy affinity that would continue during future visits to Athens.

It was indeed awkward with Meris. Her room was small, and she shared it with another student so privacy wasn't possible. Vowing to leave at least a day earlier than I'd planned, the two of us walked to the main part of town hoping to decompress. At a candy store we discovered a new delicacy—chocolate stars—whose consumption now provided much -needed succor. We went to a movie, had a late dinner, and after I introduced her to Benson she started to relax with the idea of my hanging around, as our mutual ease with him provided a social context that we evidently needed. In Benson,

Meris and I experienced the first feeling of mutual friendship we'd known since Boston. The next afternoon we attended a football game, a point of significant departure from our life last year in the Hub, where recreation meant walking or playing Frisbee. Her thoughts weren't difficult to read:

> *What do we have left? Do you really want to be with me?*
> *I still love you but what will you do here? It's different now, I don't*
> *know. What will you do here?*

My draft physical was scheduled for the following Thursday so I hit the university's ride board and was soon gone on the last leg to the coast Monday morning, arriving in New Jersey for a reunion with the *Abhain* brethren, who seemed unambiguously delighted to see me. Some reported struggling with their readjustments to high school, but not as much as some of *Abhain's* teachers, one having suffered a breakdown shortly after school had started. These people, staff and kids meant a lot to me. Seeing them again, even if after a period of only a few weeks, had fortified me for the next morning's ordeal. We adjourned to a nearby park where we schmoozed in the early autumn colors and for frisbee-tossing. They asked me about my travels, and insisted that there was no way the army would take me. I marveled at them, bewildered by how much more open and disclosing they were than my own peers and I had been during high school.

There was no need to arrange transportation to the induction facility, as Uncle Sam would pick up all invitees by bus. I boarded the vehicle promptly at 4:30 A.M. and headed into Newark, where I joined my fellow *69ers* whose number had quite literally come up. I was immediately taken to an army shrink, who predictably informed me that my discharge from the navy didn't preclude the army's interest in me. I remained mute in the absurd hope that the lines in my brow, along with the tenseness of my body would provide enough reason for the shrink to carefully consider his options.

What ultimately disqualified me from service though was my failure to pass succeeding tests of army classification involving mechanical reasoning. The years of paying dues to Herman's never-ending frustration over my inability to assemble or disassemble objects had finally paid off! I was interrupted after the fourth test (each one involving a more elementary skill set), by the increasingly beleaguered corporal. He tapped me on the shoulder and gestured for me to accompany him to a Fellini-esque room occupied by a score of men in their underwear. I waited for my time to turn and cough, and then approached the chamber of the arbiter where I was summarily informed me that I had been rejected for military service. I tried to look mildly disappointed, retrieved my clothes and exited the building into the bright sunshine of Newark. Looking for the nearest phone booth, I called Clara and Meris. Relieved, my mother's follow-up question about my plans went unanswered. I ambled around the city streets in subdued euphoria, thankful for the outcome, but knowing that others on that bus and in that facility wouldn't be so lucky, that some will die or suffer some dreadful physical and/or mental wound in this pointless war. I received my 4-F from the army during a visit with Meris a few weeks later.

Chapter 8

RESTLESS

I had moved into the West 85th street apartment near Broadway with aspirations of obtaining a hack license so that I could drive a cab in the city of New York. In its infinite wisdom, however, the Bureau of Hackneydom had determined that my psychiatric ineligibility for military service also meant that I did not possess the necessary emotional stability to ferry passengers through their boroughs. Finding other work meant having a modicum of motivation with the result that I spent far too much time visiting *Abhain* brethren across the Hudson.

Meris and I conducted an expensive long distance phone relationship. A counterculturally based workaround existed that involved the vertical sliding of a gum wrapper in a pay phone's receiver slot which mimicked the placement of coins. I'd heard about this procedure from one of the candlemakers, some of whom were now ensconced uptown in Washington Heights. Loath to attempt the maneuver because of rumors that FBI and phone company agents patrolled the streets of Manhattan, on the lookout for such consumer chicanery, I only sparingly employed the scheme even though it worked famously. The savings, however, hardly seemed worth the psychological cost of looking over my shoulder for approaching G-men and goons. My paranoia was not wasted, however, because during that winter when the apartment had been burgarlized, my grandfather's watch was stolen. Herman was convinced that I had pawned it.

Meris visited, dropped off by her driver, a male student who I recognized from my visits with her, someone I thought might be her type, and someone with whom she'd just spent 12 hours in a car. It hadn't occurred to me that her having brought him upstairs to say hello made less likely any concern she'd cheated. Unable to suppress a flash of jealousy for which she took me to task, our long weekend failed to get off the ground. My room was as small as my ambition. Later that year Meris would quote her mother's horror over the prospect of her daughter transferring to school in New York where we would live together *"in that room."* My girlfriend might have considered living together and going to school in Manhattan if I had managed to get something going, but I was disinclined to apply for a conventional job or even arrange to substitute teach. I preferred to put my name in at temp agencies and was referred to short-term office jobs. Committed to classic underachieving, nothing would deter me from this ongoing lack of focus. Ostensibly, I wanted to ramble in a New York minute, but truthfully, I had no place in mind to which I might settle. My stance was unwarranted. Meris would eventually decide on studying next year in Italy.

I auditioned at high-end clubs in the Village on open mic Monday nights, the Bitter End and The Village Vanguard. There were always agents in the audiences, and I had hoped I might get noticed for my singing or songwriting. Nothing materialized. I didn't join the musician's union local, due to its New York cost. The scene was rife with singer- songwriters hoping for recognition as the next Bob Dylan in the wake of the icon's retreat from touring.

The solo albums released by the former Beatles had recently enhanced the lure of solo careers as well. The key to success lay in writing and performing original material, and if you couldn't make that happen then you would toil in the labyrinth of Top 40, (Of course, you could do that regardless.) The first choice seemed unattainable and the second undesirable, so my music remained in as much limbo as the rest of my life.

The truth:

I had no real interest in the music business, but that didn't stop me from acting as if I did. I was going nowhere, but not alone, as the concept of upward mobility had also failed to resonate with a large segment of my peers. The counterculture's ascendancy had implied that money mattered less than anything , that if one earned enough to cover basic needs then things were copasetic. The period's aphorism, "Dope will get you through times with no money better than money will get you through times with no dope," defined the code, whether one partook or not. My cohort also had eschewed marriage. An unencumbered existence now occupied a position of status, even if the reality was lonely. Moreover, the stirrings of feminism had begun to challenge traditional gender roles. A corollary of confusion now existed re monogamous expectations.

Meris and I would neither break up nor make our relationship work. Despite our hassles, though, we also experienced the warmth and familiarity of an established love. Not enamored of university life in general, she nevertheless lived the more or less structured life of a student. I visited every several weeks, hitching rides to and from Ohio. While there I'd stay with Benson whose company smoothed over these comings and goings. Unlike my Boston friends he was humanities-driven and emotionally open.

* * *

The May Day protests took place in Washington on the first anniversary of the Kent State shootings. The war raged, and opposition had reached an all-time high. Since the government hadn't stopped the war, the May Day tribe advanced the idea that the people stop the government, starting with the disruption of morning rush hour traffic in the nation's capital by means of human barricades. The previous weekend, the last one in April, the largest demonstration against the war to date had gathered more than half a million people in front of the Capitol. The crowd had included many middle and upper middle class professionals and business people, not just the perennial student and twenty-something protesters. The movement had come a long way since the Mobilization eighteen months earlier.

The surreal intensity of the event was evident from the moment several of us had stuck out our thumbs en route to Washington. Our small conclave- Meris and I, along with a couple of the candlemakers, were soon chased from the New Jersey Turnpike by the State Police, who appeared in no mood to allow easy passage to the nation's capital on their major arteries. We instead slunk back across the Hudson to take a bus, eventually arriving at the Esplanade on the Potomac, which served as headquarters for the event. On Saturday there were rumors that bands seen at Woodstock were set to perform, but as the day turned to evening they failed to show. Some luminaries did appear, however; e.g., Phil Ochs, Charles Mingus, and the Beach Boys. The musical range from Mingus to the Beach Boys demonstrated the widening demographic of protest, and the presence of the Beach Boys themselves, the real life link between the nerds and jocks, further emphasized just how mainstream the level of disgust with Nixon and the war had become. The festivities went on into the night. As the assemblage finally prepared to bed down in anticipation of Sunday's preparations, hopes for sleep in the shadow of the Jefferson Memorial were vitiated. At six a.m. the bullhorn amplifying the voice of police chief Jerry Wilson admonished us to vacate the premises or suffer arrest. Divide and conquer, we reasoned, yawning our way to McDonalds for an earlier than anticipated coffee and breakfast.

Meris and I lolled about the Mall until the strategy sessions commenced. Neither of us felt all that comfortable with escalating the protest from marching in a demonstration to street action, but here we were. The candlemaking collective had issued its own directive- *aux barricades.* They then relaxed by swapping leftwing stories with interstate comrades, while Meris and I quietly wondered whether we might not experience a more meaningful sense of belonging at a personal growth setting such as the Esalen Institute three thousand miles west at Big Sur.

Opting for the less confrontational street maneuver, she and I elected to place, or if necessary shove, leaflets into the hands of frustrated government employees idling on their stalled commute to work. We avoided arrest, although I had a close call when approaching a vehicle with two plainclothesmen, one I noticed holding, possibly fondling a billy club. The officers politely declined my offer of informational materials while inquiring if, perhaps, I'd like to get in and go downtown with them. Able to hastily beat it on down the line, I experienced an undeniable gratitude for the momentary cloak of protection.

Later that afternoon, word reached us that the candlemaking collective had unexpectedly returned to New York to 'regroup'. Radicals in retreat to fight another day, we surmised, appreciating the irony that we remained the only members of our contingent still standing and on hand for the events to follow. With the exit of the candlemakers, Meris and I now needed new accommodation for the night. Aaron, now a law student at George Washington University then stepped forth. Coincidentally, he had volunteered to be one of hundreds of legal observers for the May Day events. Donning a white armband designating his role he dropped us off on Tuesday morning at the plaza situated between two bastions of American government, the Internal Revenue Service and the Justice Department. Exiting his car our attention immediately turned toward the gathering thousands standing in front of us. A massive and unauthorized, non-violent sit-in demonstration was about to begin. In full view of these government behemoths, its employees now distracted from their assigned tasks peered down at the we- who -were -about –to- be-gassed at the hands of Washington's finest. Our locking of arms was short lived, as we hastened to cover our burning eyes, the ante now having been considerably raised. Suddenly the gas ceased and the police began arresting protesters one by one. The spectacle of several thousand unarmed young people under siege in the presence of several hundred government employees—witnesses, bad press- had shifted the tactics of law enforcement.

During the several hours that followed one couple exchanged marriage vows as the police cordoned off the area eventually arresting every last demonstrator, packing us off to spend the night at the Washington Armory. Once there we were intermittently fed baloney sandwiches and also unintentionally entertained by the hourly changing of the National Guard when new soldiers replaced their counterparts to stand at parade rest on what was the blue line for hockey games. We would shake each other awake to applaud the arrival of the substitutions. Both the police and guardsmen, we noticed, were fed McDonald's hamburgers, the only time that I can recall such food occupying a higher place in a hierarchy of culinary quality.

Our mass arrest had solved the problem of accommodations for Tuesday evening. Bleary-eyed on Wednesday, separated by gender, we first spent quality time in a D.C. holding cell. That afternoon I appeared before Judge Washington (sic) pointing out to my government-appointed lawyer that the signature on the field arrest form did not match the badge number of the arresting officer, a fact that my lawyer happily related to the judge. My reward came in seeing His Honor cast a disgusted look at the prosecution as he dismissed my case.

I walked out into the afternoon haze of a spring Washington day looking for Meris, herself now strung out from her overnight incarceration, her own case dismissed an hour earlier. Whatever relief she felt regarding my acquittal was overridden by a greater irritation. She had accurately observed a flirtation I'd allowed myself the night before in the armory, a behavior that I minimized but didn't deny. My Don Juanism remained alive and well, I glumly acknowledged as we left Washington later that day.

* * *

With much relief and heartfelt gratitude toward the city of Boston and specifically towards their hack bureau, I resettled in the Hub as spring arrived. Draft status had not been an agency-related concern in Boston, home to legions of disaffected male college graduates ripe for cab-driver plucking. I would report for my four p.m. to midnight shift with the McNulty cab company, a mere stone's throw from Fenway Park armed with a Herman Hesse novel for those lulls between fares. If not exactly a dream job, driving a cab provided the combination of solitude and unpredictability so valued in the young adult mind that conversely despised authority and routine. Working in spurts and taking frequent sabbaticals made the hack life suitable at least until the job's virtues devolved into isolation and boredom. I made steady income from this enterprise, and life was easier. I resumed my friendship with Mal and others. Still, I couldn't shake an unsettled spirit. The very cozy confines of Back Bay and Allston reminded me that I had failed to take that next step, *the moving away from everyone I knew phase*, that still troubled me from the challenges of the previous summer.

Meris prepared for her junior year abroad. She had thrown more than her share of pots in the western foothills of the Appalachians. Now she wanted to move to Florence where she could immerse herself in that city's artistic treasures and also find a way to shake me once and for all.

I'd missed it and now she's leaving me. Having failed to take the next step, she'll do it for both of us, only I'll be the more miserable for it. The signs hadn't changed—my attraction to other women, the May Day flirtation, a dalliance in New Haven while hitching to Boston—but I still paid no heed.

Now that she'd made her decision these escapades ceased. My obsessions spiked. Regret returned with a vengeance. I made the unadvisable, dumb ass decision to return to *Abhain* for the wistful or delusional purpose of self-soothing. Unlike last fall when, facing the draft, I drank from its fountain of support, I found now the well had run dry, validating what the Celts were known to say, that, *you can't step in the same Abhain twice.* They had become awfully serious during the intervening year. The candlemakers had apparently won. I took my leave not as the heroic figure of the previous summer, but as a sheepish and misapprehended shadow.

* * *

Slinking back to the Hub I hooked up with Subway Tom, a guitar player I'd met earlier in the summer in the New York's 59th Street underground at Central Park. He lived in Boston, Jamaica Plain, with his roommate. The three of us motored up Route 1 and over the border into Canada, my first time out of the country, and not in the role of draft resister. At dusk we arrived at the Bay of Fundy in New Brunswick. A full moon over the Atlantic cast its light on the world's strongest tides. The moonlight reminded me of California, now almost exactly a year ago, Meris and me along the Pacific coast four time zones west when everything still felt possible. Adrift in speculation and anomie, I now imagined having arrived in Canada instead as a draft evader. Would my life have worked out better living on that particular edge? While the price of exile would have been high, would I have discovered more meaning than on this increasingly aimless path? I exited this reverie under the cover of nite bewildered by the line of thought. I needed that level of stress to attain a purpose-driven existence?

Onward to New Scotland we trekked. My mood swung from elation -the beauty of the shoreline -to despair, the latter prevailing even amidst the beauty of Cape Breton Island. My intention to return to Boston by means of my thumb now caused my fellow travelers concern, but I crossed the Cabot Trail and began the thousand -mile hitchhike back to Boston, watching the two of them continue eastward. Better for them, I thought. The two old friends could now enjoy their vacation without having to deal with my current misery.

My guitar and I attracted rides through Canada easily enough. At St. John, near the US border, I bunked in a hostel where a traveler's guitar was stolen during the night. Luckily not mine, I think, but too close for comfort. There I met Cornelius from Quebec, en route to visit friends at my alma mater. He and I hitched the rest of the way together, only getting stuck once in Downeast Maine. Also a musician, Cornelius and I worked up a few songs for an open mic session at 700 Commonwealth Ave, a BU dorm Karlinsky had long ago dubbed its trio of drab thrusting towers, *Cases' Last Erection*, in homage to the university's then recently retired president.

We performed well but Cornelius was on his way to D.C. Friends from the road return to the road. *I have to get off the road*, but doing so resembled the effort involved in kicking a drug. I needed desperately to settle down, but I was about to run into a string of bad luck. First, my Martin was stolen. At an early autumn jam in Cambridge, near Harvard Square I connected with a lithesome acquaintance from my student days, Dark-Eyed Debbie. There was a hanger- on at the jam, who the next day sought out Subway Tom's roommate claiming that I'd sent him to bring me my guitar. The latter's gullibility sealed the separation between my guitar and me. Maybe having left the two friends in Cape Breton held greater implications than I'd thought at the time. I moved on to other digs in Cambridge with friends I made when having performed for the Vietnam Veterans Against the War. Here I waited for the insurance money to replace that wonderful guitar, the gift from my father, his present that had accompanied me through my relationship with Meris, at *Abhain*, and the magic of Sproul Plaza.

Dark-Eyed Debbie, meanwhile, had found my distress at having my guitar ripped off extremely unattractive, and dismissed me. The Washington St. apartment in Cambridge was a happier place, occupied by a couple of Vietnam vets and their high-spirited girlfriends. I admired the vets' resiliency of spirit. They were determined to make up for lost time having fully embraced an idealism that had lost its moorings among the rest of us over the two years post Woodstock. Then I heard from Meris, who was now missing us. My reply was heartfelt: *come home, and we'll start again.* But before mailing it I received another note, this one a break up letter. Writing and ripping up replies, I eventually mailed one that I immediately unsuccessfuuly tried to retrieve, pleading with the postal authorities for its return. I saw friends, hacked, and played the occasional gig, living in a daze wondering what to do and where to go. Marion, one of my housemates, a kind soul with whom I had been carrying on a casual and platonic intimacy, affected words both genuine and ironic: "You're not going anywhere." I couldn't disagree, and was both oddly comforted and annoyed…

CEASURE

…Had our parents' generation, recently referred to as 'the greatest generation" switched places with our own don't you think history would have turned out out pretty much the same? Don't the times dictate the flow...?

Chapter 9

CRASH

...1972 had some some very bad apples. The certainty of Richard Nixon's re-election now hung over both the counterculture and mainstream liberals, like sour breath from the mouth of a silent majoritarian on a three day bender. Democratic frontrunner Edmund Muskie had been done in by the dirty tricksters of the Nixon campaign. Folkie Eric Anderson had released his downer album *Blue River*, and I was literally crossing highways. I'd gone to Maine in early January, that's right, January, at the urging of and along with one of the VVAW buddies who had a musical connection living there, a mandolinist. The two of us could gig together at apres-ski locations, a notion that had more appeal than did driving a cab in the Boston winter, which provides an idea of how unappealing driving a cab in a Boston can be. After a month of bitter cold and snow among the Maine stoics, I snapped. There was no drug that could account for the sudden onset of this bizarre mental state, but there was plenty of alienation. I found myself in the throes of a major bummer. Jack of the VVAW had turned drill sergeant once he and I had arrived in western Maine, where he daily castigated me for my apparent unsuitability for the very environment he had been sure back in Boston would work like a tonic. I felt as claustrophobic and isolated as I had since my days at the ironworks, too close quarters with the wrong cohort.

Seargent Jack departed to resume life in the city, but things didn't improve. I struggled to adjust. Never quite having established a proper relationship with the woodstove, why I didn't leave sooner can only be explained by my hope that Tommy and I could work out a repertoire and gig in the area so I could support myself through the winter ski season. I didn't like the addition of long underwear to my daily wardrobe and didn't understand these people, hard and disinclined towards conversation, in short, as cold as the weather. After living with Tommy and his girlfriend in what was a delightful cabin suitable for the two of them, I moved to a room at an inn situated in the village of Kingston. He and I were slated to perform there on Saturday nights but the concert room still needed finishing. It was in that building where I began to feel myself going crazy.

The inn too, plain and sparsely furnished, lacked warmth. The innkeeper, a transplanted Long Island lantsman, sized me up as a reluctant shtetl exile. He shook his head when he'd see me—"Meshuganah," he'd laughingly and repeatedly remark, unaware, that what he lacked in empathy he more than made up for in diagnostic acumen.

Initially, I thought my alarming state of mind would be brief but not so. At the onset, I literally had experienced myself as a lost small child. This was frightening and my accompanying agitation pointed to the inescapable realization that I was in trouble. Increasingly self-conscious, I engaged in what was quickly becoming an absurd litany of continuous apology for my demeanor with these unfamiliar and unavailable people.

My agitation made it difficult to sit still and like a landlubbing Captain Ahab I took to the highways in the dead of New England's winter. Thinking that I needed to return to the familiarity of Boston, only to cross the interstate heading back to Kingston I found no solace, eventually taking to heart the innkeeper's words, "You should go home to the ones who know you best." I stopped in Boston and then New York, but when even among friends I saw no change in my mental dysfunction that's what I did. Having run out the string, I landed back in Boonton.

It was strange being home—the first few days characterized by a suspension of judgment on everyone's part. I'd provided my parents no advance notice of my arrival. My astute mother assured me that they would help, a notion that in that moment scared me not a little, as I wondered what form that help would take. My father made a reasonable effort not to give me too much trouble but my state of mind challenged him. A week into my stay he remarked that when he had occasion to visit *his* family as a young man starting out in the world, he would arrive home with gifts for his parents.

I found a swing shift job at a knitting mill that minimized proximity to him at least on weeknights while allowing me some one-on-one with Clara during the day. The catalyst for professional help was the termination of my employment. The mill's owner, a concentration camp survivor known for patience with his employees, declared as he let me go, "*Usually in America everyone is entitled to a second chance, in some cases a third, but not usually a fourth.*" Getting help, of course, had never been far from what remained of my own mind.

"Remained of my own mind" was a phrase that accurately described my state. I lacked motivation and felt such shame for having blown it all that I found it toxic to see anyone or have anybody know about my state of mind. I didn't seek counseling on my own, but by default agreed to let my parents find me a psychiatrist. The doctor recommended that I be immediately hospitalized. I resisted, overwhelmed by the financial cost to my parents and the consequent emotional cost to me, but acquiesced, having no confidence that I might know my best course. So I sojourned on the psych ward where I took some warm baths and started on medication, a problematic treatment plan because during the early seventies virtually no difference existed between what medications were dispensed to depressed patients from what were administered to psychotics and schizophrenics. Thus, my new friends, mellaril and stelazine, did little to improve my mood. They were intended to keep me from becoming agitated, which as far as I could tell was not an issue given how many hours I slept once I returned home after three weeks in the facility known as 'Franklin Five'. The attending psychiatrist, a Dr. Hammer (no kidding), described me as he sent me on my way as one of the 'most nervous guys' he'd ever met, how helpful.

There had been one attempt at intervention prior to the hospital. The local rabbi, a youngish fellow, not long out of seminary, had seen, after a couple of visits I had with him, an opportunity to cut his family counseling teeth on our family. The location for our session was the kitchen in Boonton's Jewish Center. He began by inquiring into how we each perceived the problem. Clara expressed a desire to understand the nature of my unhappiness, but was soon interrupted by my father's glaring assessment that "there is a fence between him and me" and that he (i.e., me,) had "built it." As an unintended therapeutic intervention on his part, his comments unleashed a profanity from me that even in my miserable state I knew was too strong and of course not helpful, but his take had brought me to the breaking point. As an ironic afterthought, it occurred to me that this was the first time my father had ever acknowledged me as having built anything, even if only metaphorically.

Well, this wasn't really what any of us wanted or needed. The only positive development to emerge from this sorry single session encounter had been my knowing that when push came to shove, I would fight in the fight vs. flight arena. Although I may have been transiently psychotic over the past two months I was basically one severely depressed young man who had given his old man one more thing to hold against him. He would hold this against me for years, episodically reminding Clara of my having 'cursed him out in the rabbi's study'. (Never, however, did he reference that session directly with me.) Under such circumstances, one could see how a stint in the hospital provided a form of respite.

I felt double bound, wanting to leave, but having insufficient psychological strength to know where to go or what to do. I rejected the sound idea put forth by my parents of finding a suitable job, buying a car, and living at home for several months until I could afford to move out. This plan though would keep me here too long. During much of the lethargic summer I stubbornly clung to the idea, that with cessation of rambling I could still resume a significant piece of my familiar lifestyle.

Clara had been instructed that I should not be left alone upon my discharge, because my attending doc had considered me a suicide risk, an interesting assessment since despite the presence of suicidal thoughts I hadn't ever engaged in self-injurious behavior. My mother greeted me warmly every morning, listened patiently to whatever incoherent utterances I produced, and made every conceivable effort to soothe and normalize what I was feeling. Exercising a patience that Job himself would have respected (God presumably not having smitten him with a depressive disorder among his many other afflictions), she fortified me, even as her heart was breaking to see me in such a state. When I heard Artie was in town on break from law school, I nervously allowed myself to see him, but wondered why I would wish in my current condition to be with friends. How could I possibly relate to the progress in their respective lives without feeling worse for the knowledge? With the prodding of both my parents, I rode with him in his Citroen into Brooklyn, to visit Hal, in med school there, Beth, and their two-year old daughter. Standing on the pier and gazing across the East River, I tried to believe my oldest friend's injunction that I would be all right. My friends telling me I looked good made no sense to me. I considered their comments a form of cheerleading, and I knew my zombie-like demeanor much exacerbated by the medication regimen had to have made them uncomfortable. Though I desperately disliked the medication, I felt powerless to stop taking it.

I found a job as an orderly. It was within walking distance of my family's house at a nursing home for the retired firemen of the state of New Jersey. I wouldn't buy a car but I would pay for my therapy. The coordinator, a kind soul, had taken more than a passing interest in me, although he never came on. His gentleness was of great help and when later in the summer it was arranged that I should go to Greality to stay with Miri, he volunteered to use his vacation time to drive me there. My sister had sent me a copy of Rene Daumal's *Mount Analogue* and had asked me what I thought of it. When I told her the medication was blurring my vision she told Clara that I should come and live with her. It became the plan.

My appointment that week had required me to take the train, as my father needed the car. On the way home I encountered Ben Granville, but he barely looked up from his newspaper when I greeted him. Departing the train he didn't look back. I'd been shunned, in his mind, a mere malingerer. This hurt, but I took it as a sign that I needed a new start somewhere away from here.

Greality it was. In addition to Miri, Aaron's sister and brother-in law lived and worked in the psychology department of the local university. While preparing a feature on Adele and Fremont for an article for Boonton's local rag, Clara had disclosed my situation to Aaron's folks. They encouraged the move west, thinking that my getting to know Fremont would prove helpful.

Wracked now with guilt over the cost of this sorry episode, I prepared to leave Boonton and this house. During my last night my father had admonished me to "not corrupt Miri." When I heard his footsteps pivoting to my room early on the morning of my departure I prepared myself for more but he just stood at the door and quietly wished me good luck.

I hugged my mother. The loving stoic woman who had sat with me each day listening to my ragtime, caring for me long after she shouldn't have needed to—it was more than I deserved. Ray drove me and it wasn't easy in the beginning.

As we approached the Delaware Gap, doubts began to grow as the country spread out before me, now filling me with dread, in contrast to my westward journey of two years past when anxious moments had contrasted sharply with joyous expectancy. We pulled over at a rest stop while Ray waited for me to decide. I exited the car, indecisive, but when I heard him say we could turn around, I told him no, let's go, let's go west; let's go to Colorado.

Chapter 10

GREALITY THERAPY

Before Greality I lived in the mountains where Miri now student taught at a regional high school. She had found a rental house nestled against the northern rim of Clear Canyon that she shared with a fellow student teacher. I slept on the living room sofa. The house overlooked a silver mine. I had arrived in September, having crossed the country with Ray who didn't stay more than an hour after depositing me with my sister. I watched him drive down the hill out towards the interstate. He'd bestowed a kindness, yet another one I couldn't repay, and one that I fervently wished I hadn't needed to accept. He'd promised to write, something that made me uncomfortable with its implication that we would develop an ongoing correspondence, a hope on his part but for me an unwanted obligation. I wanted this chapter behind me even as I knew that had he not volunteered I likely wouldn't have managed any other way to get here.

I chucked my medication after my visit from Sid, now teaching in a Denver suburb, who had recently settled in an adjacent mountain town. Walking through the old west town those first few days, I let the mountains enfold me, newly experiencing some long needed mental calm. Within a week Miri and I had scored a gig at *The City Dump*, a local bar that had hired us to play both Friday and Saturday evenings. We continued there until just before Thanksgiving, the longest house gig that I ever played. Performing with my sister was good. Not only did we have musical chemistry, but also compared to the East, the audiences were downright friendly. Plus, the Dump had a separate music room away from its bar, where people who wanted to listen could congregate. I wrote my first song in over a year, a somewhat hopeful ballad with a lyrical nod to the healing powers of my environs. Our repertoire also included Miri's own "Song of the River" with its inspired lyric:

You look at me as though I'm troubled,
You look at me as though I'm sad
But you don't know that sadness is deep within your own mind,
And Baby, it's been keeping you behind,
Baby, it's been keeping you behind...

And when the sun shone down on the river
And when the rain showered honey through the trees
That's when I knew my soul was alive again
And alive is all I ever want to be; alive is all I ever want to be.

My sister's comfort level with other musicians made me rethink the wisdom of performing solo. I needed other musicians, that having been my intent when setting out for the disaster that had been Maine. Our duet was comfortable and musically rewarding. Versus a solo act the only mixed aspect of performing with my sister was the occasional decline in flirtation from women in the audience who were convinced Miri was my significant other.

I needed to make more money than what the gigs paid, so I signed on with a construction crew building condos up the mountain. The national migration into Colorado, now underway required more housing in mountain towns near the ski areas. I signed on for the task of digging postholes in Silver Lode, a Victorian burg just below the Continental Divide. My tenure, however, lasted only as long as the 1972 World Series, an exciting seven-game affair between the Oakland A's and Cincinnati Reds, my shoveling duties made less unpleasant by the presence of a like-minded contemporary. I was terminated when the foreman approached me one afternoon to tell me that he "could dig more dirt with a teaspoon than I could with a shovel."

I had no answer for his comment on a content level, but marveled at the man's unexpected capacity for metaphor, wondering if he'd composed it on the spot or had held it in reserve for just this occasion. I invited my colleague, who had momentarily contemplated quitting as a show of solidarity, to meet Miri. The two hit it off and carried on a liaison for several weeks, a development that I took some small pride in having facilitated. Just before she had arrived in Clear Canyon my sister had ended a relationship with the second love of her life, a singer songwriter from Greality who had let her down hard.

Like many of her Greality cohort, Miri had recently embraced the cult of a corpulent thirteen-year old Indian guru. Shortly before my arrival she had undertaken a pilgrimage to western Colorado where she and her similarly enthralled buddies sat at and/or kissed the feet of this pubescent spiritual marvel, who had imparted something called *knowledge*. Now, away from her fellow devotees, known more precisely as *premies*, and hanging out with her brother and his former labor comrade, she took to knocking back a tequila sunrise reentering her own zone of normalcy. We were enjoying ourselves, something I hadn't been sure would happen, worrying in the early going that my presence would burden her.

Every so often I gazed westward toward the Divide, and thought of California. When Berkeley bound travelers crashed with us for a few days after seeing us play at the Dump, I considered joining them, but wishing them luck I chose to stay behind. Whether it was because I didn't yet trust myself or because life here was good I couldn't say. I soon met a contingent of exiles from Flint, Michigan who had rented a house nearby. We spent election night together, and watched as Richard Nixon won, incomprehensibly, forty-nine states against the civilized George McGovern, who only carried Massachusetts. We faced another four years of Tricky Dick. Our general state of lamentation, notwithstanding, I experienced long overdue succor in the person of Rosanne in whose fine company I spent much of the next month.

The crowds at the Dump swelled with the advent of the colder weather. They liked our covers of songs like "The Ballad of Easy Rider," "Wild Horses," and "Ripple". Our originals were also well received. The skiers would soon be arriving, with the possibility of our earning more money during the high season, but Miri's placement was ending at Thanksgiving and so too would our run of gigs. Rosanne and I decided it had been fun, but there was no next step. I left for Greality. Mountain life had been a welcome but temporary tonic.

* * *

The thermometer had failed to rise above freezing those first two weeks in December. The extreme cold also had the unfortunate effect of ramping up the odor emanating from the Mountfort Company's feedlots north of town, Greality being home to the largest stockyards west of Chicago. My sister flew home for the holidays while I settled into the college town on the plains. The ensuing solitude felt welcoming. The campus had emptied with the end of the term. I read, played guitar and hung out in the music store, whose owner I had jammed with during my previous visit.

Leaving his store one evening, I took note of the movie marquis next door. *The French Connection* would show in a few minutes, and as I wasn't all that enthused with the prospect of walking the five blocks in the now single degree weather, I purchased a ticket. Not long into this crime drama, the first to win Best Picture as an R rated film, I experienced a dizziness and nausea that caused me to bolt into the freezing weather, where I expelled the soon frozen whatever it was that ailed me (in all likelihood the unadvisable second and third shots of tequila I'd imbibed earlier), onto Greality's holiday-adorned Main Street. My sensibilities restored, I pondered the curious juxtaposition of Advent with the showing of a film about heroin trafficking, ultimately concluding that the zeitgeist had reached even Greality.

All of this suggested that the time had arrived to call on Adele and Fremont, who lived in a small house between my present location and Miri's rental. With the temperature now zero degrees a journey home in stages seemed advisable anyway. A large exuberant man opened the door, greeted me warmly and hustled me in from the cold. A welcome cup of hot tea appeared. I recounted the tale of Main St to their bemusement. Although Adele was from Boonton, and Aaron's sister, because she was five years older, I barely knew her. In the present context we were *lantsmen,* not unlike our forbearers who encountered their old neighbors in lands far from their birth. Profoundly relieved at the ease of our interaction, (I only now realized how much I'd been depending on it.) I relaxed in their company amidst the sheaf of manuscripts that comprised their works-in-progress, their books and articles in the field of humanistic psychology. Fremont possessed a balance of wit and compassion I'd not yet experienced in any male. His ebullient, often provocative professorial style had made him a favorite of students and colleagues, while also raising eyebrows in administration circles. He and Adele had similar philosophies, disparate personalities, and a complementary relationship. Leaving their home towards midnight, I allowed myself the thought of pursuing a Masters degree in psychology.

* * *

Our recently reelected president had decided to celebrate his victory by destroying the infrastructure of North Vietnam so that the raised expectations for the war's end could be met. His charismatic national security advisor, Henry Kissinger, had, after all, stated during negotiations in the fall that,"peace was at hand". Working against the deadline of a heavily Democratic Congress convening in January, (Tricky Dick had carried forty-nine states but the electorate in their wisdom had voted in a strong counterweight.) Nixon saturated North Vietnam with bombs for twelve days, mostly to demonstrate to the South Vietnamese that America would not abandon them. By mid-January a treaty was signed, and the marquis on that Main St. movie theatre read *Peace at Last*, at least for a day or two.

I asked few questions of Miri when she returned from her visit home. We resumed our musical association, adding a singer -guitarist, a transplant from upstate New York. Our trio was known as Yankee Folly Road, named for a street in Darwin's old haunt of New Palz. Three guitars, three voices, with accompanying three-part harmony made for interesting musical exploration. Miri and I composed songs, three or four-chord tunes whose lyrics spoke to personal, psychological, and spiritual concerns. We gigged at the university and at local clubs. A nice scene developed. What with these gigs and the odd job I paid my share of the rent, utilities, and food, although on occasion we availed ourselves of food stamps.

Darwin's buddies were older than both the college set and me, and I liked socializing with this more diverse group. Life proceeded with an easy rhythm. It was spring in Colorado, a bipolar weather pattern featuring days of sixty-five degrees followed by a foot of heavy wet snow that then evaporated just as suddenly, along with the vestiges of my depression. I made strides in forgiving myself. There was nothing I could undo. Kierkegaard's "Dreadful had already happened." I lived more in the present,

With real spring came the unraveling of the Watergate cover-up, as the Ervin committee chipped away at the iceberg of the Nixon Administration's abuses of power. We woke daily to the televised hearings from Washington that, with the two-hour time difference, would be underway. The disclosures kept coming, dramatic and damning weeklong testimony from John Dean that neither Nixon's highest aides, John Erlichmann and Bob Haldeman, could refute when it came their turn. When the news of Nixon's taping system emerged, a Rubicon of sorts was crossed. For almost another year, insisting that the tapes belonged to the executive branch, Nixon refused to release them, but even the edited versions had further eroded his credibility. The hearings gave hope to many that the country might be redeemed from the agonies of the last decade that some measure of balance could be restored by Nixon's eventual removal from office. It was closing in on ten years since JFK's assassination.

* * *

Bianca did not appear to be my type. A petite black-haired brown-eyed woman of Greek background, she was also extroverted and cheerful, qualities I found, if not quite discomfiting, then at least unfamiliar in a prospective girlfriend. Slow to realize that she had feelings for me and convinced I desired only her friendship, I saw other women, unsure I wasnted the role of being the first love of her life. Together we followed the Watergate hearings faithfully. Plunking on the living room sofa, we'd sip our coffee and munch on the Winchell's donuts she'd routinely bring, taking in the cadence of the exemplary Senator Sam Ervin's homey North Carolina drawl. We were cheered as he wore down first one and then another administration official, regarding as Howard Baker, the ranking republican member of the committee, put it, *"What did the president know and when did he know it?"*

The growing friendship between Bianca and Miri was good for my sister, whose closeness with her older friends had begun to fade. This added to my hesitancy to reciprocate Bianca's feelings. Rocking the boat seemed ill conceived: better to remain romantically uninvolved with someone whose friendship I valued, and to avoid complicating Miri's world. Pursuing other women, however, failed to solve the problem. There was no way to integrate anyone new into a scene that had suddenly become so vibrationally complex and enmeshed. Bianca hung in but I wasn't ready.

* * *

My parents now finally got to attend their first college commencement. They pulled into Greality in a spanking new turquoise 1973 Pinto to present to Miri as a graduation present. We hadn't expected their arrival until the following day, although my sister had urged me to clean up my space just in case. Now Herman found me sprawled across my bed in my unkempt room in essentially the same prone position I had been in ten months earlier when we had said our goodbyes in Boonton. His groan of displeasure had been the first sound I heard that morning. Though glad to see me, Clara didn't hesitate to express her displeasure over the admittedly awful appearance of my room.

The laxness with regard to sprucing up my quarters may have represented a preemptive indifference toward their arrival. I had intended to be absent from the festivities. Still, I shouldn't have pissed off Miri. Unconscious memories involving the aftermath of my cancelled graduation had likely been in play. For a few anxious hours during that day I felt my recovery was in jeopardy and so made haste to visit Fremont. We discussed the relative wisdom of my showing up at the dinner that he and Adele would be hosting for my family later that day, deciding I'd best stay away.

When our parents departed equilibrium was restored, minus a smidgen of guilt. Proximity had facilitated our music process. Darwin lived in the basement apartment next door with his girlfriend, and Alvin, a bassist in the other folk trio in town. Keeping the web going Alvin and Miri began keeping company. When I asked my sister how she felt about my continued presence I didn't get the feeling she wanted me to move out. Most of the time we laughed, never more so than when Bianca was there. The accidental discarding of a month's worth of food stamps followed by my heroic dive into the dumpster to retrieve them yielded recurring glee. Ease found its way into our lives, and Miri told me on more than one occasion that she was glad I was around.

* * *

Yankee Folly gigged a lot that summer. With our harmonies tighter, our songwriting improving, we played locally two to four nights a week. Visitors came to town, first Sol and his will-of-the wisp girlfriend on his motorcycle en-route from a cross-country trip; then Meris had passed through en route to her new home in Southern California. *Meris*: It had been nearly two years since I'd seen her. She'd stayed in Italy, in Firenze for about six months, returning home in May of '72, having decided that the cultural chasm between her and her Italian paramour could not be bridged. Meris, perhaps the one person who could have reached me during those hellish months, had eventually learned of my hospitalization, but now told me she hadn't known then if she should have contacted me, as afraid of seeing me, I imagined, as I was afraid of life.

She slept on the couch and left the next morning. I permitted myself the luxury of thinking I would likely have reached out had our situations been reversed, but who knew? My attention now focused on Bianca, and I overlooked my discomfort as her first love. I'd imagined a second relationship wouldn't start without bells and whistles, but I was finding out differently, and realized something I'd not grasped with Meris, that love was not only a feeling but also a decision. My new composition, "Sitting Here with You", written in her cabin addressed my hopes for a shared intimacy based in an attraction that had evolved from friendship. A fragile intimacy grew between us.

Now as the night comes upon this country home
I'm feeling something so deep in my bones
With the time that's gone by, and the tears we have cried
Will we ever find out why, we are even here at all
Sitting here with you
What we've been through
Your love so new

Bianca and Miri had moved into a shack five miles out on the Plains, but in September, on the day of the military coup in Chile that overthrew the government of its duly-elected president, Salvador Allende, Bianca, at home alone, was assaulted by a migrant worker who had come to her door asking for water. She had avoided rape—her Spanish speaking may have helped, -but she'd been handled roughly, and had been afraid for her life. Our cadre took turns staying with her and Miri at the rental until the police caught the suspect, based on her description of the man's truck. When she learned the accused had a family, she didn't want charges to be filed. Sympathetic to the plight of the migrant workers, she had aspired to work with them after she graduated. The suspect was charged and now she was reluctant to testify. We vigorously debated the subject with me advocating in favor, a position she decried. She was finally persuaded for the protection of other potential victims, and the suspect was convicted. She'd been through hell.

We scouted for a place where the three of us could live. We found a great old four-bedroom house in town but we needed a fourth to make the rent. In Sterno, we found a compatable fellow traveler so we signed the lease and moved into this expansive domicile with a huge carpeted living and dining room, a sizeable kitchen and three bedrooms upstairs. The fourth was downstairs off the dining room. We drew lots for the rooms.

Location Location—the fragile intimacy between Bianca and me faded. She and Sterno were in adjacent rooms. From downstairs I easily and not infrequently heard the exchange of words in the hall and easily imagined a likely liaison. Karma had reared its head.

Apparently usurped, I threw my energies into the band. The trio was bursting with creativity. With each week Miri, Darwin, and I brought in new tunes. We played a gig at the university opening for a Fifties Revival band, where our forty-five minute set featured several enthusiastically received songs fortifying my desire to find gigs in Denver and in the mountains. Miri and I spent a couple of days doing just that scoring two weeklong dates in Breckinridge for early December.

Bianca's status with Sterno remained unclear to me and I preferred the ambiguity. My freelancing, however, soon accomplished something I never thought possible. While lunching with a young woman I had dated occasionally, Sterno happened by and I awkwardly asked him to join us. Within a few minutes, the woman's roommate showed up. Right at that table love was born that went on to marriage within a year.

* * *

Yankee Folly Road sang inspired three-part harmonies, largely attributable to Darwin's facility for vocal arrangement. A one-time high school art teacher from Yonkers, who had once proudly showed off his letter to the *New York Post* (They had titled his letter, "Art Critic.") which excoriated the paper for its superficial critique of a Jackson Pollack painting, Darwin had been a veteran of several bands. He impeccably guided our voices to present the most enriched sound possible. In turn, my sister and my songwriting inspired him to begin writing his own songs. By November we had enough original material for a hypothetical album, had we the money to afford studio time.

We did the next best thing, heading off to play those dates we'd arranged in the mountains, a week at an inn followed by one at a well-paid bar. There we breathed much fresher air than in Greality, but Darwin was miserable being away from his girlfriend and their cozy nook in Alvin's basement, the seasoned musician having lost his enthusiasm for the road. The thin crowds at the inn also dulled our performances. I wasn't sure Darwin would last one week, let alone two. A saving grace appeared in the form of five lads and one woman from Boulder whose folk-rock band Huzzah Creek was gigging across town. We partied with these lean hungry-looking minstrels whose demeanor stood in stark contrast with the few red-sweatered ski bums we had been entertaining. Extending a complimentary description to us as "Zap Comics on stage," we repaired nightly to their chalet, where we fortified ourselves with smoke and drink. Their drummer, a mustachioed and bespectacled upstate New Yorker, rolled joints for a smoking procedure he described as a "knife hit," wherein product pressed between tips of two red hot kitchen knives would yield smoke then subsequently sucked through a funnel. A precursor of the contemporary vaporizer, the knife hit provided a cleaner inhalation than a bong or pipe. I gave the drummer the handle, *Yosha Knife-hits.*

Our camaderie got us through that first week and for me formed the basis for long-term friendships We partied hard, knowing that Yankee Folly wouldn't be making any more road trips. What this meant for the trio wasn't immediately clear, but some air had most assuredly escaped. Miri, feeling the need for a break between the two gigs, left with Alvin for a couple of days. Bianca had made her feelings known with respect to the haze I'd been in for most of the week. She'd come up Friday and left Sunday, suspicious that I might have been up to my old tricks. She wasn't exactly wrong.

Sometime during our second week stint, a much lower-key affair, Darwin indicated he'd had enough, and not only with travel but with the band. He disclosed new aspirations to make music for the Divine Light Mission of the Corpulent Adolescent Guru. I recalled my sister's escape from premiehood but intuitively I knew things had come full circle. No such tequila sunrise deprogramming effort would deter Darwin. It was a loss. We three had been good.

Jamming with my synthesizer-playing neighbor Jeff soon became a creative outlet that provided new direction. A songwriter to boot, Jeff turned me on to the compatibility of the acoustic guitar in contemporary British head rock bands like King Crimson, Emerson Lake and Palmer, and The Moody Blues. I returned to my latest odd job as a lot boy at a local car dealership, where I washed Ramblers, Sportabouts, and Jeeps with increasing diligence and heightened finesse. Grateful to its owners for having let me off for two weeks for the mountain gigs, Miri and I subsequently attended the company's Christmas party held in its showroom, where a tall lanky redheaded salesman's pre -kareoke rendition of "I Don't Like Spiders and Snakes," put us in stiches. Before she journeyed east to visit her family on Long Island's south shore, Bianca gave me a book of Dylan's lyrics. She inscribed it *I'll keep it with mine,* the title from one of his finer love ballads. I would do the same.

Chapter 11

HEAD ROCK

The journey from northern Colorado to the Bay Area contains long stretches of dull desert wasteland, but riding shotgun with a driver nicknamed after marijuana rolling paper, hell bent on a Reno based liason for later the same day, I could take comfort in the fulfillment of the prophecy of 1970-I'd returned fucked up. Moreover, my second arrival in California had coincided with the kidnapping of Patty Hearst.

"Zig," as he was affectionately known to his eastern Colorado brethren, had rented an east bay house in Santa Lupita that would be home to the band, and I, his designated passenger now accompanied him in his crimson corvette across the salt flats and deserts of the Great American West to said destination. For starters, Zig was not the most interesting conversationalist. Talk might have helped ease the pain of leaving Bianca before dawn, while alternately contemplating the desolation of Wyoming and the likely end of our volatile couplehood. Zig did, however, like to drive fast, and it seemed that we reached the Utah border rather more quickly than expected. This man of few words now hunkered over the steering wheel, eyes peering straight ahead single-minded in purpose to reach Reno by midafternoon. Having slept through that desert city four years ago, I couldn't adequately appreciate his enthusiasm for the place, but I kept my own counsel. Silence reigned as we hurtled past the Great Salt Lake and through the Bonneville Salt Flats. When we reached the state line of Nevada, Zig shared his hope that he'd scheduled our itinerary for a punctual arrival in Reno, a curious utterance since once we reached the Nevada line we paused so he could play the slots. Once underway again it became immediately clear that any vehicle in our lane traveling under eighty miles an hour would make more problematic that now somewhat smaller window of opportunity.

I pondered the fact that this individual's long-term friendship with Jeff didn't hold out a lot of promise for the latter's social judgment. Hopefully, he and Bill, our drummer had already arrived in Santa Lupita with our gear. Fighting off the worry that just maybe another life blunder had left the gate I closed my eyes to contemplate how I would spend this unanticipated layover. Fortunately, I had plenty of time to prepare as the three great milestones of the Silver State: Elko, Battle Mountain, and Winnemucca all loomed before us. Surely, I would come up with something in the time it would take to traverse these stimulating burgs.

* * *

Yankee Folly Road had died with the New Year. With Darwin safely ensconced in the bosom of premiehood, Miri and I had confronted the fact that neither of us wished to continue as a duet. Moreover, my sister had tired of Greality. She planned to return east to aid our parents in the transition to their newly purchased condominium on the outskirts of Amishland's northern tier, not far from where Herman had purchased yet a third ironworks. The Boonton house was up for sale. My mother had remained to sort through and pack up the twenty-five plus years of our family life. Miri, assuming the role of paternal caretaker, would housekeep for my father until the sale of our childhood home would bring Clara to eastern Pennsylvania.

The band's passing had caused me also to want to move on, an especially ironic fact since Bianca and I might now be able to work out our thing. I wasn't prepared to consider graduate school an idea that Fremont had thought might serve as a rational next step. I craved another band, and Jeff had provided the vehicle. The only rub was that he wanted his shot in California. Really, how could I deny him? Bianca was enthusiastic, intuiting that my staying in Greality without the trio wouldn't hold enough for me. She was right but I was already missing her.

Ah, Reno, so uninteresting this Wednesday afternoon that getting out of the car to grab a bite had less appeal than the thought of nodding off for an hour while Zig, that transplanted stud from the Great Plains, twirled with his damsel upstairs in a casino named the Kitchen Sink. I drifted off for almost a minute and a half before, *lo and behold*, the Zigster, so soon home from the hunt, revved it up and we set sights on Tahoe and points west.

* * *

The Symbionese Liberation Army, a mesmerizing collection of sociopaths, would occupy the country's attention for almost the next four months, from their kidnapping of Patty Hearst until the shootout in Los Angeles that ended in the deaths of most of them, leaving the now participating Patty (aka "Tanya") on the run for the next few years with fellow travelers Bill and Emily Harris. During the initial four months of her captivity, the SLA had blackmailed the Hearst family into providing free food for the poor of the Bay Area, brainwashing "Tanya" to their cause and into participating in the bank robbery for which she was later convicted and sent to prison. It had been a long way down from Mario Savio.

We settled in, Zig, Jeff, Bill and me, and soon Nina and Nick, guitarist and bassist respectively, having arrived from southern Colorado. A suburb of Oakland, Santa Lupita's main streets housed an equal number of churches and massage parlors. As there were only so many hours of the day that could be absorbed playing and practicing music, my thoughts often wandered north to Berkeley and San Francisco. Before Nick and Nina's arrival Jeff, Bill and I had auditioned at the Boardinghouse in SF, a club being made famous by *Old and in the Way* and Steve Martin, but visiting Berkeley proved to be surreal. While my memory remained strong, the sheen of the place had considerably dulled. Telegraph Avenue looked somewhat marginal. Walking up Dwight Way to what had been Dark-Haired Gina's apartment building, I paused in its courtyard in an attempt to make sense of that which had once seemed so profound only to discover that memory's power is eclipsed when one is actually in vivo.

I'd been writing songs at the rate of one or two a month for the last year, and had hoped to increase my output with this quintet of aspiring British-ish rockers. Influenced by the early seventies head rock our music featured acoustic guitar, keyboards, bass, drums, and electric lead guitar. I was odd man out re social history. Jeff and Bill were Zig's buddies from the eastern plains, having been friends since childhood. Nick and Nina had been a longstanding couple from southern Colorado who our keyboardist had met and jammed with before the beginning of our musical association. Nina and I sang lead. She was a forceful guitar-player, influenced by King Crimson's Robert Fripp and Yes's Steve Howe coupled with a strong blues presence. Nick's loping bass, reminiscent of Paul McCartney's best work on "With a Little Help from My Friends" provided a strong compliment to her melody lines and improvisations. Challanged by how well these four played their instruments, I came to accept that a rhythm guitar player and bard fit this ensemble. The shift to a rock band challenged me. I'd never before played alongside electric instruments or for that matter a rhythm section. Nina, Jeff, and I wrote the tunes and the musical sharing itself, though lacking the intimacy of Yankee Folly, proved stimulating, but Rock Symphonique, under considerable financial pressure, needed gigs pronto.

And dates were hard to come by in a mid-seventies California overrun with bands that having long been here had established networks. Zig had been patient, but needed help with the rent. Enter Manpower, the work agency for those in-between jobs or just generally unsuited for permanent employment. For one labor -intensive week Jeff, Nick, Bill and I unloaded a boxcar of napkins for Denny's Restaurants. We worked alongside a middle age drifter who quixotically referred to us as 'goddamned democrats'. Things soon got more lonely. Nick and Nina had each other, or so it seemed, and Bill had taken up with an ex girlfriend of the Zigster. That left Jeff and I to contemplate our respective romantic and/or domestic dilemmas. He also had left his girlfriend behind in Greality. That prairie town was now idllyic in comparison to this east bay suburban enclave that I experienced as hollow much like most of the rest of the state,

I suspected. Had I unconsciously known that my first time around as well?

Our electronic keyboardist had evidenced less interest in looking back, although his schizoid personality made it difficult to know his emotional process. Our duets in Greality had excited me a great deal, but now I wished we had built on what we had there. Too many changes in too short a time weighed on me, but Jeff was determined to stick it out. Making new friends here involved much more effort than I had imagined. Wistfully, I realized that this California dream belonged more to my younger band mates than to me.

We hired a business manager who did next to nothing for us, although he showed up at Casa Zigster faithfully three afternoons a week doing his part to keep up our spirits up doling out Three Musketeer bars. We paused in our viewing of *The Mod Squad* to accept his offerings, while waiting to hear about the little he'd accomplished on our behalf. He did get us a gig opening for yet another Fifties Revival band at a local college, where I set a record (no fault of his) for breaking strings, *three* in a half hour set. He suggested we commercialize our act so that he could introduce us to the inestimable Van Nobleduke, a Vegas contact of his, the subtext suggesting that our fortunes might be better made out of the East Bay or without any reliance on his buisness acumen.

All this moved me to place a call to the Columbia Records office in San Francisco. I saw the name John Hammond, Sr. under the Columbia listing in the phone book. Incredibly, on a Friday afternoon, with expensive day rates applying, I reached the renowned producer who had discovered Billie Holiday, Johnny Cash, and Bob Dylan (*Hammond's Folly,* as the latter was initially known by executives in that record company). After listening to me describe my circumstances for twenty minutes (and it was on my own behalf that I called, and while speaking with him couldn't believe he had nothing more pressing), he indicated that he'd accept a demo that, if suitable, might let him book me at USO clubs at bases in the Pacific. He'd generously given me his time, but I had trouble mustering enthusiasm, even though it was looking like my bandmates and I might be entering a period where it was becoming necessary for each of us to think of ourselves first. Years later, when I first visited Kauai, I wondered if perhaps I'd dismissed the scenario prematurely, but I reminded myself that such far flung locales as Guam or Okinawa would have been the likely postings. Still, that might have been all right, a possible steppingtone, a steady income, and one very highly placed contact.

Zig had now determined that it was time to move on, and in, with one of his many female admirers. Before doing so occurred an event of literally explosive magnitude. Jeff, who routinely stayed up late tinkering with the many sounds of his synthesizer, usually in a considerate enough manner such that the rest of us could sleep, apparently had consumed more than his usual amount of drink. Suddenly enamored of the train whistle option, he incrementally raised the volume for such a protracted interval that the nominally constrained Zigster lumbered into our preoccupied keyboardist's personal space, grabbed him by the collar, and put him through the translucent window next to the front door. Then, the muscular mesomorph turned to look at the four stunned bleary eyed musicians, nodded his head, and went back to his bedroom while we tended to our comrade who was so drunk that he was oblivious to what had just happened to him.

Little conversation ensued over the next couple of days. Rehearsals, as one might expect suffered. Nina and Nick had secluded themselves, only emerging from their room to eat what little food was available. Jeff and I thought they were preparing to bail. Bill moved in with his girlfriend, only showing up for rehearsals. Employing my well-developed skill at matching my reading selection to context, I began *The Exorcist*, and Jeff, well, in combing the neighborhood for social contact, had met the Jesus freaks.

Our keyboardist's contact with the Jesus set embodied both a Darwinian exercise in adaptation and a timely exemplar of Grace, for the band's cupboard was bare. Some modest excitement had occurred in the immediate aftermath of Jeff's *good news,* when I having correctly named the title of a Dylan song for a KSAN radio contest promoting the seer's first tour in eight years, soon basked in anticipation of receiving one, perhaps two tickets for his upcoming San Francisco show. Thrilled at the prospect of seeing him live for the first time, I subsequently learned that my prize instead consisted of his entire discography on vinyl, and that I could claim my winnings whenever I could get my lucky ass down to the station. Never mind that I already owned nearly all these albums even if they weren't currently with me. So Nina and I trekked to the city to fetch the sacred texts. We crossed over the bay where I pointed out the magic spot of Sproul Plaza. Still a happening place, though, as between us Nina and I sold ten of the twelve Dylan albums within fifteen minutes. Only *Self-Portrait* and *Dylan* remained in our hands, the discerning Berkeley avant -garde having dismissed Dylan's rendering of covers with the same rigor that they had embraced his original pieces. We departed for Santa Lupita some seventy and change richer, able to feed the band for the next several days.

Jeff's new Jesus friends had professed much excitement with the prospect of breaking bread with us at our earliest opportunity. We were certainly sheep in need of feeding, and even I, acknowledging the need for a decent meal, was willing to put up with a couple of hours of proselytizing. "Not to worry," our keyboardist reassuringly noted, "one of the brethren is a Jew for Jesus", Rock Symphonique walked to their place that evening gingerly sidestepping Zig, now intently focused on window repair.

The meal's noteworthy moment came when Grace was offered by a bearded member of the brethren whose features breathed a visual history of surfer burn and drug abuse, a man who had been through it all, a western hemisphere Siddhartha-like believer. He intoned,"We pray Thee, oh Lord, to have mercy on these minstrel souls trucking through life, searching for gigs." It took considerable willpower, but I restrained a bellow, lacking faith (so to speak) in my colleagues' ability to see the humor in both the remarks and his delivery thereof.

The more was the pity that we accepted the brethrens' invitation to spend an afternoon on the Santa Cruz beach the following Saturday, where we would each be worn down by our own personal zealot. It was a validation of the age-old axiom that there is no such thing as a free lunch, or in our case, dinner. Predictably, the Semitic-looking gentleman had been designated especially for me. I countered his religious probing with stories of my non-Jewish girlfriend and my plans to rejoin her in Greality, lest I lose her to another man who might not share my qualms about living in sin. We agreed that loneliness was a terrible thing and that I should hasten to her side.

Bianca, though, beat me to it. Early on the following Tuesday, I awoke to see her at my bedroom doorway. As in a dream she lay beside me providing validation of yet another axiom, that if something looks too good to be true then it probably is. She had driven twelve hundred miles to tell me that she had slept not once but twice with someone named Buck, that she still loved me, but felt unsure if she wanted me to come back, what did I think? Obviously faced with a most difficult decision, and given how encouraging the band's fortunes looked here in Santa Lupita, I hinted at returning. "Ok," Bianca said with minimal enthusiasm adding, "but I can't promise anything."

Only the previous day there had been band discussion of relocating to Vegas. This would entail finding a way to perform pop tunes for the elusive Mr. Nobleduke, who might then lend his considerable weight to rectifying our perilous career path. I was outvoted three to two. Bill's relationship with his significant other had now made him a stay at home drummer. In my best William Jennings Bryan manner, I informed my colleagues that I did not come to California to play music only to be crucified on a cross of commercialized fluff on the most garish strip on the continent. Like Bryan, I lost (although only once to his three election defeats). Jeff, Nick, and Nina, constituting the thinnest of majorities prevailed.

We left in the highly capable hands of our candy-carrying business manager the task of finessing the details, seeing as we had no money for and minimal inclination towards making a demo. Would the good nobleman find a way to hear the band live, and furthermore, seeing as we had no gigs, could he come to our lodgings to do so, before we packed up and slunk back to an adjacent time zone? We didn't think we were asking for too much, and, as our manager's efforts had been something less than productive to this point, we thought he might relish the opportunity to redeem himself. The snort that emanated from his giblike nose offered little encouragement. Walking the Santa Lupita streets at midnight, several hours after Bianca's departure, the realization that I was again unlikely to become a Californian entered my consciousness. Nothing held me here. I should just up and go, but rejected that course of action, as I was, of course, broke, and also of no mind to abandon my comrades while they were down. The solution involved getting the three who remained at La Casa Zigster to join me in leaving. The key was Nick and Nina, who, I rationalized, could always return to Pueblo and pick up musically where they had left off. I couldn't believe these rockers were desperate enough to want a Vegas gig. Persuading our keyboardist was hopeless. Here he now stood, hanging with the Jesus people while simultaneously pining for a gig in the biggest sin city in the country. The duality that would soon form the bedrock of the Republican Party already setting up in his brain, I expected Hosannas to blare from his synthesizer at any moment. I certainly hadn't envisioned this present state of affairs.

What I did next was without contemplation and with a complete lack of anticipation of unintended consequences. I dialed the house and attempting to disguise my voice, introduced myself to Nick as Mr. Van Nobleduke, ostensibly just finishing a drink at a downtown club, and wondered if I could mosey on up to to give the band a listen. It was 12:30 a.m, no way would they buy this. Shaking my head, I started my walk up the hill to crash for the night assuming that the worst that would happen would be that the others would scold me for having pulled their collective coats. But why is Bill was running towards me at breakneck speed, yelling that Van Nobleduke is coming to hear us play. Everybody was dressed. We had to tune up and run through a song. We only had five minutes before he would be there. *Hurry, hurry...*

...They all looked so good dressed to the nines, the footlights shining, making Nina look especially gorgeous as they awaited the knock on the door from Mr. Nobleduke. I gave them but a glance as I headed quickly for my room, feeling as poorly as they imminently would, I buried my head in my pillow, bracing for their ire, and wondering why I persist in the belief that the creativity of musicians automatically translates into a capaicity for irony and/or a self-depreciation. Was it really my fault that they had swallowed it whole? I'd played on our conjoint desperation and for that I plead guilty.

While I hoped that we'd leave together, I hadn't intended for our departure to occur in this manner, if for no other reason then for the next two days I went through hell in the form of their silent treatment. I was grateful that on the third day the news of the demise of a significant portion of the SLA in a shootout with the LA police had trumped our collective misery. A gig at a local dive finally paid enough for us to return to our respective homes. Bill agreed to drive the gear back in a few weeks, but would ride along now for a brief visit. Once back home, Nina informed us that she'd wrangled some studio time from a former band mate who had owed her. We cut four original tunes that got us into Ebbets Fields, a noted Denver club, slated to open for Tommy Bolan. This would have been terrific had it not been for the fact that our gear still sat in Santa Lupita, a sad fact providing evidence for the third and most salient axiom, that when one contemplates change, making more than one at any particular time demonstrates exceedingly poor judgment.

Chapter 12

RAPPROCHEMENT

Both of us worked at night, this impeachment summer, Bianca waitressing at a country club while I plied my bachelor's degree working on a custodial team that cleaned up after hours at a bank. During my five-hour workdays, I often looked forward to discussions with my supervisor on the subject of Jane Roberts' *Seth Speaks*, a proto-New Age series of books regarding the Soul's journey. It proved refreshing to feel at one with the cosmos while vacuuming the offices of the bank's president, board chairman and numerous other officials. I emptied the wastebaskets, moving down the hierarchy towards the work- space of the tellers where I often paused in acknowledgement of our respective, if quite not parallel, domains.

Bianca had not quite called it off with her Buck, a strikingly handsome and decent enough chap who having behaved so graciously upon my meeting him that I felt nearly put to shame for thinking that the two of them didn't belong together. Yet, she had not determined that our splitting up was at hand. With understandable misgivings, Bianca let me back into her life. We lived together through that summer and into the fall. Truthfully, she seemed more deflated by the demise of Rock Symphonique than did I, because had the band survived in California, then she could have moved on. I missed the band some but not California. Had there been sufficient interest among the four of us I would have been open to gigging here, but Nick and Nina lost touch and Jeff chose, round about, to go back to California. Had we built the band in or near Greality, as opposed to the California of our collective dreams might we have fared better? In any event Richard Nixon would morph into a whirling dervish before I joined another band. I contemplated performing as a soloist, but felt no rush to pursue even that. My interest had moved to the possibility of a self-designed program within the university's educational psychology graduate program. I applied in September, and was accepted for the winter term starting in January.

The slow summer's pace suddenly broke when unanamously the Supreme Court ordered our imperial president to hand over to the House Judiciary Committee the transcripts of sixty-four "privileged" White House conversations. One of these transcripts revealed that Nixon had approved the Watergate cover-up—the so-called "smoking gun." Three days later the HJC voted the first of three articles of impeachment. Within days it became apparent that our beleaguered chief executive would fail to muster the support of more than one-third of the U.S. Senate required to remain in office, so the old Red-baiter from Southern California resigned the land's highest office on the ninth of August. Who would have thought that two nineteenth century relics, impeachment and assasination would reappear in the present day?

Our new president was Gerald Ford, appointed less than a year before to replace the previous vice president, the right wing attack dog Spiro Agnew. Ford declared, immediately upon assuming office, that "our long national nightmare is over," a comment that caused me to wonder just when he thought it had begun. As a member of the Warren Commission, hadn't the new president participated in the nightmarish rush to judgment regarding President Kennedy's assassination? Did he mean to suggest that these were two separate, very bad dreams or really one eleven-year long and continuing one? As for Mr. Agnew, the disgraced former vice president had resigned his office the previous October after pleading *nolo contendre* to charges of tax evasion. History had bestowed true kindness on the country not only for Nixon's removal but also for the fact that Agnew hadn't replaced him. The one-time Maryland governor had castigated Vietnam War protesters as "an effete corps of impudent snobs" and, having showed considerable alliterative flair when he had likewise described dissenters as "nagging nabobs of negativism." Despite Ford's pardon of Nixon, an act that cost him the 1976 election, Agnew's elevation to the Presidency would have constituted a new national nitemare.

Bianca and I watched the impeachment drama unfold just as we had followed the Ervin hearings some sixteen months before, singing our songs of experience and innocence respectively. We were hanging by a thread, but hanging nonetheless.

* * *

Clara had moved to Amishland's northern tier by summer, my parents having decided instead to rent out the Boonton homestead for at least a year. They settled into a spanking new condominium in a unit that nearly approached the minimum standard for establishing and maintaining personal space for two. After two years in the West, and in the aftermath of Nixon's fall, I visited my parents and Miri there. Over the eight months that Clara had lived in Pennsylvania, and particularly during the impeachment summer, my sister and I had periodically discussed the advisability of my coming home. Miri had gone to work for Herman in his recently purchased ironworks during part of that time, having helped out in the office and in the foundry's paint shop. She spoke of working alongside the castings painter who often chose to remind her that the building across the street was 'that factory where they make the girls' panties, you know'. In need of money for tuition and a car, I determined that the most feasible way this could be accomplished involved my asking Herman to work for him for for two months. He agreed and I flew home towards the end of October. The cramped quarters of the new living unit notwithstanding, an unexpectedly joyous reunion ensued, as Clara provided a banquet of chocolate in the forms of baked and purchased cakes and cookies, chief among them the highly addictive Entenmann's chocolate chip cookies and the aptly named killer blackout cake.

Judging by the eye-catching Victorian character of the ironworks' neighboring towns, Nazareth, in particular, home to the Martin Guitar Company, I wondered why my parents hadn't purchased a living unit there, the location being closer to New Jersey and consequently more convenient for my mother's visits to her sisters in Greater New York and her Boonton friends. In any event, these trips were now a half hour longer each way as the living unit was located on Allentown's west side. For Herman, however, the further away meant the better. When he confided that, "this (the condominium) is the one place I refuse to take seriously," I grasped that domestic contentment would forever elude him. Would that he could discover another bunkhouse, his expressed wish "to die in the sand pile" only emphasizing his consistent longing to dwell forever in the world of iron men. Only Blanco, my father's high-strung German shepherd, could take his mind off the flaws of others.

Blanco should have been more accurately named Gris, since during the workday the dog spent his time chained to a sorry-looking stand-alone tree on ground covered with bits of industrial coke, bricks, and the shavings of scrap iron that had been employed to fuel the ironwork's cupola. The canine would consistently howl for Herman's attention although at times the foreman would be bold enough to free him from his chain that he had managed to wrap around the tree throughout the course of his day.

Marta was now the family's only far-flung correspondent, having commenced her senior year at the University of Arizona. Upon her graduation, and unlike her siblings, she would demonstrate a greater degree of self-reliance and independence through gainful employment in her chosen field of study, journalism and communications, by means of the imaginative career choice of rock deejay. It should be noted that among the three of us only Marta was ever fired from the ironworks, a testament to the clash-of-the-titans-like temper battles that historically had intermittently erupted between her and my father. In a further differentiation from her older siblings, Marta also had purchased her own first car, unlike Miri, who received hers at graduation, or me, who had now quite unexpectedly became the recipient of an orange '74 Pinto because, as my mother related to me, I had *chosen to come home.* To say that I felt shock was an understatement. This went against my entire understanding of my place within the family, having been a pariah for the last five years. Whether my parents' move to Allentown had signaled a new chapter in our family history or because time had mellowed him (a notion I soon realized was not the case), the seemingly impossible had happened in that my father had forgiven me. There was also a third possible explanation, that Herman had acknowledged I had shown some initiative, however modest, towards making my way in the world, thus allowing for a thaw in our cold war. He had provided confirmation of this when upon bestowing the gift, he declared, "I can see you're not a Bolshevik."

Truthfully, accompanying my stunned disbelief in receiving the automobile, I had also suppressed the awareness of an unexpected lost automony. I had genuinely expected to earn the money for my own car, thinking that my doing so would maintain a suitable boundary between us. While glad for the wheels, I was now more confused with respect to what possible paternal expectations for me may have been renewed. Moreover, I anticipated that Bianca's reaction to my father's unexpected generosity might further complicate things between her and me. When revealing the news to her, I perceived in her tone the belief that I had likely embellished my difficulties with Herman. I suspected that her revised perception of me from that of the disaffected bard that had initially attracted her to the less appealing *fortunate son* would only grow. Still, I longed for the Christmas holiday that would bring her back east to visit her family, to be followed by our cross-country journey back to Greality in the new vehicle whose standard shift transmission I would now enjoy thanks to her long-suffering instructional efforts. Bianca had taught me to drive a stick shift in the Greality Kmart parking lot.

I thought my mother would be sad to leave Boonton, and perhaps she was at times, but mostly she seemed happy in the new digs. She and my father rowed as ever and as often as before over the most inconsequential matter. At dinner one night at a Pennsylvania Dutch-inspired eatery, Clara said something of such little note that Herman's subsequent weeklong silent treatment completely baffled us. Given the possibilities, it likely had referred to a description of some Amishland feature she'd seen or visited, the description of which put my father on the defensive, feeling his provincial sensibilities were an object of spousal scorn. The unit's kitchen, really an oversized pantry, was often the locus of many a skirmish. During such conditions that zone deserved a designation as a hard-hat area for non- combatants. Nevertheless, I sensed that the move had agreed with Clara in some indefinable way.

My combatant status was unpredictable. The cause often defied understanding, but the unsettling effect left me drained. My father's employees had learned to live with his mercurial temperament, those that continued to work for him at least. He was, after all, their boss and on other occasions could be ebullient and solicitous. I, however, struggled to retain any sense of equilibrium when on the receiving end of an inflammatory verbal thrashing, wherein I was labeled as lazy, incompetent, and/or parasitical, his Randian perspective never far from the surface. Understanding that as a scion I merited no preferential treatment, I nevertheless refused to respect his unwillingness to leave it at the ironworks, on occasions telling him and on others tuning him out, the latter requiring considerable effort. How Miri had dealt with his temper over the months she had lived and worked for him before Clara's arrival puzzled me, though that subject didn't come up for discussion between us.

Incredibly, when in more convivial spirits, my father had volunteered that, should I choose to return and work in the business, he would purchase a condominium for me adjacent to theirs. The ensuing red flag, what I would come to identify as *bad boundaries* had reared its head in my enmeshed family constellation. It was a harbinger of events that in hindsight should have been easily predicted.

* * *

My first nominally normal family Thanksgiving in six years came and went without incident, with my great Aunt Yetta, Anna's only surviving sister, in attendance. Family legend had told of the existence of an imaginary line through the middle of her refrigerator in the apartment she had shared for many years with her sister, recently deceased. They had lived spinster-like in Weehawken, a city across from Manhattan, not far from the historical marker denoting the locus of the fatal duel between Aaron Burr and Alexander Hamilton. The family now passed around a tape recorder so that each of us could express greetings to Marta, still in Tucson. When Yetta's turn came, my understandably technologically challenged, elderly aunt, her lips a bare inch or so from the machine's internal microphone, tentatively uttered, "Hello, Marta…I can't hear you" to our collective uproarious delight.

When Marta arrived from Tucson the personal space meter went decidedly clinical as the five of us made every effort to maintain equilibrium in the living unit for the last two weeks of 1974. On Christmas Eve, my sisters and I journeyed into the near-deserted center city of Allentown to view the recently released cinematic masterpiece, *The Towering Inferno.* Starring Steve McQueen and Paul Newman it was the latest entry in a genre including such classics as *Airport* and *The Poseidon Adventure.* That this film won an Oscar for Best Cinematography and also for Best Song, the heart-stopping "We May Never Love Like This Again," as well as a nomination for Best Picture is a hint that even during film's Golden Decade all that glittered was hardly gold. Nevertheless, this represented the first outing in a long time for my sisters and me, and it proceeded with much laughter as we collectively reminisced evaluating the wisdom of our parents' move to the northern tier of Amishland. That issue we couldn't resolve, but we easily agreed as to the movie's mediocrity, the last time the three of us would be in sync about anything for many years to come.

Bianca briefly visited the living unit primarily for the purpose of seeing Miri, something I understood but whose weirdness factor I could not help but register, the two of them more in sync than my girlfriend and I. This contributed to my readiness to hit the road. Shortly before New Year's, I departed from my parents and Miri in an emotional farewell, something we had been deprived for the past five years. The navy, the cancelled graduation, the counterculture, major depression and the resignation of a president all now begged for release and expiation. We hugged, and I drove away, tearful, grateful, first east to Long Island to retrieve Bianca and then westward again.

Chapter 13

BERTHA

I had to move, really had to move.
That's why if you please, I am on my bending knee
Bertha don't you come around here anymore.
(Hunter & Garcia)

The orange pinto rolled into Charlottesville, home to the law school where Artie had enrolled. Having since survived his encyclopedia-selling adventure in Dixie, my old comrade was now in his third year of law school. He greeted Bianca and me from the porch of his rental house, the very picture of Southern hospitality. His forever Cheshire grin, accentuated by his curled mustache now evoked the memory of his delight in the foil of the Ruptured Duck a decade before.

He and I entertained Bianca with yarns of our youth as we relaxed in his cozy digs, that second day of the New Year, our first and hopefully last stop on our imminent journey through the heartland. She and I planned to share the driving and plow straight through to Greality. Bianca and I had spent an entertaining weekend with her warm and good-hearted parents. Her father's relentless determination to watch the Miami-Oakland playoff game from a standing position, having ignored all demands from wife and daughters to sit, put me in stitches. Her mother's repeated assertion that what the country needed was a "good five-cent cigar" had provided the conservative counterweight to her dad's liberalism. In her family the political persuasions were gender-reversed from my own, but with less disparity, less intensity, and seemingly less at stake.

Artie recounted for Bianca our great moments: from our childhood through high school- from how he, Hal, and I had been instructed by our rabbi to clean up the altar during which time my friends asked me, in their best Bob Newhart manner, if I were aware I'd unplugged the Eternal Light, through our New Jersey teenage rite of buying beer in New York state, where the legal age was only eighteen. Returning from Greenwood Lake, the alcohol procurement zone just over the New York line to Artie's house, we downed multiple cans of the water-like Big Cat Malt Liquor. As the one least able to hold his alcohol, I found my queasy dizziness then trivialized by Hal, convinced I was exaggerating. Only moments after he left for home I vigorously vomited, emphatically stating to Artie, 'Well, I guess *this* shows Hal.'

Later, she and I experienced a passionate reunion and hit the road the next morning, traversing the coal- mining regions of West Virginia and eastern Kentucky. Greeted by a snowy landscape in Missouri, we were subsequently hit with an arctic mass that had enveloped eastern Kansas. It took all our concentration to plow through. Taking turns at the wheel I awoke past Salina to hear her tell me, "You look like shit."The farther west we drove the more ephemeral seemed the brief spirit of Charlottesville, the gales hitting our windshield signaling a change. Once we arrived in Greality, Bianca disclosed she couldn't live with me anymore. I moved out and into a house close to campus, fortunate to find a fine roommate in Steve. He had graduated college here and was now employed in a local print shop. I began my three graduate-level psychology and communications classes as Bianca and I entered our endgame.

I excelled academically. The intellectual environment was therapeutic and I made friends with two sharp-witted colleagues, Big John from Canada ('from the soggy shores of Mt. Zion to the Zuider Zee,' when initially denoting the disparity in our respective ethnicities), and the highly empathic Tim, he from our own Colorado mountains. Enrolled in the experiential School for Educational Change and Development I was expected to submit a proposal by the end of the quarter. If approved, the project plus course work would earn me a Masters in Education. My project idea involved some ill-conceived highly idealistic scheme to investigate separating art from commercialism. The closer I got to crunch time, the more I realized that the zeal of my inspiration far exceeded my interest in developing a concrete proposal. Thus, I took a sabbatical after the quarter during which I'd done well in three well-taught courses. I postponed any decision regarding withdrawal until seeing what Boulder might offer in facilitating the stalled project.

I ended it with Bianca, a difficult decision, unsure if either of us truly wanted that. The new mileu helped and scoring a two-week solo gig at the local Holiday Inn looked to provide some diversion. I went full tilt with that gig. Steve printed up cards that I passed out to many new and old friends, including Bianca in a chance encounter. She nodded. Afraid she'd recognize the gig as a self- rehabilitation project, I quickly moved on.

Opening nite rocked. Nearly a hundred supporters had showed up through the evening buying plenty of beer and wine, so I arrived the next night full of piss and vinegar, only to learn my services had been abruptly terminated, ostensibly because my audience had *only* consumed beer and wine. Ignoring my contract the manager informed me that, "ninety hippies swilling beer won't cut it here." While no mathematical wizard I wondered aloud how the usual few cowboys and double-knitted suits knocking back a few cocktails would yield a greater bar take.

It was difficult then to claim the fiasco for the badge of honor it eventually became, what with the pre-gig media blitz having involved not only the cards, but also a promotional picture appearing in the Greality paper, but Steve found me a gig at a more suitable venue, essentially a honky tonk. Tim subsequently gave me a handle that lasted for years, christening me *Dr. Petey.* He and I were fellow travelers, he the reincarnated Rhode Island Eric. Like me, he had spent a good part of the last four years in rambling mode. Our conversations visualized an alternate universe of endless repartee at the Med on Berkeley's Telegraph Avenue. During my quarter in grad school we were often inseparable. When he decided to move to Boulder after the quarter he invited me along.

What Tim possessed in intellect and empathy, Steve had in kindness. After finding me that gig, he rallied his friends to show up until my audience found their way back. The engagement paid a lot less, but rocked also in its own way, and all the more so when Clara came to visit. She met and conversed with my fellow students, covering more than a few drinks. Her charisma shone through. It was evident she enjoyed this first ever visit to her son's environs. Away from Herman, without having to be concerned with whatever damage control she'd have to perform had my father been present, my mother relaxed, enjoying the company of my contemporaries.

We made the rounds, dining with Adele and Fremont, and then with my Communications professor, a thirty-something who had captured my imagination with a class that proved to be the most stimulating of my protracted and non-continuous graduate career. The course delved into the meta-communication research conducted at the Mental Research Institute in Palo Alto during the sixties, and included a provocative and brilliant analysis of Edward Albee's *Who's Afraid of Virginia Woolf* from the perspective of communication theory. My discovery that the subject of relationship pathology could be studied with nearly the same level as it could be experienced was most illuminating.

Although I had no shot with her, the fantasy nonetheless provided a welcome distraction from Bianca who during my mother's visit had dropped by to be remembered to Miri. The moment was awkward, although my mother was, of course willing to pass along Bianca's best wishes, even as she marveled at what she perceived as her *chutzpah... couldn't she have called first?*

I moved to Boulder in April with Tim and his undergraduate girlfriend, the three of us sharing an apartment behind Kmart in the northeast part of town. Fremont and Adele, I'd recently learned, planned to move on themselves. Next academic year they would be sharing a professorship at an even smaller college in rural Georgia. I wondered about the likelihood of ever visiting them there, the Deep South of all places, but leaving Steve was the real heartbreak. A gem of a human being he'd had my back. We lost touch after he visited once to Boulder, my new home that with the exception of its inclination towards the deification of sprouts, beans, and lentils, I found more suited my sensibilities. I had departed Greality.

* * *

In ancient times Boulderado had no pedestrian mall. At Pearl Street's west end stood a bar where on weekday afternoons the under and unemployed jockeyed for optimal position for viewing the daily afternoon fix, the original *Star Trek*, now entering its fifth year of syndication. While not in attendance every day, I dropped in on occasion, drawn to this nascent media and cultural phenomenon. The show's cancellation six years earlier had resulted in such a firestorm of protest that its subsequent syndication can be heralded as one of our generation's more enduring victories. The hosting entity for this daily rite, Shannon's, embodied an ambience that would find no home on the mall that would complete construction three years hence. This was no fern bar. Little did we know that we dwelt in the last days of a pre-corporate Boulderado.

Little did I also know that Steven King, a local resident for the past six months, would having soon returned to Maine, complete *The Stand*, which had featured Boulder as the destination of his 'good people.' His novel had described many Boulder points of interest, including Eben G. Fine Park nestled at the city's west end at the very foot of the mountains. Here I encountered Daniel on one cool spring afternoon. He and I had first met at a jam held in Greality during Yankee Folly's heyday, in the autumn of 1973. Now popping up here, I find to my delight that he lives across Iris in those Sheriff of Nottingham Court apartments, close to my digs behind Kmart in the newly constructed Hackleberry complex. We arrange to meet forthwith, so the next day I meander to his digs, which he shared with his wife and their handsome black lab, Abraxas. We break out our instruments, fiddle and guitar, and commence our musical association. He also plays mandolin and we are a very good vocal mix. Over the years Daniel will help expand my repertoire from folk and rock to include bluegrass, both traditional and progressive, especially "Dawg" music from the brilliant mandolinist, David Grisman, and then later to the gypsy swing guitar of Django Reinhardt. That first day we had to have played some Dylan, and perhaps a Dan Hicks tune to whose music he turned me on. Elated, and leaving to call on a neighbor, another guitarist he strongly felt would fit, Daniel re-enters with Trent, the acoustic guitarist from Huzzah Creek, who lives directly downstairs with his wife, Alma, that band's bassist, and their seven-month old daughter. Trent offers that their child's conception coincided with the sojourns of Huzzah Creek and Yankee Folly during those Breckinridge gigs of December '73.

As went Yankee Folly, so apparently did Huzzah Creek, only in their case it was because Trent and Alma became parents, not for any reason so exotic as guru fascination. The three remaining members, Paolo, Franco, and Yosha Knifehits had recruited Ernie John, an extremely talented Chicago blues lead guitarist to help form Solar Boogie, a hard-driving rock and roll blues band. The band lived in a farmhouse east of town. An instant musical community had thus become available in the still semi- liberated zone at the foot of the Rockies. I found very part-time employment at the Boulder Free School, where I taught guitar to a smattering of students. A bit of intrigue arose when the school's new catalog, released before summer session, had described my guitar technique as "Einstein picking," a never-before-heard-of style-of-finger-picking, unknown because no such method actually existed. The author of that phrase has remained cloaked in mystery despite my attempts to track him/her down. *Dr. Petey and his Einstein picking*—sounded like good enough snake oil to me.

Local pickers and singers "showcased" their wares at an establishment on Pearl Street known as Fred's, but the audience preoccupied with culinary concerns, usually managed only marginal interest. I played there once, but scanning Pearl Street for other venues I discovered an unlikely musical opportunity, not at a bar suitable for rock bands, nor at a coffeehouse for folkies, but at the Sobriety Ice Cream Shop located below the now-closed Boulder Theatre. Here I played for tips and all the ice cream I could consume, my favorite being its stellar chocolate chip mint. This mammoth intake of calcium may have been genesis of the kidney stone that emerged four years later. With musical buddies sitting in during my twice- weekly appearances, some decent music happened in this most improbable of performance settings. *The ice cream dates* demonstrated that a gig was a gig, and the tips derived thereof kept me in burgers at the Aristocrat, a greasy spoon located a couple of blocks away. Its long-term presence would be noteworthy among the influx of health food establishments.

* * *

On April 30th came the end of the Vietnam War with North Vietnam overrunning Saigon, renaming it Ho

Chi Minh City. The evacuation of the American embassy commenced. The television now brought disturbing images of South Vietnamese citizens pounding on the American embassy's gates in the hope of escaping what had been their country. Tim and I watched the helicopters evacuate the last of the American personnel. Terrified South Vietnamese were pushed back onto the roof. For the first time America had lost a war, faring no better in Southeast Asia than had the French, except that we had actually lost the country. Seeing those images of desperate Vietnamese filled most Americans with anguish regardless of their view on the war. The right wing quickly and predictably took aim at anti-war protesters for the loss of South Vietnam. It must have been our collective lack of military knowledge, I suppose, to which they were referring, since none of us had stepped forward with any constructive suggestions to help our military leaders successfully prosecute a guerilla war. Now, in defeat came the end of that nation's arbitrary division and the overthrowing of a corrupt South Vietnamese government. Vietnam would three years hence facilitate the end of the killing fields of the Khmer Rouge in Cambodia, a tragedy created in part by our own government's bombing incursion into that country.

By mid-May securing yet another day job had become unavoidable. It had been a good run, really since January, but *as sand through an hourglass*....Ancestral Boulderado essentially ended at Twenty-Eighth Street, just a down slope, Canuck-driven, wind-spitting distance from my Hackleberry digs. Venturing east in search of employment took me past Thirtieth, a dirt road forming the city's outer rim beyond which lay farms and ski manufacturing factories dotting the interstellar region between Boulderado and, well, the terrestrial equivalent of Alpha Centauri, our nearest solar neighbor, Kansas City. Not far from the outer rim I chanced upon the Loveless Ski Company advertising for a sandblaster, an individual willing to don a surgical mask and spend his/her day guiding ski edges through a machine whose dust-raising capability over the long haul would doubtlessly result in eventual major respiratory illness. Fortunately for the more skilled and experienced employees, the blaster's work-station sat in a walled off area, thus keeping the swirling chronic duststorm sufficiently distant from their labors.

A gamer for two weeks, I requested and received a couple of days off before Memorial Day weekend so that I could visit Marta in Tucson. I had mentioned the disgraceful working conditions to the plant's Scandinavian scion. With emphasis I pointed out my deeply held conviction that a real effort be made to clean up this unacceptable situation, lest I avail myself of my New Deal-given American right to contact an appropriate official of the Occupational Safety and Health Administration. Sven nodded agreement, indicating he would look into it, and off I went on the long journey through the Southwest to visit my younger sister, now just months away from her own graduation.

Popping a Dexedrine south of Colorado Springs had helped make more palatable the sounds now emanating from the Pinto's AM radio. The speed had a nitrous oxide-like effect although it had been so long since I'd visited a dentist I had some trouble identifying the sensation. Driving through the nite as the Colorado Plateau spread out before me, I was privy to the likes of "Get Down Tonight," by the inestimable KC and the Sunshine Band; "Thank God, I'm A Country Boy," by Colorado's own laureate of pap, John Denver; and a whiny offering by someone named Minnie Ripperton, entitled "Loving You" (although it sounded more like *Lahahahahving You*). Fortunately, the amphetamine that Tim provided had peaked by the time Ms. Ripperton's mimicry of orgiastic ecstasy had reached my ears. Reminded now that my car had not been factory-equipped with a tape player, I couldn't help but also recall how Herman had suggested I get my own tape deck if I wanted one, in a possibly unconscious, possibly intended reference with respect to his ongoing attitude towards whatever musical aspirations I might yet harbor. Not so, however, for Miri, who in the spring of 1975 had begun a stint in a show band in the Pocono Mountains north of Amishland.

A Vegas band- what has God wrought? "Cut the Cake," a proto-disco number by the aptly named Average White Band accompanied me as I climbed Raton Pass and entered New Mexico. Perhaps, I reasoned, someday Miri's path and that of the Nobleduke will cross in Vegas, that city placed in eschatological opposition to Boulderado in *The Stand.* The moonlit desert landscape made me now recall the road trip I had taken with Bianca last summer that enroute to her sister's home in Malibu had covered some of this same ground. That journey had occurred in the wake of Nixon's resignation, and we were Greality bound when the Pardon had come down. We had stopped in Santa Fe on an early morning, the plaza deserted. Remembering this I had avoided the state's capital city this time around. Barreling through New Mexico I finally rested near White Sands towards dawn. After sleep and breakfast, I resumed heading south on I-25 to the intersection at Las Cruces to I-10 where I turned westward, thankful that even after some shut eye and food there remained enough speed in my system to tolerate the Captain and Tennille's reminder that "Love will Keep us Together."

The sun blazing and well into Arizona, my eyes had suddenly taken in the unnerving sight of liquid black sealant in the crevice of the driver's side door. How can this be? Will I still have a door when I reach Tuscon? AM radio is the least of my problems now. (Like my Pinto-owning cohort, I was over two years from learning about the car's potentially explosive gas tank.) I watched the sticky liquid congeal on the carpet, and apparently onto the orange exterior, if the alarmed looks and curiosity I received from passing motorists were any indication.

* * *

Having been assured by qualified personnel that my vehicle was still roadworthy I proceeded to my sister's digs with only a hint of the black-on-orange tableau, relieved, yet also disappointed that the full panoply was not on display for her. Marta had rented a trailer in a park that, aside from her, housed exclusively septuagenarians. Her principal recreational pastime had consisted of as she put it, "sitting around listening to the hardening of the arteries." We had spent little time together since my high school graduation and I knew little of her life. When I'd been sick in '72 she'd dragged me to see 'The Godfather', in one of the few outings I could tolerate at the time. I had always trusted Marta. During our visit we yukked it up plenty. Like me she had an edge, a trait that we shared with Clara. Unlike Miri and me, Marta had little inhibition in giving as good as she got. There was a melancholy though in her hat I felt went deeper than my own despite my episode of major depression. She carried that sense of being the fifth wheel, a notion Miri and I sheepishly had laughed off over the years.

Although a male friend of hers had showed up that first night, Marta labeled their status as platonic. She'd had no viable love interest for quite some time. Soon she would be angling for a full-time disc jockey gig, having cut her teeth on the university radio station. On Saturday she drove me through Sabino Canyon and that evening we attended a concert in a great old theatre downtown. In my sister I saw a potential present day version of Clara, who, unlike our mother, would imminently complete her degree in journalism, then follow a career path as an FM jock, a medium I desperately wished at this moment I had access to for the long journey home.

* * *

Upon my return to work I was stunned by the sight of a new sandblasting machine in a now squeaky -clean work area, amazed at the rapidity with which management had acted on my request. In true esprit-de-corps Loveless the Younger stopped by to inquire about my thoughts regarding the new equipment after which the blond scion guided me to the door and wished me the best of luck in future endeavors. I left with mixed feelings, having hoped I could have made it for long enough to put away a little money for the summer's rent. Still, I took satisfaction that my sacrifice had not been in vain, that succeeding sandblasters at Loveless would experience a new breath of clean air, and would not, consequently, perish from the earth in a storm of dust. I would leave Tim and Hackleberry at the end of the month having concluded my second consecutive ninety-day living arrangement. Looking for a soft place to land, I moved into the basement of the farmhouse occupied by Solar Boogie and also officially withdrew from school in Greality.

* * *

To this point in my life there had existed no greater expert practitioners in the art of hanging out than the members of Solar Boogie. Their domicile, an old east Boulder County farmhouse, faced the majestic peaks of the Front Range. At dusk, hundreds of bats emerged from the attic-roof for their diurnal exercise and food procurement regimen. We were consistently amused by the antics of the farm's two resident black cats, Nemo and Bird. Bird had an uncanny knack for sticking his head into a glass jar but with significantly less ability to extricate. Rounding out the farm's menagerie were two dogs, the no-nonsense boxer, Captain Hook, who belonged to the band's flamboyant live-in business manager and chef, Jerry, himself a far cry from Rock Symphonique's J.C. Penney style candy-dispensing booking agent. The mild-tempered mutt, Magnolia, officially belonged to Rich, the band's one-time bassist.

The band consisted of more transplanted easterners. This three-story mansion on the edge of the Plains housed Paolo, lead and rhythm guitar and a New Englander; Jerry, Brooklyn-born and bred; and Yosha Knifehits, drummer and financial pipeline from upstate NY all who lived upstairs. Jerry's footfall on the stairs signaled the commencement of the day's activities, rarely before 10:00 a.m. Off the kitchen sat Ernie John's room, the Delta Picker from Chicago, a man who in addition to his sublime blues playing had also demonstrated superior functioning in the arena of the practical joke. Forever on the lookout for new opportunity, during the Yom Kippur holiday that September, the iconoclastic musician had fooled no fewer than three fasting Jews, having turned the kitchen clock backwards by two hours at the agonizing home stretch hour of 5:00 p.m. Keyboard Franco, also from New England, occupied the west-facing small bedroom off the TV-viewing area whose window afforded fine views of the Continental Divide. Upon awakening at his customary hour between 3 and 4 in the afternoon, he typically encountered his mates watching the tube as he trudged to to self-ablute. When Rich moved in that summer, he claimed the only remaining sleeping space, the large closet off the great room, as I was already ensconced underneath it all in the spacious subterranean quarters of the unfinished basement. The band's current bass player, Gersh, a diminutive fellow with a work ethic worthy of John Calvin, lived off-campus with his wife, a woman who had been banned from the house due to personality conflicts with more than one band member. On one occasion the usually soft spoken but tight fisted Gersh had exclaimed with indignation, "Band money for shoelaces?" upon learning that Jerry had assented to such a request from Ernie John.

My move into the band's basement coincided with the release of Bob Dylan and The Band's' iconic *The Basement Tapes*, a collection of songs mostly composed and recorded in the basement of the legendary Big Pink house near Woodstock during the icon's recovery from the fateful, career-changing motorcycle accident during the summer of 1966. The folk, country and blues tunes, both original and traditional, bore a down-home authenticity, a sharp contrast to the dominant psychedelic rock of the 60's. Twenty-four tracks, representing only a fraction of the total cuts, had now been released to instant acclaim in a double album.

We adopted "Lo and Behold" and "Million Dollar Bash" as themes songs at the farm.

From my basement digs I soon wrote "Speak of Survival," a song highly regarded by my fellow musician friends both then and in the future, not only for its David Crosby-inspired melody, but also for its lyrical description of itinerancy:

Speak of Survival and tell me what's true
Speak of Survival and tell me of you
All of us here we just want to get by
Why for others that means nothing less than the sky...

Solar Boogie gigged with some regularity that summer. When they toured to such exotic locales as Lander, Wyoming and Goodland, Kansas (the latter date having featured a police escort to the Colorado line), Rich and I would enjoy the farm's quiet. He and I jammed and dropped in at a few open mics in town. He hailed not far from my neck of the woods, relatively speaking, a few hundred miles west of Amishland, near Pittsburgh. After sitting in at the Sobriety, he and I contemplated putting our own band together. An unexpected call from Nina catalyzed that idea. Now living with her parents and having split up from Nick, she wanted to put together another ensemble. I was interested as long as Rich would play bass, as much for his friendship as for his bass chops.

First though, in keeping with our devotion to film, especially those intellectually driven and foreign, Rich and I had traveled to Denver to view the new Ingmar Bergman offering, *Cries and Whispers*. Joining us was a female friend whose interest in him he hoped to shake by having me along.

I mistakenly thought her hairy legs would be the visual low point of the evening, but those features were soon upstaged by the film's early scene featuring Liv Ullmann's character plunging a shard of glass into her pubis. In déjà vu fashion I left my seat in the throes of major dizziness and coming to on the floor in the aisle, gazing upward at a host of attendees, bearded men and palefaced women now visibly concerned for my wellbeing. Up went the houselights and blank went the screen. "Are you all right," someone asks? *Am I all right? Aren't you the ones so numb to genital mutiliation that you aren't also made ill? How can any of you be all right?"* My friends and a reluctant usher then removed me to the lobby. Enroute I note not only my last similar episode in Greality but also the more distant occasion when I had passed out in the Boonton High School auditorium during a compulsory viewing of a pre-prom movie graphically depicting the perils of venereal disease. Closure for this evening soon came with receipt of two free passes for the upcoming premiere of *Fiddler on the Roof.* Whether this honorarium came my way due to coincidence or because the theatre manager had recognized my ethnicity, I could not adequately determine. I derived, however, from this on-the-fly example of customer service, the message that I should stick to pathologies involving my own kind. Hence, the three of us wandered downtown looking to see if *Love and Death* was showing anywhere.

* * *

Nina's family lived in a suburb of South Denver, closer to Boulder than the southern Pueblo area haunts where she and Nick had long stomped, but still more than an hour from the farmhouse, making for long drives to rehearse in their cottage off their house. The bonding among the three of us proceeded easily. I was delighted to synthesize these two musical chapters, the folk and blues of my recent association with Rich and the doomed but compelling head rock effort of the year before with Nina. One day the guitarist had proposed, in a ritual unfamiliar to me, but apparently a staple in her old school code, that we *kidnap a drummer.* Towards that end, the three of us drove deep into the mountains to attend her target's gig, and present him with an offer he could not refuse. The trip through the Sangre's evoked repeated peals of laughter that so frequently characterize band honeymoons before the onset of hassles. The drummer stood no chance, for Nina's charisma, persistence and talent were legendary among her peers. A rarity during the mid-seventies, a female lead guitarist bore a not insignificant burden inherent to invading the domain occupied by the likes of Messieurs Hendrix, Clapton, King, and Allman. That girl could play.

Initially gratified that she had wanted to resume a musical association, I thought we might recreate the originality of Rock Symphonique, but our developing repertoire soon invoked more of the predictable pop. I adapted, however reluctantly, but couldn't help but feel puzzled as to why she chose me, of all people, to join her in her lurch towards the mainstream. Entertaining the thought she was exacting revenge for the Nobleduke fiasco, I made a mental note to share an account of my Nobleduke caper with Ernie John, anticipating probable approval.

Rich had expressed dissatisfaction, but the two of us didn't bail. A weekend gig at a club in Colorado's most southern city, Trinidad, a town that in future years would become famous as the world capital for sex change operations both paid and was not altogether unsatisfying.

Meanwhile, big news broke at the farm. Yosha Knifehits was leaving the band with his new love for upstate New York, where he would take his place as scion in his father's business. A similar lure had been creeping into my own thinking, especially so since the fact of my own familial rapprochement. I could see no point, however, in making that leap without my own helpmeet. Unlike my drum-playing buddy, and disinclined toward an interest in business generally, I doubted my prospects of either finding a woman suited to my sensibilities and/or sufficiently long-suffering to partner through such a transition. But I also had the more pressing concern of having drifted into a no longer desired itinerancy. I needed to make a bold change or risk some repeated version of my earlier troubles.

In the end in the wake of Nina's decision to abandon us and run into the arms of, no kidding, an agent named Dick Dollar, Rich and I saddled up the Pinto in preparation for a trek east, he to Ohio for a visit with his sister, and I bound for the Manheim Industrial Grind to enter the cauldron of the ironworks.

Chapter 14
RIPTIDE

Rich and I vacated the farm's cellar and closet on a late September morning in my orange automobile. Rich, with his uncanny physical resemblance to a darker-haired Harpo Marx, had over the summer become the closest thing I'd had to a younger brother. Articulate and smart, he had been great company through the ups and downs of the Nina miasma. We now hurtled through the Nebraska night, immersed in dialogue regarding the relative degree of primal energy represented by guitarist John McLaughlin and pianist McCoy Tyner. Banking on the notion that the increasing distance from Boulderado would translate into closure, I acknowledged that intentionally or inadvertently, Nina had indeed exacted her pound of flesh for the Nobleduke caper.

Rich did express a cautionary skepticism, however, with respect to my sudden decision to attempt scionhood. He was right, as I had not thought it through with the necessary consideration, instead having reacted to Nina's musical abandonment as I might have the breakup of a love affair. Back at the farm, when Jerry had asked, while putting the finishing touches on his much-loved gazpacho, why I had to go back east simply because things hadn't worked out with Nina, I answered, "I can't explain," to which he rejoined, *well, then you have to go.* Mostly, it was my sense of having failed in establishing a minimum living standard through playing music, but the farm's changing vibes had also become a factor. Yosha Knifehit's departure had made it necessary for the band to find a new drummer. The replacement then had proved polarizing for the group, (They would break up early the next year.) so the domicile no longer felt conducive for ease or self-reflection. Wanting to visit his family and needing transportation Rich and I had hit the road. What other set of circumstances would provide a more reasoned and balanced context to consider entering one's family business?

Depositing him in Athens, Ohio, Meris' old stomping ground I headed across PA without a sense of what lay ahead. Whether hopeful because my father and I had reached a sort of normalization of relations the year before, or due to a delusional belief that we had reached a sort of normalization the year before, I could not be sure. He wouldn't be pleased, I imagined, that in the previous nine months I had accomplished little more than dropping out of graduate school after only one quarter. Breaking up with Bianca, and having failed to get a leg up in the music business hadn't exactly done wonders for my self -esteem either. My once folkie sister now pulling down nearly four digits a week in a show band not only boggled my mind, but also made more painfully difficult continued justification for itinerancy. Driving a spanking new VW van ferrying our father, she now pulled up next to my well -traveled Pinto in the living unit's parking lot. Immediately evident was Herman's air of smugness as we exchanged greetings. I barely recognized my sister now coiffed and well heeled. Miri has joined the parade. Struggling to remain on this side of the event horizon, the distinct liklihood that I had again stepped into the same abhain twice reared its unpleasant head.

My parents were preparing to depart for a two-week vacation to Israel, a happy fact for them and a convenient one for me, as it meant I would have the living unit to myself during my adjustment to life back east and to the ironworks specifically. My father's willingness to undertake this trip had surprised me, as it went against his attitude toward vacations involving travel generally, which he had previously summed up with the declaration, "If you don't go, you don't have to come back." Notwithstanding that intriguing but depressing point of view, now with Marta's imminent graduation making tuition payments a thing of the past, my parents had at last reached the milestone of travel for which my mother had longed yearned. Herman and I had agreed that I should start working before their departure and continue in his absence. Being broke I had little choice unless I found some other employment in the meantime, something we both acknowledged made little sense.

He had wanted me to sign legal papers regarding a partnership he'd set up, a tax shelter, something he'd mentioned to me the previous year. On my way out the door my mother provided a heads up, 'five percent'*with the remainder to be gifted later* apparently according to my father, *when I had demonstrated sufficient maturity and responsibility.* It was plain she'd gone against his instructions in choosing to inform me of my remarginalized status, her disclosure now representing an entirely inadequate effort at damage control. Plan B would now require formulation. I'd need a few hundred in my pocket before I could leave again. I dutifully visited the attorney remaining mum upon my return. Eventually my capricious father asked if I understood the message. *Oh, I got it.* I drove them to the airport, wished them a bon voyage and returned to Allentown simmering over why Miri hadn't had my back. Marta hadn't been heard from yet, and I wondered what stance she might take.

Miri's show band played Albany the following weekend. I saw her but faltered when it came to expressing my feelings, conflicted because of our history. I resigned myself, however, to the notion that if she wanted most-favored-offspring status with our father she was welcome to it.

I signed to stall for time. Had I raised a challenge I would have needed to make a hasty exit from Allentown with no place to go and no resources at my disposal. Worse yet would have been any attempt to bargain with the old man under such duress. Neither of these options made as much sense as working for a couple of weeks while he and my mother sojourned in the Holy Land, and wait for their return to tell him where he could stick it.

Sometime during that second week though I stopped showing up at the ironworks altogether. On the night before I picked my parents up at the airport, I drove to my Aunt Paula's home, (She and Uncle Doug had separated.) where we watched the sixth game of that year's World Series, between the Big Red Machine and Boston Red Sox, a game that went down in history as one of the greatest, ending with Carlton Fisk's dramatic home run hitting the left field foul pole in dear old Fenway. After bringing my aunt up to speed, she acknowledged what I had more than suspected, that I would be in for one rough day tomorrow. Then came a recollection. At her and Doug's old house when I couldn't have been more than eight, with my parents and mother's extended family present, I had made the unadvisable comment with regard to how little I felt I had in common with my father, a statement that resulted in the latter's having gone ballistic. Apparently, I had wished I could relate to my father with the ease that I then felt with my athletically minded uncle, a desire so strong that my young mind had failed to adequately evaluate the disclosure's humiliating impact on him.

Paula wasn't wrong. My parents looked well rested emerging from the jet way. I held off speaking until we put the bags in the trunk, even until we reached the airport exit, but once I pulled onto Route 22 all hell broke loose. He lost it when he realized I'd left the ironworks with no family member present in his absence. Keeping my eyes on the road, I didn't react except to say I didn't like being set up anymore than he did and that it had occurred to me over the course of the last few days that my life was no more fucked up than anyone else's I knew. Once depositing them in Allentown I would forthwith be on my not so merry way. I was fortunate, however, that our chinwag continued inside the living unit, where he paused in his tirade to read Marta's letter. Having enclosed the partnership form unsigned, she explained that unless the shares were equally distributed she would have no part of it.

* * *

Club owners are generally not all that interesting, let alone elegant, but from my first meeting with Eddie I sensed a lightness of spirit and a welcoming, profound gentleness. Miri had clued me in to his club, the Fox, on the Delaware River. I would have had little interest in the area if not for him, for although home to many jazz musicians, some well known, Delware Water Gap's provinciality had initially unsettled me, its too small population making me immediately aware of the inevitability of gossip. Eddie hired me for a gig right after our first handshake. The date was successful enough for a return engagement. Over the next year I played at least once and often twice a month on Saturday evenings. Eddie loved musicians. He valued them. Even with the occasional piss poor crowd it was almost a pleasure to play music on his stage.

Delaware Water Gap, an hour north from Allentown, gateway to the Poconos, was a vacation spot for New Yorkers and a weekend respite from the Manheim Industrial Grind. Overlooking the Delaware's wondrous water gap that served as the border between Pennsylvania and New Jersey, I could view the Jersey rest stop across the river, the place where I had told Ray to push on west some three and a half years before. Recently, the area had absorbed an influx of its own belated countercultural holdouts, river squatters who had protested the construction of the Tocks Island Dam by the Army Corps of Engineers. The squatters had been removed by Federal marshals in February of 1974 around the same time that Eddie had bought the Fox. Eddie's energy helped synthesize the countercultural elements with the Gap's more traditional jazz community. It was a good time and place to be playing music, and as a number of other clubs existed in the area I managed to eke out a living.

A divorced father determined to quit the rat race and sign on to the age self discovery Eddie had provided a shot of inspiration. Now in his early forties he'd finished working on his own"Maggie's Farm," his lifestyle shift having demonstrated that the cultural shifts of the last several years might actually be sustainable, a reassuring thought. As I came to know him it became evident that his gentleness of manner was accompanied by a wicked sense of humor. He had once shared a birthday card he intended for a family member whose lines read, *When I Think How Small Am I When Compared to the Vastness of the Universe I Can Only Wonder if You Understand... Just How Small You Are Too.* More than this, though, Eddie was a unique activist who engaged in his own version of street theatre. Upset and irritated by automobiles speeding on 611, the Gap's, Main Street during afternoon school release hours, he would, on occasion, remove a chair from his bar, and after placing it in the the middle of the street sit himself there in an effort to force drivers to slow down.

This was the year of the country's bicentennial, and the nation's collective unconscious now grappled with the process of integrating the sixties into its historical fabric. Nixon was gone, if pardoned. His departure had signaled another death -blow to McCarthyism, to which the disgraced ex-President had hitched his wagon early in his political career. Vietnam had ended badly, but ended, as had the draft three years earlier. Jimmy Carter had recently won presidential primaries in the South as a non-racist. Things were both looking up and calming down.

One of the joints where I gigged across the river in western Jersey, the old Hainesburg Inn, was located only a few miles this side of Wasigan. Clara had shared that she and Herman had often driven from camp to the town to procure ice cream both during their courting days and early on in their marriage with me in tow. Twenty eight years later, fortified by blackberry brandy, I now rendered the tunes of Jackson Browne, John Prine, Dylan, and a few of my own to the inns' assembled fans of acoustic music. I still hoped for normalization with Herman, thinking against most indicators that he'd eventually come around to some modest acceptance of me. Living in such proximity to him and Clara, I visited monthly, my ongoing itinerancy a point of contention notwithstanding. When my mother wanted discussion, serious or otherwise we would meet at Ye Olde Diner out on Highway 222. Here, as we enjoyed the tasty Pennsylvania Dutch selections, she expressed her own concerns regarding my lack of motivation towards obtaining financial stability. She often concluded our meetings with a smattering of paperback fiction, Robert Ludlum novels among her favorites. My mother's capacity for adaptability had served her well during her first few years on the northern tier of Amishland. She served on the board of the Allentown symphony and had established new friendships of her own. Determined to build an independent social network as a buffer against her marital dissatisfaction, she indicated that, "your father will have to pay a lot more than he thinks if he wants me to go away." The concept of no-fault divorce not yet having reached the Commonwealth of Pennsylvania made any prospect of a permanent legal parting a non-starter for either of them. His miserly payoff proposal of twenty thousand dollars she swiftly dismissed with the derision it deserved. Right out of the Ayn Rand playbook, my father had clung to the cherished belief that only the 'creators' of wealth, its 'producers', should call the tune when it comes to any and all substantative issues, civil or social. Since his life partner of nearly thirty years did not, in his mind fit that category, having merely raised his children, he reasoned she should be grateful for whatever he "gifts" her in the form of walking away money. The holiness of wealth creation demanded no less.

For Father's Day I had bought him something I mistakenly thought he might read, *Zen and the Art of Motorcycle Maintenance*, Robert Pirsig's philosophical narrative and family drama describing the author's struggle to meld the world of opposites, the intuitive and creative with the mechanical and analytical. Herman had placed it on the end table next to his reading chair. As far as I could determine from its consistent position and the lack of wear and tear on its cover he never once picked it up. I suppose I had harbored the hope that the book might provide him an intellectually stimulating and non-political glimpse into the world I inhabited, something in which he had absolutely no interest. Leaving the house that Father's Day, I experienced another uncannily metaphorical misadventure. Not quite halfway to Delaware Water Gap, in the midst of a severe thunderstorm, the hatchback of the orange Pinto inexplicably shattered, leaving its rear interior completely exposed to the rain, thoroughly saturating the carpet.

The well-traveled automobile had recently been given a name by my new guitar-playing buddy, Roland, a Pocono native. He and I sporadically gigged in a five- piece band, a musical entity which I had strangely named, Band on the Half Shell, in a tip of the hat to Kurt Vonnegut and his recent book,'"Venus on the Half Shell." On a weekend date in Scranton we played our typical rock set which had featured tunes by the likes of the Kinks, but were terminated after the first set when the owner indicated, "Bluegrass doesn't go over that well here". With stubborn determination Roland then unsuccessfully implored the clubowner to pay us for the nite's work, not the one-third remittance we were eventually issued.

Roland had dubbed the car "Pinto Acres Estates," in recognition of my rambling history and propensity. An insightful name, for I still felt very much at loose ends. Instead of finding a decent rental house, I had continued to live with Eddie above the bar after he moved there, having left the rental house he'd invited me to share in scenic Cherry Valley. The bedroom above the bar offered little privacy, the apartment having become a fishbowl, but I could not bring myself to either rent for myself or find a roommate in a more suitable setting. By now I couldn't help but consider my refusal to do so an exemplar of a character flaw, this profound shiftlessness, a kind of monkey on my back, not so different from ones I saw all around me involving drug and/or alcohol abuse. Rambling fever still constituted my drug of choice. Like many substance-dependent people I minimized its corrosive affect. It might not kill me, but it assuredly would not make me stronger.

I should have settled somewhere and found a tolerable means of income by now. Teaching would have been the likely candidate, but I'd shown little interest to get certification, let alone go back to school for a master's degree, a prerequisite for a substantial position. I could always substitute but my inclination towards sleeping late, a priceless benefit of my marginal and itinerant musical career, had precluded that possibility. Nevertheless, had I made some effort to make use of my college degree now nearly seven years on, I might not be facing my present predicament —the unpleasant recognition that women preferred spending time with men who had money.

Reality was breaking up that old gang of mine. If I needed artistic justification for making some changes (and

I did, of course) it came in the lyrics of Jackson Browne, whose songs I prominently featured in any set I performed. I frequently sang "The Pretender" and "Running on Empty," which spoke to two emerging and salient issues: the inevitability of compromising authenticity with the need to survive, and the declining capacity to rely on friends to help one get through.

Bicentennial summer in Delaware Water Gap proceeded lazily, its only drama having involved news of my father's boat running aground in New York Harbor as he and his guests viewed the tall ships sailing through that July 4. I heard from my mother that he'd considerably exerted himself swimming to dislodge the *Lady Clara,* but still had needed help which came from nearby boats and the Coast Guard. I couldn't say I exactly missed being there, but contemplating how such a cool event had turned to shit in literally a New York minute made me sad for the old man. It seemed that when he wasn't doing this to himself, the world stepped in to do it for him. He had asked me to accompany him on day excursions out of Sandy Hook, but I dodged these invitations, recapitulating, as my rationale, the five percent solution he'd imposed last fall. I had no trouble being the black sheep again, finding the role strangely liberating now.

On one summer day I drove to Wasigan in the company of a young woman I'd met while gigging at the Hainesburg Inn. Ten years after the camp's last summer we traversed the dirt road and beheld the lake with its small stone skyward jutting tower. Sold only a year ago to a Pakistani doctor who had built a mansion on what used to be the girls' hill, the Wasigan property remained beautiful. I'd been nearby on several occasions, but hadn't been able to bring myself to make the journey alone. Though Clara had indicated the new owners would welcome visitors, especially family, we chose not to enter, content to view the shimmering lake and remaining buildings from a distance. Memories flooded me but I didn't really regard the scene as some lost Promised Land. I mainly missed my grandmother. I described the general history of Wasigan to my companion. Taking a last look, we drove past the entrance and away.

* * *

Towards the end of summer I played my first wedding. Yosha Knifehits and his bride tied the knot at his family compound in upstate New York. I sang 'Today', by Jefferson Airplane at their ceremony where I also partied with Jerry and Paolo, the event's musical highlight, of course, sung by us all, Dylan's "Million Dollar Bash." A year into scionhood, Yosha looked happy, on his way towards becoming the scrap metal mogul of the region. Paolo, now back in New England, looked to be at loose ends without the band, more or less as rootless as me. Jerry had been doing sound for other bands, and soon to be employed in Yosha's company, also missed Solar Boogie, and particularly Ernie John, who had packed it in for Sweet Home Chicago where he now pursued his musical career. Franco and Rich had remained out West, and no one could say for how much longer.

Andrea was Yosha's first cousin who I had first met the summer before when she visited the farm and Paolo particularly. Not unlike her sibling and cousin, she had showed some interest in the family business only to be stifled by the fact that her father and uncle had eschewed women in management. We hung out in the wake of my aborted attempt at ironworks existence. Before meeting Eddie and then moving to Delaware Water Gap, I had briefly lived in New Brunswick where I contemplated the low probability scenario of graduate school at Rutgers. Ten years before in this same town I had experienced my four days of fame as one of 'tomorrow's leaders' at Boy's State. During this present interval I had worked part time for, if not the most exciting governmental agency, then certainly one of its friendliest, the Soil Conservation Service. Created during the New Deal to prevent another Dust Bowl, the local office had needed someone to stack and file documents four hours a day, five days a week. Who was I to decline this opportunity?

She and Paolo no longer an item, Andrea and I had arranged to meet in Manhattan and drive to the compound over Christmas. I welcomed the companionship. She and I were platonic, and I could think of no better way to get through the approaching holidays than to spend it with her upstate in Old Smithy, New York. One of the regional lakes, the fourth, to be precise, had long ago achieved literary notoriety as the setting for Theodore Dreiser's *An American Tragedy.* Andrea was the family's academic, finishing a master's in archaeology. Her high-pitched, slightly histrionic speaking voice possessed an endearing quality. Still, the closer we got to Old Smithy amidst the snowdrifts and the cold, the more anxious I became. Altogether unexpectedly, I began to experience my familiar dissociative symptoms. There had been a confluence of stressors. First, the cold and snow were reminiscent of the miserable winter in Maine now almost four years ago. Of greater import, though, was the imminent visit with her family, one that despite its own issues and my friend's protestations sounded enviably less dysfunctional than my own. Her brother, a recognizable fellow traveler had, before Yosha, found a way to work in the family business, had married, and according to Andrea didn't appear to be any the worse off for either choice. I was twenty-seven, with nary a pot to piss in. The recognition of the disparity had brought on symptoms.

Now these several months later during Bicentennial summer we walked along First Lake, glad to be in each other's company. If we had contemplated moving our friendship to another level neither of us acted on it, but Andrea's acceptance of my symptoms along with the comfort she provided at the time had been instrumental in making those panic-driven dissociative moments the last of their kind.

* * *

A second friend who had eventually made a successful transition to scionhood, and with whom I shared a strong affinity was Rob. He was a painter who had been enrolled in Greality before transferring to school in New England. During my pre Yankee Folly days the two of us walked the town streets (*wide streets and narrow minds*) engaging in repartee. Reconnecting now, I sensed his war of attrition with respect to entering the family optical business. His dad, his benevolent parent, was someone who could be needy but not rejecting or judgmental. His parents had divorced when he was twelve. First in the stone house he had rented in Bucks County, and then in his Morningside Heights apartment, we hung out at more or less regular monthly intervals. The move to Manhattan had been his capitulation to working for his dad, not all that bad an environment, I thought, in which to surrender.

These were restoring visits. I continued to gig in Delaware Water Gap, but I needed more intellectual stimulation along with an occasional dose of ethno cultural familiarity. I didn't require a broad base of such interaction, but a hint of recognizable tribal identification yet proved satisfying. During these years Rob became my closest friend as we shared that dual affinity. With the city as the backdrop we'd pass the time communing and commiserating. During some early on point in his scionhood, we had meandered through Central Park, where fortified with marijuana we debriefed from the movie *Alien*, both of us having experienced profound difficulty in ejecting that horrid penis-like monster from our minds. Many contemporaries would subsequently attest to that bizarre creation as being the most frightening image in that film.

* * *

That November two significant events transpired. First, Jimmy Carter was elected President, the first Southerner to win the White House since before the Civil War. Second, my father had rewritten the partnership agreement, having equalized the shares among my sisters and me, thus providing a mutually face-saving opportunity for me to try the business again. I held off for several months, but in early March I made the decision to give the ironworks a serious try. So I went to work for Herman.

I rented an apartment in Allentown and and continued to gig in the Gap. The first few months proceeded well enough except that, often exhausted but vigilant, I would fall asleep early in the evening, and then awaken and begin getting dressed for work at 3:00 a.m., not able to orient to my actual schedule. One Saturday afternoon I had inadvertently kept a female visitor waiting at my door for an hour because I'd fallen asleep after having worked that morning. Amazed that she hadn't departed after ten minutes, I wondered if my gainful employment might have constituted an independent variable. Appeal to women was, after all, one of the primary reinforcement of such apparent stability.

Like most scions I started at the bottom, but unlike most I stayed there. Although the business would eventually pay for me to take a course in Industrial Management at a local community college, my father was nowhere near ready to delegate anything managerial to me, his trust in me minimal. Since I harbored considerable doubts as to whether I had the disposition, aptitude or inclination for management, I only minimally protested the unskilled labor I was assigned. Some weeks I worked in the cleaning room grinding castings for six and a half hours, and then if I were lucky enough, be called upon during the last ninety minutes to help the molders during the pouring of the iron. Along with other designated employees, I shifted the weights from each poured row of molds to the next, first by removing weights and brackets, placing them on the succeeding mold, ad nauseam. Intense heat emanated from the cupola. Performing this task on hot summer days could be dizzying. I needed to go outside for air on one such occasion, much to Herman's chagrin and disapproval, but in cooler weather an undeniable rhythm proceeded from the iron pouring that I found almost agreeable, sometimes Zen-like, although this being the last task of the day, it's timing just as likely accounted for its appeal.

On July 4th the ironworks shut down for its annual summer vacation and I went to hang in the Poconos for a few days. It was a good break and I appreciated the fact that I didn't have the usual money worries that I'd experienced when I had lived there. After my return to work, though, things began to get weird. Herman started calling me on several weekday evenings for no apparent reason. My being away for more than a weekend had evidently caused him a distress that only his making contact with me would ease. This was not a good sign. He'd also succeeded in sufficiently wearing me down such that I agreed to the long postponed Sunday boat excursion. This meant awakening at dawn's early light on my one full day off, dreaded before and lamented during. After a relatively mild sail out we came about near the Verrazano-Narrows Bridge, where within moments we were caught in a riptide. The return trip, which in normal conditions might have taken an hour, thus became a five -hour ordeal. An epochal struggle ensued, my father ordering me to assume the helm while he furiously manned the sails in a desperate attempt to get us moving. He exploded in frustration with the sorry state of my navigational abilities. "Steer for the tower on the shore," he repeatedly yelled, as if I could draw on the years of my now non-existent nautical experience to comply with his order. This continued through the remainder of the afternoon, although the interaction soon generalized from my shipboard incompetence to the more familiar themes of my inadequacy as a son. He only quieted when I had finally found the words to tell him that if he'd taken the time and had shown enough patience in teaching me anything during my boyhood, perhaps things wouldn't have developed so poorly between us. After a brief silence, he mumbled just loud enough for me to hear that I was a 'good kid'. Undoubtedly the most affirming comment I'd heard from him over the course of my life, it was nevertheless one I'd worked for way too long to get. Not unlike many fathers from his generation, he didn't believe in the value of praise or encouragement, stipulating that his lack of a negative comment meant all was well. *A good kid at twenty-nine,* I sighed, fully realizing I still had many knots to go before leaving my own version of Captain Ahab.

Part of my duties at the ironworks had included delivering castings to factories in New Jersey. Almost always grateful to be away from the ironworks for the day I was surprised one Friday morning in August when he came along. Out of nowhere, on the way home, he lit into me, the afternoon's theme my apparent lack of initiative. Exactly how this could have been displayed I had no clue since his instructions had uniformly involved me minding my own business and doing what I was told. Something else had to be driving this present rage, but who knew what? An intense thunderstorm then arrived as we lumbered homeward west on Route 22. He pulled over when it became impossible to see through the windshield, and I opened the cab and got out, walking along the shoulder in the pouring rain, watching him inch forward as the light changed, another occasion now where he wouldn't know what to do. At that moment not only was I determined to walk or hitch all the way home in these conditions, but I also resigned myself to the possibility of a lightning strike that would end everything once and for all.

Marta's move to Long Island from the Midwest where she'd cultivated some renown as a rock and roll deejay soon lifted the old man's spirits for a brief period. Apparently feeling he could spare my workmanlike efforts for a couple of days, he entrusted me with an envelope of cash to deliver to her to help get her started. She was hoping to break into the

New York market, recently having been hired locally. While visiting her I related the story of my phone call with John Hammond, Sr., a tale that left her curious and non-plussed. Within a few months, though, she herself left New York, moving back to Kansas City, the Apple's lure apparently not sufficiently strong.

When Elvis Presley died in August, my father provided his own brief commentary regarding the fallen icon. Pulling up beside me in his yellow pay loader, and having barely dodged the hyperactive Gris, he removed the stogie from his mouth, (He neither smoked nor chewed, but apparently enjoyed biting them.) and extemporized about Elvis having been responsible for "most of the hysteria of your generation." Shaking my head as he rolled away, I realized what Presley must have signified to him, the king of rock bursting forth twenty years earlier when my father was in his early forties. He would have been freaked by the idea of a white male modeling a black man. Add the hip gyrations, and the poor man might even have experienced an apoplexy bordering on transient psychosis. When a few weeks later I suffered a deep cut on my right thumb from an accident in the grinding room, the old man actually seemed pleased, as if not being able to play the guitar for awhile might be just what I needed.

I had promised myself that I would give the ironworks a year, and as awful as Herman's moods could be, I wasn't ready to quit after only five months. So on Labor Day weekend I returned to Old Smithy in hopes of gaining some semblance of perspective, a basis of comparison, so to speak, if such a thing were possible, and if not that, then at least to enjoy a few days away from this hellhole.

Chapter 15

SATURN'S RETURN

I had no idea on my way to the compound that Andrea would accompany me back to Allentown for a few days. We had spoken only sporadically since my visit last summer, but our ease as friends remained strong. She had completed her masters and at loose ends, so she thought that a few days visiting the Manheim Industrial Grind, while not the most desirable of locations could offer a respite from her own clan. My invitation was spontaneous and based at least in part to my aversion of returning to the Grind alone. Her parents, however, had reacted as if I'd Andrea and I had named a date. This gave me pause. Gone from the shtetl too long, I had failed to recognize them as Old World, having underestimated how eagerly they wanted their daughter to get married. In any event Andrea's visit confirmed that what we were was friends.

So autumn came to the northern tier of Amishland, Allentown, and the ironworks. The Yankees and Dodgers had resumed their historic World Series rivalry for the first time in fourteen years. The last time these teams had met in the Fall Classic had been only a month and a half before JFK's assassination. Reggie Jackson's third home run in as many swings in Game six which gave the Yankees the title, certainly got Herman's attention. He called me with a level of exuberance I'd not heard or seen from him since our 1963 trip to the Polo Grounds when Duke Snider, so long of the Dodgers, had put one out of the park for the hapless Casey Stengel-managed Mets. Only the birth of the new national league franchise in 1962 had galvanized my father's baseball interest. He had never been a fan of the Yankees, even and especially during their heydey of the fifties and early sixties. The Mets' miserable performance during those first years afforded him an unexpectedly therapeutic relationship with the team that to this day holds the record for the worst single season winning percentage in baseball history. As with many alienated fathers and sons of the time, baseball had formed a predictable, if narrow, bridge between us—or baseball, plus in our case, the Shel Silverstein song popularized back in '69 by Johnny Cash, "A Boy Named Sue." Witnessing a home run or hearing that song could get us by when nothing else could. The Mets had also inspired Clara to write a song for the team, a ditty that subsequently received honorable mention in a contest sponsored by the club to find a team song. She was awarded an autographed baseball from the '63 squad that she gave to me several years later and which I still own.

Allentown, on the main artery within the Manheim Industrial Grind had been a hub of iron, steel, and truck manufacturing for generations. Like Philadelphia and Baltimore, its residential areas were comprised of row houses, my apartment in one of them. A blue-collar town of the rustbelt, within a decade parts of it would resemble the urban blight of Flint, Michigan, as major industries shut down, migrated to the non-union south or moved overseas. Not that it looked all that good when I lived there, but at least the industrial mainframe was still in place, if unsure of its future.

Entering a laundromat in that gritty city early one autumn evening my life literally turned on a dime, in the form of a coin that had stubbornly refused entry into a dryer despite the many attempts of the hassled attractive dark-haired woman to place it therein. I volunteered my services and quite unexpectedly came to her rescue. We exchanged names and numbers, although she indicated she was seeing someone. The encounter was pleasant enough, but I needed to be on my way. Many similar chance meetings had fizzled, and although Jenna would be nice to see again, later for her and for her two adorable little daughters, fairly sure I wasn't ready for all that involved.

Getting into Pinto Acres I recalled prior random encounters. Most had gone nowhere because of what I came to formulate as the Billie Holiday principle—those that have, get; those that haven't, well... Being in a relationship often makes one more attractive to others. Conversely, when one is without, the vulnerability can be costly for the unattached person to risk pursuit, and the same vulnerability often makes one that less attractive. Wasn't there some other, safer way to meet women? I thought it over as I fell off to sleep.

Jenna and I talked every couple of weeks and I eventually asked her out, although her current romantic involvement (with her therapist, good luck with that) had precluded taking things further. Despite that curious and concerning fact, as well as her status as a divorced mom with two small children, she had continued to make steady appearance on my radar over the next several weeks. When she called after Thanksgiving, suggesting we meet the first Saturday in December, I agreed without hesitation.

Her apartment, a hovel not unlike my own, but located in a seemlier neighborhood, was a twenty-minute walk away. We had the day, a cold gray Saturday together. Jenna had moved to Allentown two years ago from West Virginia seeking refuge from her family of origin in the industrial North in the aftermath of a divorce. Parts of her narrative reminded me of the folk and bluegrass songs that have long chronicled the migration of mountain people to the cities of the North to find work, the living-in-exile syndrome. Certainly her wistfulness was the same, but her sadness and her daughters' tragedy was her ex-husband, their father. He had wanted an open marriage, to which she reluctantly assented, but he could not handle her involvement with another man. Ten months after divorce he suicided.

In mid-afternoon we walked in the snow. Miri who lived nearby happened to drive by, and seeing me walking arm in arm with this unfamiliar companion honked the horn as she slowed momentarily. Her peripheral presence prompted me to recount our Colorado adventures. I wanted to take my sister's brief appearance as an omen, but whether it signaled a blessing, a warning, or patience, I didn't know. Jenna was compelling, representing something completely different, but I half-supposed it was probably for the best that she wasn't more available, her story as spooky as the hollers from where she came.

* * *

Slogging through Advent was made more palatable by my first of several viewings of *Close Encounters of the Third Kind*. Spielberg's new film implied a process parallel to my own, an emergence from dormancy into a renewed self-knowledge. The power of this movie had extended into the ironworks' cleaning room, where a most peculiar coincidence then occurred. The calendar picture adorning the wall in the patternmaker's workspace was of the aliens' landing site itself, Devil's Tower. Still unaware of the concept of synchronicity, I nevertheless felt something afoot. If such a powerful coincidental symbol could extend this far into my distressed environment, then didn't that prove that something was working at a higher level? An invitation from a Greality associate, an aspiring writer now living in California suggested I might have a way out of Allentown if I so chose, a hopeful thought, but also a low probability event given my history with that state. Having not heard further from Jenna, I fought against false hope from that quarter.

Amidst this flux Meris had reappeared. Earlier in the year her family had moved to of all places, the capital region of Amishland near its southern tier and not far from the old ironworks. She had accompanied me to a gig at the Fox during a brief September stopover, where she observed me buying a round for the bar, the generosity of a man who is flush from an excess of blackberry brandy. Now back for the holiday break from her southern California home, she had come to my Allentown digs for the long Christmas weekend where we would assess our prospects of resuming a relationship now nearly eight years gone. Her comfort with me I attributed to my gainful employment. My comfort with her reflected my awareness of that basis. Two former lovers trying to see if they could get it back together in a different context. Did she really believe she would want to sign on as the helpmeet of a reluctant prodigal son? Did I? It was hard to imagine; the culture shock alone of the requisite move to the Manheim Industrial Grind from Santa Monica seemed prohibitive. Moreover, unable to provide a guarantee that I would remain in the ironworks for the long haul made me wonder where we would land in the increasing liklihood that I left.

These issues were on the table when Jenna called to extend Christmas greetings. Curious, my first love wanted to know all. She wasn't brought down, not annoyed, mostly intrigued, and probably relieved. Enough had transpired in both our lives to elicit bemusement on both our parts at this unexpected intrusion; however, there was no mistaking the change in momentum. For three days Meris and I had pondered the possibility of renewal. In the wake of Jenna's call, the scenario disintegrated. Too much and not enough had passed between us. On this Yule, karma had left its calling card.

* * *

Miri's move to D.C. in mid-December made sense for her, but had unsettled me as the New Year rang in. She and her Kenny Burrell contest winning guitar player, and sometimes on, sometimes off boyfriend were set to gig in that area and had relocated. Once there she rented from a woman she thought I might like. Miri was relentless in her attempts to find me a girlfriend! In early January she introduced me to Brenda and I subsequently invited her to Allentown, Jenna's holiday greeting appearing to be merely that.

With the bleakness of January on the northern tier of Amishland, my *joie de vie* quotient now settled into the dull-normal range. Dodging Herman's mercurial temper now constituted a war of attrition. Outside of the occasional visit from Roland, often with a Gap buddy in tow I had no social life of which to speak. My writer friend's invitation, though difficult to imagine accepting, looked better with each passing week. Doing so would mean the end of any real thought of financial security, but remaining in the ironworks meant forever being linked with Herman. My father's ongoing assertion that he had no plans for retirement at the very least represented an indefinite lifestyle choice (insofar as the words "lifestyle" and "Herman" could be placed together). Finally, the reemergence of the Loveless ski scenario involving the liklihood of a major respiratory illness reminded me that I too, might die in the sandpile if I didn't find an alternative way of life.

Brenda had provided the catalyst. Visiting Allentown as planned she had arranged a return flight to D.C. from the local airport for early Monday morning. As we breakfasted, concluding what had been a pleasurable couple of days, during which time she had reintroduced me to the power of Beethoven's *Eroica*, I cogitated over an unexpected Sunday evening call from Herman requesting that I meet him at the living unit early the next morning and drive with him to the ironworks in his truck, something about the Mercedes needing a tow, and that he was unwilling to leave his pickup overnight at the foundry. With Brenda in tow I now complied. In his pickup we sat, my father, my weekend companion, and me, each of us contemplating how best to initiate safe conversation. Brenda, I was to discover, had her own problems, but in this awkward situation had behaved with poise. She most assuredly had not, upon my return to work deserved being labeled the object of my 'whoring.'

Was this new installment about my having a life of my own or did it owe more to the woman in question? Did he even know that my companion was my sister's landlady, as I now recalled his admonishment of years ago that I "not corrupt Miri"?

I showed up through Wednesday, the full finality of my fatherlessness taking a couple of days to sink in. He remained on the warpath with everyone during those couple of days. On Thursday I slept in, awakened by the phone that I then ignored. Since caller ID had not yet been invented, I could only surmise that he was on the other end wanting to know when I was coming back. When later that afternoon I forced myself to call the office for my check I got the bookkeeper, relieved that Herman had not answered. I was done, but didn't choose to tell him. We were way past that. Updating Jenna I indicated that I'd be spending a few days in D.C. hoping to see her before leaving for California. Then Pinto Acres and I beat it on down the line for a visit with Brenda and Miri, a visit extended when the blizzard of 1978 blanketed the whole of the Northeast corridor, thus delaying my return to Amishland.

In itself that would not have necessarily been unpleasant except for the unanticipated effect of Brenda's subsequent bender, at which time this otherwise intelligent and refined woman turned into a nasty drunk, a version of Edward Albee's "Martha" in his masterpiece I'd so enthusiastically studied in Greality. We had been visiting friends of hers when after a couple of bourbon and waters, she unexpectedly and in a most mundane manner, disclosed certain proclivities we'd shared the previous evening. I fled, thankful that for me at least these people were strangers, and so much for a sit-by-the-fire winter romantic getaway. Once with Artie and Aaron I conveyed the events to my sister, who did, after all, live in Brenda's house, presumably now not for very long.

When the roads cleared Miri and I looked at each other as I prepared to wrap things up in Allentown, not knowing what would happen next, to which she replied that I'd "probably be amazed," making me wonder how she herself had become so familiar with the Devil's Tower landing site.

A week here at the most, one last gig at the Fox, then I'll be as gone as Johnny Cash's "wild goose in winter." I parked outside Jenna's apartment. I knocked firmly on her door, wanting her to finally let me in from the cold.

Embraced and enfolded, I encountered her girls, Lara and Gita, six and five, who take my hand while repeating the *Orange you glad I didn't say bananas* joke they'd been yukking up with me at the laundromat those few months back. Like Richard Dreyfuss guided onto the mother ship I am gently led around the living room. *It has come—whatever this thing pending—it is here, if I know it, and I know it, but do I know it steadily, in every minute, or am I merely permitting myself a peek into something unfathomable? Or both? My God, Jenna, here we are. Where are we?*

She put the children to bed and we stood in her kitchen where, after disengaging from an initial kiss, she backed off and stared into me, through me, and I moved towards her and took her face in my hands, kissing her, touching her hair and caressing her with a new and unfamiliar passion. She kissed me deep and hard stroking my face, her own revealing a stark, primitive beauty covering a grief both enduring and desperate.

The transfiguration of the Industrial Grind into a crystal Eden had followed me home, the snow once so bleak and gray now pulsating and the subfreezing cold irrelevant. I entered the apartment knowing my days here are down to very few, stretched out on my bed and fell asleep.

She accompanied me to the gig. Eddie, outside the club having a smoke broke off his conversation. He ushered us in, predicting a light crowd. I asked him if we needed sound. He and the barkeep then arranged the tables for a more intimate gathering. Playing to perhaps ten people for the next three hours, but mostly for Eddie and Jenna, the bookends of my life in Pennsylvania, I channeled, albeit more intimately, the transcendent Berkeley nite of the decade's beginning. No gig, this—just the real thing, the unwinding of song after song in the quiet joy of *being with*, having been blessed with another communion. I drank in every second. He looked at us warmly and thanked me for the evening.

On our return to Allentown she caressed my shoulder. Down the mountain and into the Grind we drove, deciding somewhere past Saylorsburg that I'd help her and her children move back to her family home in Morgan Bridge, and then go myself to California. "Are you sure?" I asked. She kissed me. I took her home, as she was an hour overdue with the sitter.

* * *

From across the booth at Ye Olde Diner, Clara inquired, "Isn't this a complication?" Poking at her shoofly pie, she was flabbergasted at my intentions, not thinking for a minute that this was a mere stopover. She had understood California, as that was where she'd hoped I'd have settled in the first place, but now this, some *holler* in whatever alternate word to Bumfuck she could think of, with a woman and her two young children and no means of support- *For how long? You don't see yourself as a coal miner, after what you've been doing here for the last year?* Clearly she struggled, beset by an uncustomary inability to speak her usual words of encouragement, the oft repeated well intentioned *I have always been in your corner,* no less true for its bromidic quality.

Jenna and I headed out in our two vehicles. She had hesitated in front of her now vacated digs and I pointed in a southwest direction and in an epic voice declared, "Go!" At an ice cream joint across from a decaying amusement park I stopped for a last look at the Grind. Caught in my ambivalence, whether to hoist a middle finger or give thanks for what the berg had so recently bestowed, and along with the recognition that I might be turned into my own pillar of salt if I didn't forthwith move my ass, I got back inside Pinto Acres and headed out of the great industrial North.

* * *

Morgan Bridge was no more than a couple of general stores with a car dealership in between. The rolling hills, woods, and river, the pastoral beauty of the greater area, were not our immediate environs. I lingered with the three of them in a house close to the old federal highway a two story two bedroom dwelling belonging to her parents, who themselves lived a short walk away. When we weren't touring the countryside in either Pinto Acres or in the Porsche that had belonged to her late ex-husband (a vehicle she insisted I drive, but was too spooked to do so more than once), I busied myself with transferring what vinyl I'd brought with me to cassette for the trip west, a journey I was less sure would still happen as the days turned to weeks. Jenna enrolled Lara in school, then she, Gita and I toured the bucolic countryside of Morgan, Hampshire, and Berkshire counties until the end of the school day, often joking that Lara was the only one of us gainfully employed. On some occasions Jenna dropped off Gita with her parents so that she and I could explore what we were about. Walks on the river, visits to an abandoned church, looking at cabins to rent…

This was getting too close to the real thing.

Instant daddyhood, so appealing when reading to the girls in the evening after dinner or before their bedtime, however, had developed prematurely. Knowing that the longer I stayed the stronger would become our attachment, a fact that in view of their father's death I vowed not to ignore or minimize. So when Lara hinted to her mother that it seemed like I *was living with* them my spirits sank with the knowledge that the meter was running. Moving them here had accelerated a process that required time we hadn't had, and that now I struggled to see myself putting in. If it had been just us two she said, she may even have come west with me, but we both knew neither of us were ready to do so with her kids. Then too, the area's remoteness wore on me, accompanied also by transitory unease whenever I saw the Porsche. I wondered about what I didn't and wouldn't know unless I took the leap here and now, persuading myself that it had all been about the rush of the rescue.

The prodigal daughter had returned with a major assist from a no longer prodigal son from another tribe and region. Her parents had expressed their appreciation by hosting dinner, a meal remarkable for both the quality of her mom's cooking and for its resemblance to the family dinner scene straight out of *Annie Hall.* That Jenna's parents were sizing up their daughter's gallant knight was undeniable, and was perhaps more benign than I thought, although I wondered whether I ought be concerned with how her dad was coping with my extended stay. Jenna responded by saying that, relative to my own father, I had little to worry about.

The notion to do so nearly jelled anyway. Berkeley Springs had a decent music store. Strumming a Martin and conversing with the store's owner, I nearly asked for a job I suspected didn't exist. Daily, I gazed down the highway over the hill, visualizing Pinto Acres hurtling westward, still failing to grasp the paradox of freedom, its inherent struggle to discover and puruse what was meaningful. Instead, I dwelt in the now all too familiar territory of Schroedinger's multiverse where everything was possible and where nothing was decided.

On a rock overlooking the confluence of the Potomac and Shenandoah, Jenna told me *that if I ever wanted to come back she'd be there.* Later that night, after the girls went to bed, I fished a little, wanting to know if she were open to having more children. She stiffened, saying she didn't think so. I added that piece of ambiguity to my cognitive ledger, getting way ahead of myself in some pointless and abstract curiosity.

Had I the presence of mind to slow things down, maybe a visit with Artie or Aaron, only a couple of hours east, I could have reconsidered, maybe moved closer to DC, found a way to give myself the space to determine if this could have worked out. Jenna suggested a visit with Eddie, but I wanted no more part of Pennsylvania. My sister was to have come for a visit one Sunday, but an early spring snowstorm had precluded that, a random act of weather that fortified my westward inclination.

I hugged Lara before she left for school that morning, sensing that I was already gone from her life as I watched her scurry to the bus. Jenna, Gita, and I then stood in front of Pinto Acres. Gita stared up at me and said, “I love you up to God.”

Chapter 16

WITH THE FURIES

I marked my thirtieth birthday standing on the Santa Monica pier. I gazed into the Pacific in a passing moment of suicidal contemplation, a spike in the depression that had settled over me now that I'd determined just how badly I had blown it. Coming west again had merely been a misapprehended stab at the familiar among friends whose own lives had since moved on. I stopped first to see Marta. Having recently resumed her life in Kansas City she only became irritated during my visit upon the issuance of a speeding ticket as we toured the city. I motored to Colorado thinking I might drop in on Bianca, but also in hopes of retrieving the beloved beat up suede jacket that I had curiously left with Sid. I soon learned that he'd discarded it just days earlier while in the process of moving, my storage options having apparently expired. Working hard not to perceive this as an omen I arrived in California fighting physical pain from what was soon diagnosed as crystallized lactic acid. The interminable hours on the solitary cross-country trip, accompanied by too little exercise enroute had been the cause. My only company across the nation, the twenty cassette tapes I had diligently made in Morgan Bridge, had more than adequately described the boat I'd missed.

Once at my friends' home another unexpected physical symptom became manifest, an allergy triggered by the almond crop that awoke me gasping for air in the middle of the night. Sleep deprivation only exacerbated the ruminating about my too short life with Jenna. A relationship abandoned out of some absurd and noble notion is how I now saw it. With the passage through each time zone I had felt her fade further away during the collect calls she had encouraged me to make. My California hosts were kind, but also perplexed. They'd seen me struggle in Greality over Bianca and the déjà vu was unexpected for them. Anxious now to rid myself of anything that would remind me of Jenna, as if that could possibly happen, I traveled to Berkeley where I traded my guitar for a smaller Martin. Then I left for LA in the hope that the ocean would prove healing, which it did for my allergies, but not for my heartache.

* * *

Roland had coupled with Babushka, a mutual buddy from the Gap, and they had moved to Marina del Ray where he now attended LA's guitar institute. I desperately hoped I'd be welcome for at least a short while when I parked Pinto Acres in front of their small shaded yard. They looked happy enough with each other, my automobile's christener and his lady, a Jersey girl who had also been one of the Delaware River squatters. They appeared to have a nice scene here in this two-bedroom bungalow. We played some music. The two of them had been here for several months, but having certainly corresponded with Eddie they likely knew of my recent adventure. Babushka provided the hug that opened the gates for the catharsis.

What had I done? Walking the beaches, the ocean now screamed at me. At night the breezes from the palm trees provided too little comfort. In the next day's mail, forwarded from Sacramento, a letter from the girls, enclosed with drawings of what they imagined my new house looked like, accompanied by Gita's question, "How do you like your new home?"

She'd buried the poster in my suitcase among pairs of jeans. It read *Orestes* and showed a young bare-chested man in loincloth being guided away by his companion, Pylades, pierced by a fire bolt from one of the Furies. Below the picture she had written of our walk in the Allentown graveyard. Then she stunned me:

What doors are open for the wanderer and which of us shall find his father, know his face, and in what place, and in what time and in what land? Where?[*]

---

* Of Time and the River Copyright ©1935 Charles Scribner's Sons Copyright renewed 1963 Paul Gifflin, Administrator CTA Estate of Thomas Wolfe

Part II

Chapter 17

GRADUATING CIRCUMSTANCES

It should now be noted that the Ford Pinto of the mid-seventies had a seriously checkered history caused by its defective fuel tank. In the event of a rear-end collision the car could burst into flames. Aware of the design flaw the Ford Motor Company had determined that wrongful death lawsuits would be less costly in the long run than retrofitting the Pintos already on the road, at reportedly a cost of $11 per vehicle. The scandal broke in the September/October 1977 issue of *Mother Jones.* "No longer a Bolshevik," I hadn't been reading lefty literature then, or I would have almost certainly traded the orange conveyance.

Having departed from Roland and Babushka in better shape than when I arrived, I trod my well-beaten easterly path towards Colorado yet again, now having achieved the hat trick for living attempts in California Where once stood Pearl St, was now the new pedestrian mall, a celebration of emerging McBoulder. Swept away were the likes of Shannon's, so as to make the town more family and consumer friendly. The Sobriety, too, was no more, although ironically its kitschy, barbershop motif would have fit nicely with the surrounding aesthetic. The box office of the now closed Boulder Theatre featured a poster advertising a debate between Timothy Leary and G. Gordon Liddy, an event I thought would yet draw a sizeable audience. At least the theatre was rumored to be reopening.

I steered Pinto Acres east to a dot of a town located south of Greality to see Bianca. She lived alone on the plains working for the Migrant Council. She answered the door suppressing surprise. She looked beautifully blue, a contrasting figure to the effervescent young woman I had met five years before. Had this been our first encounter, I would have been immediately attracted. So tentative was our reunion, however, that after a cup of coffee we visited mutual friends, rather than risk extended conversation. In the safety of their company our two moderators filled in the awkward silences. Back at her home we parted, making no plans to meet again. I experienced no surprise and only minimal disappointment, merely mystified at how much mental energy could be spent on the contemplation of things that were not going to happen.

* * *

Within a week I found myself in Dallas, Texas. Why not? Reliable rumor had it that gigs galore awaited in Lone Star country. Given that my recent journey through the past had yielded bupkis, I decided that I could hardly do worse than trying out new turf even if the locale in question was in the city still associated with the horrible events of 1963. I went first to infamous Dealey Plaza. Every landmark of the setting cried *conspiracy*, from its School Book Depository and Dal-Tex building to its Overpass and Grassy Knoll. Standing at the infamous picket fence, I felt myself at the epicenter of our generation's maelstrom. I noted the three hundred degree turn from Houston Street on to Elm, which had slowed the presidential limousine, a choice of route with no inherent logic given the more easily negotiated alternative of a continuous route down Commerce St. History might have turned out differently had the motorcade's planners employed the principle of Occam's razor. During that summer of 1978 shortly before my arrival, acoustical tests conducted in the plaza had failed to establish the existence of a fourth shot. A noise had been discovered on a policeman's fifteen-year-old dictabelt recording from the plaza at the moment of the assassination. Initially thought to be the recording of another gunshot, the investigation concluded it had merely been a backfire from the patrolman's motorcycle. Conspiracy hopefuls were frustrated yet again.

Gigs could be had in Dallas, so it was not hard to get by. I earned a living there, but was also at the point of knowing that success in this racket involved more than the procurement of steady gigs. I was coming to accept that use of my intellectual faculties had been on standby for far too long. In the wake of the Three Mile Island nuclear accident in Pennsylvania, in March,1979, I started performing for the anti-nuclear movement, coming into contact with more academic and political types. My thoughts turned again to graduate school, and/or a move to Austin, the state's acknowledged liberated zone. There would be fierce competition for gigs in that city, the *Outlaw* antithesis to country music's capital of Nashville, but there would also be much more intellectual and social stimulation there than here in the underbelly of Texas' *nouveau riche.*

It was with these thoughts that I looked out of my apartment window that spring morning to see Pinto Acres Estates in its new mortally wounded glory, freshly totaled from a sideswipe, another casualty of Dallas. A patch of blue streaked across the top of Acre's surviving gas tank, the signature of the offending automobile. The end of an era, I surmised, acknowledging that the driver of that offending blue vehicle deserved an assist for pointing me to graduate school.

In what can only be described as an example of historical irony, exemplifying incredible competence and efficiency the Dallas Police within twenty four hours had located the offending vehicle, in curious contrast to fifteen and a half years earlier when they had been unable (?) to prevent the murder of Lee Harvey Oswald at the hands of Jack Ruby in the basement of their very own headquarters.

* * *

The passing of Pinto Acres Estates propelled me to purchase my sister's now four-year-old unnamed but highly roadworthy vehicle. Doing so required a perfunctory stop-over in Allentown to retrieve the car, where I arranged monthly payments to Miri, herself soon to depart for gigs in the Northwest. *Zen and the Art of Motorcycle Maintenance* had not moved from its original site next to Herman's chair. My father may have even hatched the idea that I buy the van, but he remained mute during my brief stay, except to remind me that without tags I couldn't go anywhere with the van, how helpful. I was quickly off to a traditional lunch at Ye Olde Diner with Clara, who I now assured of my intention that this time I'd complete a masters degree at the college in the very Deep South where Adele and Fremont had set up shop, she a professor there and he a psychotherapist in private practice. Then, perhaps because I knew my route there would involve traveling through North Carolina, I suddenly remembered the high regard that Clara held for

Thomas Wolfe. Remembering Jenna's poster brought on a sudden sorrow so I segued and soon left. After brief visits with Eddie, and Rob I turned south for another stab at an M.A.

* * *

I picked up Aaron in DC for the drive to Carrollton where he would visit with his sister and brother –in-law. As we left the beltway I recounted my memory of events at Steven Geller's bar mitzvah in 1961, a tale in which Aaron had been the inadvertent foil.

Steven's bar mitzvah had followed our own by several months, having occurred in the fall. The food at the reception had been cold cuts, a memory forever fortified by the several sandwiches that Aaron had deftly thrown out the window. Hal, Artie and I had admired his shiftiness, and were soon caught up with the bar mitzvah boy himself, in convivial rowdiness.

My contribution was a behavior that I can only attribute to a profound lack of imagination. I commenced turning the lights off and on to the understandable ire of the assemblage. One highly placed denizen of the Jewish Center, a certain Mr. Rosenberg, also a proud sponsor of one of Boonton's Little League teams, soon accosted me by the shoulder, and sat me in the alcove next to the *Coca Cola* machine where he instructed me to remain until he had called my parents. Vainly, I inquired what price Aaron would be paying for his indiscretions while sullenly waiting for Herman to fetch me from this unpleasant turn of events. Fortunately, I soon learned that my father didn't care much for Mr. Rosenberg, his car dealership, his little league sponsorship, or his general demeanor. When it came to Aaron and his unpunished shenanigans, Herman had merely offered a shrug of the shoulders. It dawned on me that he had no dog in this fight, that forces were at work I didn't quite understand. Herr Rosenberg's assessment had apparently constituted a pissing contest unworthy of my father's engagement. That I would avoid a reaming for my ill-advised behavior was a relief, but more important, I recognized that when it came to the uptight cabal of our local synagogue my father had no status. He was an outsider, *and it was good.*

* * *

Aaron and I wound our way through Dixie. It had been a long time since I had traveled with a friend, and it was just fine having company. I'd wanted to fill him in on the missing years. Skirting the areas of western Virginia I recalled my recent and final contact with Jenna, having phoned her from a booth in Stroudsburg to learn she'd married and, for good measure been *born again. Jesus,* was all I could think, rightfully so. Since her conversion marked only the first among family and friends that would occur over the course of the next decade I had no idea that her news might be the harbinger of the end of secular humanism as I'd known it, but it also had a revelatory effect of another sort. Leaving Morgan Bridge may not have been all that unwise, the local culture evidently as insular as I'd intuited. I had not yet worked out my own beliefs, but I was no bible literalist. I had long been fascinated by the description of the messiah as the 'son of man,' words suggesting the long held yearning for a savior, but not one necessarily divine. Nor could I in any way sign on with those fighting evolution and/or clinging to the belief that the world was no older than some six thousand years. It was sad to think that the once Vonnegut-loving muse might wind up thinking along those fundamentalist lines, but only myself to blame. I had to wonder though, if any of her account were true, fantasizing her story to be a test in the manner of the folk tales, like Joan Baez's "John Riley," wherein the heroine conducts a ruse to prove her devotion to the love she hopes will return. Right.

Aaron filled me in on his life and loves. My friend, the Mayday legal observer of eight years ago was now an attorney, who owned his own home, manifesting an atypically stable status among my peers. He also played and sang in a D.C. area bluegrass band of local and regional renown. He lamented his own heartbreak, now several years past. His mother had disapproved of the love of his life, also a shiksa. His mother had passed away within the last year, but over the past decade he continued to date only non-Jewish girls, acknowledging that while this might qualify as an example of closing the barn door after the horse's departure, it nevertheless provided some satisfaction with regard to thwarting those maternal marital aspirations.

We wound our way into Georgia. At one point the van seized up with a vapor lock in stop and go traffic outside Atlanta. I assured my friend not to worry. This had happened only a week before in a much more inconvenient location: midway across the George Washington Bridge. There, I had absorbed the frustrated epithets of exasperated drivers en route from New Jersey, some choosing to add the distinctive hand and finger language so characteristic of the region's motorists. The more cultivated Atlanta area drivers hurled not a single untoward remark our way during those tense moments before the car recalibrated. The shaking van on the vibrating G.W. Bridge had left its mark, though, a bridge phobia, a white- knuckle psychosomatic occurrence that required my eyes to look only straight ahead while crossing bridges of any substantial span.

* * *

If a certain Congressman had been granted tenure at a certain western Georgia college during the 1970s, then the course of American history might have mightily benefited. The college's fateful verdict, however justified, unfortunately resulted in putting the educator on a path to politician and election to the House of Representatives. There the Republican Party assumed control of said legislative body under his leadership in the mid-nineties. His speakership was a forerunner to disaster. Our country's current economic crisis owes in large measure to his party's penchant for deregulation and its celebration of unfettered greed. If Reagan was this political philosophy's patriarch then educator-turned-Congressman Gingrich was its attack dog, thus begging the question, why couldn't the college have bent its tenure requirements just this once, to have spared the country.

Adele and Fremont lived in a roomy Prairie Style house they'd purchased in old Carrollton, where I lived for several weeks before school started. I minimally supported myself through the summer picking peaches in the orchards outside of Carrollton where, alongside descendents of the old Confederacy, I quickly strained many muscle groups. When the term began, along with two grad students, a Gregg Allman-looking Kansas native and a Swahili-speaking South Chicagoan, I rented a shack that called to mind the dwelling place of Dylan's 'Hollis Brown.' Its landlord, a white-haired and bearded professor of undergraduate psychology, had in his own substantial backyard, established and "maintained" a *Corvair farm* where one could view the ruins of these death traps, automobiles first manufactured in 1964 by General Motors, and the subject of Ralph Nader's famous expose, 'Unsafe at Any Speed.' The *farm* was a cross between genuine conceptual art and one of those roadside attractions featuring gigantic plastic dinosaurs.

Aside from its rundown exterior, the shack's principal liability was its home to mice, a categorical demonstration, to paraphrase Mr. Nader that made it feel unsafe at any time. Certainly true for my Allman doppelgänger colleague and myself, and sufficient to motivate us to seek girlfriends in town with whom we might begin keeping serious company. Tatenda boldly held down the fort, employing mousetraps, seemingly undeterred by these unwelcome squatters. Every few days when I would stop in to retrieve my mail I'd look in on him during what sometimes felt like visiting hours at a quasi-detention facility.

* * *

Myrna and I had met as colleagues while delivering pizzas for the newly opened Domino's franchise. An articulate fellow psychology grad student, she had waxed rhapsodic about the "battered psyche of the Southern woman," sometimes in general terms, but also at times more specifically in a barb aimed at Jana, a fellow former student, who Myrna was convinced had not only her sights on, but, also, a hook into me as well. True, Jana and I had shared one unexpectedly interesting evening following a dinner she had attended hosted by Adele and Fremont. That encounter had occurred on the tenth anniversary of Woodstock when her boyfriend was out of town, and had replicated more than one activity associated with those late festivities in upstate New York. I met Myrna later, but apparently these two had history as rivals, history that Myrna was determined not to repeat. Consequently, our relationship began on shaky ground and stayed there until, a few months later when we parted as friends, a relational denouement that heretofore I had not experienced.

* * *

Had I entered the humanistic psychology program a few years before, I might have signed on with a great deal more overt enthusiasm. I began my studies self identified as a rogue coming in from the cold. I enjoyed the courses and had strong admiration for several professors. My intellectual curiosity was stimulated and satisfied, but I was more anxious to finish my degree so I could begin experiencing the wonder of earning steady income than in being a devotee of any particular school of psychological thought (Watson and Skinnerian behaviorism were not even candidates.) The program borrowed more from philosophy than from experimental psych, the latter having constituted the boring courses I'd taken in my undergraduate years, so I was much more predisposed towards the subject matter. The emphasis ranged from the existentialism of Camus to the Buddhism of Alan Watts, from the British object-relations ego psychologists Winnicott and Fairbairn to the New Age transpersonal writings of Ken Wilbur. It was a compelling curriculum of study.

* * *

With November came the merciful end to the sweltering humidity that envelops the nation's southern region from April onwards. Many of my fellow students had eagerly snticipated the release of Francis Ford Coppola's *Apocalypse Now*, the final piece of Hollywood's unofficial Vietnam trilogy. Preceded by *Coming Home* and *The Deer Hunter*, Coppola's film was an absurdist Vietnam commentary, based in part on Joseph Conrad's *Heart of Darkness.* Its release amidst much media hype, however, had been eclipsed by real world events—the taking of American hostages in Iran by the Islamic revolutionaries who had earlier toppled the Shah. A pall descended on the nation when it became clear there would be no imminent release, our nation's superpower status seemingly irrelevant towards achieving that end, the mood only deepening when the Soviet Union invaded Afghanistan in late December. Tensions heightened between the superpowers to their highest levels since the Yom Kippur War six years earlier. At a New Year's Eve party in Myrna's hometown of Augusta, an opinion I suspected was being similarly shared among my countrymen was uttered by a son of the South who declared, "We will probably be up Russia's butt hole by the end of next year."

The seventies were ending right on schedule. Starting late, with Nixon's resignation, and ending with turmoil in the Middle East, it was easy for people over thirty (the age bracket we purportedly couldn't trust just ten years earlier), to think the coming decade would resemble a fifties redux. Certainly, by the end of 1980 that thesis did not look to be all that incorrect. With Reagan's election the possibility of an encounter with the anal cavity of the Soviet Union might not be all that improbable.

* * *

Marta had relocated to Atlanta where she continued her successful, if increasingly dissatisfying, career as a rock deejay. It was a wonderful occasion when Clara visited Georgia and we all convened at Adele and Fremont's home. Also in attendance was Dorinda, a friend from the program, more or less engaged to her significant other. Charismatic, Dorinda was someone I would have contemplated dating, had she not already fixed me up with her sister, in school across the state. Besides the fact that this would have been bad form, I didn't really believe that Dorinda and I could make it, apropos the previously outlined Billie Holiday axiom, but my affinity with friends from the wider world clued me that I was unlikely to remain in Carrollton after completing my degree.

The assembled sat down to one of Adele's delicious meals, quite a few of which I'd had the pleasure of consuming during that year. The two had often hosted faculty and students, and many relaxing hours were spent in their company. Now, as on numerous occasions, the imposing Fremont burst into operatic song in full expression of his joie de vie, which easily surpassed that of any person I'd yet encountered. His energy was boundless, and inspirational because he had overcome dark periods of his own.

My mother provided the highlight of the evening. Dorinda was describing the plan for her "relationship celebration" with her significant other to be held on Florida's Gulf Coast later that year. Careful not to describe the event as an actual wedding, Dorinda had piqued my mother's curiosity with a convoluted description of just what she and life partner-in-waiting were committing to. Putting down her fork, my mother bluntly asked, "Why don't the two of you just get married?" Dorinda, if not quite taken aback, was nonetheless speechless.

* * *

Within a few weeks of my mother's visit, notice of an official wedding did arrive. Miri announced that she planned to tie the knot with a classical pianist from the Northwest whom she had met while performing in the region. She disclosed in the same letter that she, too, had been 'born again', also imploring me to follow suit. The full import of that injunction would have to wait. The immediate rub was the requisite trip to the northern tier of Amishland for what could only be an uncomfortable few days in the living unit. Marta and I flew to Allentown together, neither of us particularly joyous.

Still, I owed Miri my attendance at her nuptials and the arrival of the groom's family provided diversion. The imminent father-in-law's Kermit- the- Frog-like disposition, presumably uncharacteristic of Christian Missionary Alliance preachers (although how would I know?) had the effect of containing Herman's inclination to demonstrate overt hostility towards me, at least when the groom's parents were present. The groom himself was a terrific pianist. Clara, who had been active in supporting Allentown's symphony, had arranged access to their facility so he and my sister could practice the piece they would perform at their ceremony. Sitting in the balcony spellbound by his rendition of "Claire de Lune," I experienced a pang having learned only a few minutes earlier that my sister's fiance shared the same birthday with Jenna. Not far from here Miri had slowed down and honked, in the van that now belonged to me. Wishing now the vehicle was at my immediate disposal to get the hell out of Jennatown, I grieved. I had worked hard to achieve some overdue now jeopardized emotional distance, as I sat watching and listening to my brother-in-law-elect, his fingers striking the ivories with romantic passion and style.

It was also my dumb luck that Miri's new religious conversion had inflated her sense of filial piety to the point that her wedding would now be little more than a party for her parents. No friends of hers would be present, maybe not even invited, just family, business associates of Herman's, my mother's relations, other adults we'd known from childhood, and fortunately, wonderful old Jersey City friends of Clara's. The lack of a peer group for the bride made me think that my sister now aspired to little more than June Cleaverhood.

All preoccupations were preempted by a crisis in the bride's dressing room. Miri had forgotten her veil. A mercy errand was needed. Anticipating that despite his up-to-now shunning of me, Herman would soon beseech me to fulfill its retrieval, I let him squirm before I stepped up. *At last I had achieved competence potential.* Satisfied that he'd had a well-deserved moment of discomfort, I accepted the keys to his Mercedes and left the Steel City Hotel on this vital mission of brotherly aid. With thanks for this reprieve, and in the momentary throes of self-efficacy I proceeded to the living unit with an inward grin. Events had conspired to force him to rely on the son he despised! Reveling, I considered some sightseeing, maybe a side trip to Gettysburg. I'd never been there, and as the groom reportedly idolized Lincoln, perhaps he'd enjoy some brochures from the national monument. Breathing in the humid, springtime, Manheim Industrial Grind air, I instead retrieved the veil compliantly returning with all deliberate speed to the hotel. Handing it to Miri, I witnessed the old man force himself to make a modicum of eye contact while speaking to me civilly for the first time in the four days I'd been in Allentown, and for that matter for the first time in over two years when he remarked,"You got it, didn't you?"

Oh, I got it all right.

My second clue regarding Miri's desire to erase the 1960's from her memory came in the form of her deliberate omission of our musical collaboration from her event. Wrongly anticipating that she might ask me to sing at her reception, I asked her anyway if she would allow me the pleasure. Reprising "Today," I felt compelled to make a statement, at least musically. Someone needed to remind a few people that not all of us longed to return to 1956.

I wished I could quit the premises with Aaron, a late arrival at the nuptials, (Miri had rented a room in his home in the wake of the Brenda fiasco.) but I had a return ticket to Georgia the following day. I promised myself that any future visits to the northern tier would be limited to lunch with Clara at Ye Olde Diner. "Please let it not be necessary to have another event like this any time soon," I said to Marta as we flew southward to Atlanta, but if she was amused by the comment she displayed no indication. When it came her time to marry twelve years later, however, she eloped.

* * *

Ah, summertime in Dixie—its relentless heat and humidity drove a fellow counselor-to-be, and I to cruise the apartment complexes in search of swimming pools. We found one to use undetected for nearly a month, and most importantly through the Republican National Convention where Reagan was nominated for the Presidency. When my wealthy friends the Milstein's, took their family on vacation I was grateful when they asked me to house sit. I joyously received many visitors, and happy to dole out air conditioning time to others in the oasis that was their home. Jana was among them, once bringing her laundry, and intimating a fantasy of playing house for a few days, something I resisted, not wishing complications before leaving, but the Milstein's house would have been good fantasy material.

* * *

With only weeks to go before graduating I had to figure out something to do. Driving to Savannah, one of the nation's oldest and most beautiful cities, I interviewed for a counseling gig in nearby Brunswick, but I couldn't see myself there, or for that matter anywhere in the South. The slow pace of life, the endless heat and humidity, and the region's conservative political climate all combined to point my compass north. I decided two things while walking the beach on Jekyll Island where I was entertained by the flying fish. I would quit cigarettes (a promise I have kept for over thirty years), with the rationale that this was the only decision over which I had any current control, and secondly, I would take my chances back in Massachusetts of all places. Overqualified for the paraprofessional position available at the Devlin School, I was thinking more long term. I needed to know I had a job in a location where I could feel familiar. I'd start in early September, beginning my career in the helping profession (admittedly as a minor leaguer), Masters in Psychology in hand and where, among other things, I would root for the Celtics.

Chapter 18

PISSAH, WICKED PISSAH

Worcester's Yippie native son, Abbie Hoffman, had resurfaced the day I hit town, having arisen from his status as an underground fugitive in the wake of a cocaine bust seven years before. I drove into his hometown seeking a living situation so I could settle in before beginning my job. The Devlin School was located in Worcester's bucolic northern suburbs, whose leaves soon began to turn, allowing me to view the splendor of a New England autumn. Achingly beautiful, and all the more so because of the season's transience, with winter menacingly waiting in the on-deck circle, one could only hope that the autumnal batter would foul off pitches forever.

Devlin School, an education and treatment center for emotionally disturbed and/or cognitively impaired children, had hired me on the spot in Carrollton where they had been recruiting. (*Recruiting,* now there's a word that should have immediately tipped me off.) Completely without professionally related work experience I had known I would need two things once I obtained my degree: a job and the knowledge that I had a job (the latter to inhibit any distractions on the way towards starting a job). My master's degree was conferred in August at a ceremony I predictably did not attend, and I headed off to this curiously overqualified position, which nevertheless had satisfied these two requirements.

Driving toward the Bay State, I first made my usual rounds in the Mid-Atlantic region.

After a short visit with my attorney friends in the capital region, I detoured west for a Morgan Bridge drive through. Slowing down at the house and continuing past the ancestral home, locus, I imagined, of any real information had I inquired. I drove away, both amazed and reassured about the relative wisdom of having not stopped. Unlike my return to Dark-Haired Gina's courtyard, where no information could be had, I had come to Morgan Bridge with at least the possibility of learning something. Caution, however, warned me off with a strong signal to let sleeping dogs lie. How her parents might react to my unexpected appearance had inhibited me. More likely, however, I didn't want to hear confirmation of her marriage, preferring instead my tangled memories. Reaching the Virginia line, I recognized that memory had chosen not to take a holiday during this particular in vivo, even if it hadn't quite entrapped me either.

* * *

I took lodging near Devlin in a small town rooming house. The building known as a "hunt club" faced the Common, as did the window in my room where in the morning hours I followed the news on National Public Radio, sipping instant coffee prepared on my recently purchased hot plate. The presidential campaign looked bad for Jimmy Carter, what with the continuing hostage crisis, the Russians in Afghanistan, and fourteen percent home interest rates.

At Devlin I worked the swing shift as a recreational therapist. I greeted the boys as they emerged from school en route to their dorms, and ended my shift well after they were (hopefully) asleep. Those first few moments of their transition from school were the best. These latency-aged kids, so happy at being released from the regimentation of their classrooms, shared that joy with staff, the momentary stand-ins for the loving parent that they had either been denied, or had lost. Highly ephemeral, these moments, as within an hour crisis intervention with one or more child was not atypical. *Hands on,* the operative phrase, these were the front lines, milieu therapy, and a delicate balance required providing a safe environment for a child's self-expression while preventing injury to himself or others—Zen and the art of limit setting.

A legendary bar, The Blue Plate, and its equally famous owner, Tiny, were located within a few miles of Devlin making for a convenient, sometimes essential, watering hole on the way home. Many folk acts had performed there, and I myself would open for the Holy Modal Rounders a year down the road. Smaller than the Fox, The Plate had been around a lot longer. Ownership had spanned at least three generations. In a general way, Worcester combined both the blue- collar features of Allentown with the artistic sensibility of Delaware Water Gap. The more I settled in, the more I understood why I'd decided to relocate in Massachusetts, rather than return to the West or remain in the South. I felt grounded here. The buffer of time (now eight years) had helped integrate my memories, and while winter hadn't yet arrived, this wasn't Maine and I wasn't worried. I found a roommate and moved again, which was fine.

* * *

In late October, a few days before Reagan's election, I met Kira, who knew both my roommate and Tiny. The occasion was a Halloween party she hosted to which my geek-inclined roommate had brought me. Kira and I began seeing each other on a regular basis soon after, although I felt myself getting involved too quickly, my desire for a relationship winning out over taking the time to figure out at what pace and with whom. When we met she was working as a caseworker for a home health agency. Within six months she'd begun training in massage therapy.

I was fortunate to begin a new relationship just as the country took this huge rightward turn, the man to whom Joan Baez had dedicated the song "Drugstore Truck Driving' Man" at Woodstock eleven years earlier having now been elected President of the United States. What a splendid generational achievement! Even Massachusetts' electoral votes had gone to him because of votes siphoned off by Independent and liberal candidate John Anderson. Incredible that the Republicans had been handed the Commonwealth! Clara herself had headed up an "Anderson for President" committee in the Allentown area, her picture shaking the Independent candidate's hand featured on the front page of Allentown's daily, but the Bonzo juggernaut proved too strong. To be sleeping alone at this nadir of American political life would have added serious insult to injury.

* * *

The stunning scenery of the early afternoon drives to Devlin gradually faded replaced by the starkness of bare trees against the sky. With the ending of Daylight Savings Time the Devlin kids, no different from kids anywhere else began their countdown to the big two of the four holidays of the apocalypse, they and the staff having barely survived the first, Halloween. With the anticipation of Thanksgiving and Christmas came memories that translated into regression, creating difficult emotional times for many of Devlin's children, not to mention for some of the staff. The few anticipated holidays with home visits, while most others fervently wished they had homes to which they could return. Things kicked up another notch the closer it got to the solstice as Devlin's children engaged in their often agitated raging against the dying of the light.

Something guided me to The Plate that freezing Monday night during Advent. Football graced the modest television screen atop a cabinet off to the side of the bar. Disinterested in the game, Tiny and I schmoozed about Kira and me. They'd been good buds for a long time, and he himself was about to undergo an incredible metamorphosis. A beloved pillar of the Worcester music scene for years, he would soon immerse himself in Buddhism, travel to Dharmasala and in the space of only two years become a bodyguard for His Holiness, The Dalai Lama. Tiny had cut quite a figure when I saw him at the Dalai Lama's appearance at Harvard's Mem Hall a year later, but more importantly to me, he and I were together this nite when the world learned from the sports announcer, Howard Cosell, that John Lennon had been shot and killed outside the Dakota, his home in New York City. We remained after the other patrons had left to absorb this latest behemoth that had been set loose upon the world. The cruelty of the crime was compounded by the discovery that the killer claimed to have been influenced by *Catcher in the Rye*, the seminal book of our generation—a novel whose troubled anti-hero saw through the shallowness of modern society. That that canon should be used by this disturbed individual as a justification for murdering an icon who himself had skewered the same shallowness was infuriating and depressing. What hope still existed that a sensibility would prevail in the face of yet another act of violence perpetrated against a creative force of our generation? Tiny and I sat stunned, my only consolation being that I could have been with a no more suitable person in those miserable hours. Synchronicity is powerful.

* * *

Synchronicity is powerful, a manifestation having occurred at a rest stop on I-95 in Virginia during the journey north from Carrollton the previous August, synchronicity on the road. That spring I'd attended a music therapy retreat in Virginia Beach where I had been ushered into the world of auras, chakras, and past lives at the Edgar Cayce Association for Research and Enlightenment. By week's end I had seen my share of auras, but once back in Carrollton it was back to only regular old heads and faces, my first experience with the power of group contagion somewhat to my regret, slipping away—a drag, re-entry. Now, pulling over to stretch my legs, when the car that pulled up was that of a North Carolina couple who had attended the *same* retreat. We had shared an affinity during the conference, their remarkable appearance now suggesting that I stick with the job plan in lieu of pursuing esoterica, a wisp of fantasy. A kind of highway Grace had been bestowed.

* * *

Christmas in Delaware Water Gap, I had decided to spend the holidays on my own. Kira wanted to come, but that would have sent a signal. Though things were comfortable between us, I didn't feel in for the long haul. I had no gig planned at the Fox, just hung with Eddie, Roland (now

Babushkaless), and other music buddies. Good to be with Eddie now, our last visit had been over a year ago. Then, as now, he'd looked to be under some strain, but didn't disclose. With my comings and goings I didn't feel I should probe. He had no compunction about complaining on topics like the liquor control board or the police, but around his personal life Eddie offered little. With his friends, he listened and lent support. The Gap's substance abuse meter, however, had climbed to a disconcerting level over the past two years. The cocaine explosion of the late seventies had darkened the atmosphere. Although drug abuse existed everywhere, its pervasiveness here had the character of an organizing principle of daily life. The appearance of white lines on tables and album covers at all times of day boggled even my imagination. My early days there seemed like ages ago, so I didn't stay more than a couple of days and was off to New York's Morningside Heights to visit Rob, now a couple of years into optician scionhood.

He was miserable, although he had a nice little apartment on Riverside Drive and was carrying on a little something with a woman in his building. I loved hearing him complain, though, and not merely because I no longer aspired to scionhood. I had no illusions of the growing disparity of our respective financial status. I enjoyed my friend's sardonic whine, certain it facilitated the regularity of his getting laid. We delighted in continuing perhaps the greatest achievement our generation had offered to civilization—hanging out.

* * *

January in Massachusetts brought my first New England winter in eight years, one cold ordeal. Before the first week was out I'd received two pieces of written correspondence, the primary means of communication in those primordial years before the advent of the information highway. The first came from Clara reminding me that January 7th was the anniversary of Millard Fillmore's birthday. She had received word of this as a benefit from her membership in the society of the same name, an entity whose primary purpose was to record, evaluate, and report significant occurrences of mediocrity wherever they might be found. The second, postmarked on President Fillmore's birthday, came all the way from Carrollton, from none other than Jana, who had taken a notion to come north to visit me should I be amenable. She had called it quits with the significant other, and now, apparently wanting to try with me, was proposing a rendezvous with the possibility I might accompany her back to Carrollton or return sometime later. I considered this, assessed my present circumstances, and failed to dismiss it. We arranged that she would spend the Presidents' Day (Mr. Fillmore, not feted) holiday in Worcester.

Kira should have given me my walking papers at this moment but did not, choosing instead to seethe and fulminate. Flabbergasted, I could only imagine my own distress if she had pulled something like this on me. What was I thinking in risking an involvement with one of the more mobile of moving targets I'd encountered during my checkered love life? Never mind rationality, I allowed myself to be caught up in anticipation, it's only downside, my need to avoid The Plate since I anticipated it might be awkward with Tiny.

How out on a limb I had placed myself I didn't recognize until the very evening of the visit. Having reconsidered, Jana stood me up at the airport. Thoughtfully, however, she had left a message on the answering machine, and had cell phones existed in that day perhaps I could have avoided the expense in tolls, gas, and humiliation. But somewhat less thoughtfully, as well as completely consistent with character, she had timed her message knowing I'd be on my way to retrieve her. Thus abandoned, I returned to my digs in Worcester and secluded myself for three days. By Sunday I'd come to the awareness that I'd reached a watershed of sorts. During that afternoon, I'd noticed an automobile cruising back and forth, its driver resembling Kira's sister on what could only be a reconnaissance mission, I initially thought. Probably not, I then realized, more of a welfare check since my roommate, in his concern over the length of my self-imposed isolation, had probably sent out a distress call.

My sheepish return to normalcy required some effort, but turned out well, for I embraced a new stoicism. Doing so was facilitated by the elements of a freezing New England winter whose conditions only fortified my attitude. Now New England was home whether or not Kira and I worked out, as I emptied Carrollton and all other haunts from the longing regions of my consciousness. Forgiveness from my Worcester social network proceeded swiftly and now redeemed, Kira advocated more strongly for cohabitation.

* * *

Her good friend, Kasia, lived with her boyfriend, Jerome, a local rocker who had recently forayed into New Age music. Ironically, he pointed to me, from my week at Edgar Cayce's Virginia digs, as one of the first influences in his transformation from punk, the only time I have received a credit for esoterica. Jerome and I had attended Boston University at the same time but had not known each other. Networked into the New Age, their home quickly became the locus for several "tarot–to-go" parties. It was so frequently filled with people that I eventually tired of the scene, but when just the two of us jammed, our significant others off schmoozing, we had satisfying times. We recorded "Sitting Here with You" and "Speak of Survival" in his basement studio. Jerome really got these songs—his lead expanded the melodic lyricism I'd imagined when I wrote the tunes eight and six years ago respectively, and his production of my overdubbed harmonies, my first experience with the technique, was excellent.

* * *

I had sustained a work-related injury when an angry Devlin child, engaging in some over-the-line horseplay in the swimming pool, bit my hand during a restraint by the lifeguard and me. Two thoughts: the first, the recollection that yes, I had received a tetanus shot within the last five years, and the second, that my aspirations for continuing in the helping profession needed to be raised. Easier said than done, as competing for professional jobs with peers who had graduate degrees from more traditional psychology masters or Ph.D. programs, and/or more professional experience posed a considerable challenge to my immediate advancement. My Devlin days concluded by the end of May, I bid an uncertain farewell. I soon canvassed the suburbs of Worcester for the citizens lobby, Fair Share, doing quite well initially only to fizzle with the heat of the oncoming summer. Strangely, I then lost my digs, as my roommate had determined that he would have to move of all people, his mother, into his rental house. I knew he had issues, but so overtly Oedipal still surprised me. Thus, I moved in with Kira under some duress resigned that we were fated to be together. I nonetheless excoriated myself for the timing, and for my financially dependent position. We endured, but I couldn't shake the feeling, that I was biding time, vowing, however, not to put her through anything like the Jana scenario again.

In the summer she prevailed on me to defer my job search to accompany her, along with Jerome and Kasia, to a healing arts festival in Maine. With no pressing commitments, I accepted, feeling I might be on the verge of embracing the New Age after all. The lack of a more suitable job suggested that perhaps, not meant for the professional world at all, I might become a rainbow tribesperson of sorts, rekindling my minstrel dharma and living on the margins for the rest of my days. Enthusiasm for such itinerancy at age thirty-three, however, was small. I consoled myself with the fact that Maine had to be a lot more palatable in the summertime than it had been the last time I set foot on its snowy soil.

The gathering itself proved to be enjoyable, especially because of the outpouring of song during the evenings, facilitated by Jerome and myself. Whatever the various healing workshops had offered during the day, the wellbeing derived from the singing and sharing of songs from the sixties and seventies still provided a uniquely undeniable catharsis, as it had before the New Age was a gleam in the eye of its contemporary holistic founders and practitioners. The communion, ease, and recognition remained as alive now as before—the truly transpersonal. The music went on late into the evenings and only ended when a critical mass of attendees tipped the balance towards sleep.

I participated in two events facilitated by an unlikely looking oracle, a feisty cigarette- smoking, coffee-drinking, sixty-something lady who made me feel more at home with the process than could have any anima-laden priestess, of which more than a few were present. The first was a past life workshop in which I self-identified as a contemporary of Mary Magdalene, but my Mary held more divided loyalties between the Anointed and Judas. She, not unsurprisingly, bore a resemblance to Jenna. A subsequent life reading highlighted the presence of two female doctors in my future, a curious and compelling notion. Any question of a future with Kira was answered ambiguously, a response I found more meaningful than had I received either a yes or no, a life reading not to be confused with an eight ball.

Interesting stuff, to be sure, but I returned to Worcester with no job and no immediate prospects. The distractions of summer concluded, the shortening of the days made unemployment untenable. Kira was supportive, encouraging me not to settle for another overqualified position. Eventually, I found part-time work taking applications for heating assistance replete with voluminous paperwork. The coming winter of 1981-82 was running smack into a recession, and Reagan's trickle-down economics had slowed to something even less flowing than its name suggested. In October, the courageous Egyptian President, Anwar al-Sadat, was assassinated by Muslim fundamentalists for his willingness to make peace with Israel. Our president himself had, earlier in the year nearly died from a gunshot wound at the hands of a mentally unstable Coloradoan, who had reported an obsession with the actress Jodi Foster's role in the movie, 'Taxi Driver.' Unlike Sadat, John Lennon, Bobby Kennedy, Martin Luther King, Jr., Malcolm X, and John Kennedy, however, he survived. Survival too for Pope John Paul II, shot in St Peter's Square in the spring by an angry Turk. He forgave his assailant. The older and more conservative leaders had lived to tell the tale while the lives of the younger progressive icons lives had been snuffed, again, interesting stuff.

* * *

I was slated to open for the Rounders at The Plate on Thanksgiving Sunday, eagerly anticipating the opportunity to perform a set at Tiny's club. On that afternoon, however, I received a call from Roland with the unimaginable news that Eddie was dead, that he had been murdered behind the Fox the day before. He had been killed with an ax amidst definite signs of a struggle. I would leave for the Gap the next day but for now I was here, and numbly went ahead with the gig. Not so numb that I couldn't appreciate the irony of my being in the same bar where I'd learned of John Lennon's death almost a year earlier and in a club whose owner had many similarly wonderful qualities as my suddenly late friend, I somehow got through my set. I even stayed to be entertained by the raunchy and iconoclastic Rounders which, given my state of mind, provided a testament to how hilarious they could be. Eddie would have loved them and totally approved.

Too distracted to drive to the Gap, on the next morning I bused to Pennsylvania to mourn with friends. Eddie was gone.

Chapter 19

EDDIE AND ROSALIE

Exhausted from the long bus ride I didn't awaken, until almost noon the next day. After breakfast, Roland and I began finger picking John Coltrane's "Equinox". Rosalie stood listening from the bottom of the staircase that led to the apartment she rented from him. The three of us embraced and sat down for coffee. We gazed out the picture window that overlooked the Delaware River, soon to be frozen over from December's impending cold. Nothing would ever be the same. Others showed up throughout the afternoon, people I'd played and hung with from the mid and late seventies. With them, with Eddie, I'd had more laughs than could be counted. This mind-numbing, mind-boggling crime had brought all of us impossibly low. Someone out there had murdered our friend. We had no idea who had done it and to my knowledge the case has never been solved. He'd been killed in the basement of the Fox and his body dragged outside where it had been found by an employee. The bulb illuminating the path to the cellar had reportedly been unscrewed. What was anybody to think? Who could have, would have, done such a thing? There were no answers. I recalled Kira's and my visit last summer. As the two of us were leaving Roland's home to begin the long drive back to Worcester, she had asked, didn't I want to stop at the Fox to say goodbye. It turned out to be the last time I saw him. I remember him holding my eyes, a faraway look in his own, having mentioned it to Kira at the time.

The memorial service at the Gap's small church overflowed with family and friends. The sun peeked through the window as a local jazz singer with a Jon Hendricks-like voice, rendered "In My Solitude," the most soulful rendition I've ever heard, the stillness upon its completion total and profound. People from across the room met each other's gaze. How many lives had he touched?

Rosalie had been Eddie's close companion and as it happened she had a gig the coming weekend at a college in New England. She suggested that I accompany her as far as western Massachusetts where I could then bus to Worcester. On the evening after the service she invited Roland, his wife, and me upstairs to look at her immense scrapbook that comprehensively documented the folk process of the fifties and sixties. For hours we poured over the clippings—of Dylan, Baez, Tom Paxton, Phil Ochs, Pete Seeger—Now, in the words of the old blues holler, I could only think "another man done gone from the county farm" that is this life. Eddie, though, had been no ordinary man-*farewell, gentle soul.* Lingering within this treasure trove until the adrenalin of the past few days gave itself up, I knew the time had come for sleep. I closed my eyes, tired enough, but the sadness and the lingering horror would not remain sufficiently at bay. Eventually fatigue won out and I nodded off.

Rosalie and I departed the next morning, Saratoga Springs our first stop. I felt privileged to ride shotgun in her renowned van, to which she paid homage at all her performances, and even more so blessed to depart Delaware Water

Gap in the company of someone so recently close to Eddie. On the road, Rosalie and I mourned our fallen friend. She asked me how I came to know him, and I recounted how Miri had steered me his way, described my early days in the Gap. I mentioned the more notable gigs I'd played at the Fox, of course noting the date Jenna had attended, to convey the musical intimacy Eddie cherished—how totally accepting and welcoming a person he was. The two of us alternated between numbness and grief. We pulled into Saratoga, and she parked the van in front of the Cafe Lena, the celebrated coffeehouse on whose stage the founding folkies had trod. No gig tonight, merely a stopover, a small sort of relief having taken hold once we had crossed the border into New York State, a milepost perhaps that life continued to exist elsewhere. Even with, maybe because of the present circumstances, my journey with her provided a touchstone to my own years on the road. I sensed Eddie's hand guiding me home, the early morning sun dissolving the mist that still hovered over the fields of early winter in the northern Hudson valley.

We crossed into Massachusetts where she would perform in concert that evening at Hampshire College. We would stay with friends of hers and I'd be on my way to Worcester in the morning. Her performance characteristically heartfelt, she sang "Ashes on the Sea," a song written by her long-time travel and performance compatriot, U. Utah Phillips. Our sojourn would soon end. That she continued to live near the Gap for another year meant I would see her again and that Kira could meet her. She would dedicate her forthcoming album to Eddie's memory, its cover a photo of the huge scrapbook she had shared with us.

I returned to Worcester by Friday evening, relieved to be back with Kira though very much shaken and disoriented. A box from L.LBean containing the inadequately lined coat I'd bought for the winter lay on the couch. For weeks, months, I awoke daily to the finality of the loss. I was back at my part-time gig taking home heating applications in the selectmen's offices of a city bordering Worcester when, on the Monday before Christmas, I received an unexpected call from a mental health center not far north of Worcester. I had been bugging them about my job application for the last four months. They now were offering me a clinical position on a day treatment team treating dual diagnosed adults to start after the New Year. Would I accept? "Yes," I answered, "I will accept the position."

Chapter 20

ROLL ON BUDDY

In early summer of 1982, Kira and I journeyed to Delaware Water Gap, where for Eddie's memorial concert I played a song I'd composed earlier in the year. The warm weather of late June stood in welcome contrast to the memory of last December's sorrow. A score of musicians played out their hearts, jazz musicians primarily, but also a healthy dose of folk and rock performers had also taken the stage built specially for the occasion. At the top end of the Gap the event fronted the health food store and faced the old inn across the way.

Kira had just left her caseworker job she'd held for five years, and like me the previous summer was now at loose ends. She wanted to get a massage practice going, but in the interim had derived income through her participation in a survey/advertising campaign inviting consumers to take the *Pepsi Challenge.* Leaving for work in her company-supplied t-shirt embossed with the effort's logo, I marveled at the change in our respective career status. I'd been working for nearly six months as a staff clinician in the day treatment facility, where, as part of a clinical team, I counseled dual diagnosed adults i.e., individuals who carried a diagnosis involving a major mental illness and also a developmental disability (formerly termed retardation). Among the older clients there were those who had spent much of their lives in the back wards of state mental hospitals. In accordance with state law, they had been de-institutionalized during the seventies. The conditions in these facilities had, of course, been appalling, but the residents were completely unprepared for independent life. To address the resultant homelessness, community residences and treatment centers were established. Our population now lived in a variety of community settings from group homes to supervised apartments. Those that still lived with family were on waiting lists for community-based placement. To facilitate the adjustment of those with the most incapacitating diagnoses intensive day treatment programs were established. This was where I would cut my clinical teeth over the next two years.

Now gainfully employed, I felt more secure, but was treading water with Kira. She wanted marriage. I most assuredly didn't, although I did worry about the possibility I might be worn down, especially now that Kasia and Jermone had tied the knot. Moving out, however, would leave her in the lurch. Her current financial difficulties required support, just as she'd shown for me the year before. Rob's visit with his new love, his demeanor hinting that she might be the one, dramatized the dilemna. The discomfort inherent in seeing another couple's chemistry was disquieting. Kira persevered in the belief that doing so would trump my doubts.

One night in August, I woke from a dream so vivid that I felt compelled to journal it as accurately as possible—the lyrics to a new song that described Rosalie on the Fox's stage where, in the presence of mutual friends, she sang out to Eddie.

...Rosalie has the angels in hand as she strikes down the chords
The full moon's hanging over that roadhouse like some sweet reward
And the night wind is blowing so softly and wonderfully free
As everyone calls out to Eddie through sweet Rosalie...

* * *

Our clinical team consisted of a clinical coordinator, two clinicians, and two paraprofessional milieu staff serving a maximum of twelve clients from 9:00 a.m. to 3:00 p.m., Monday thru Thursday, on Friday until noon. There was counseling and continuous milieu i.e, terminology for enriched therapeutic setting. Expressive therapies art, dance and music, had recently been gaining in stature so I facilitated a weekly music therapy group. As with the autistic children at the Devlin School, the integrative value of singing and playing music for people with major emotional and developmental disorders was evident. Mood improved; eye contact increased; and overall demeanor normalized, barring some episode that required a participant to be removed. As a precaution, I did not bring my best guitar to these sessions! One client, a great fan of "Nine Pound Hammer," could be counted on to lead his compatriots in the rejoinder,

Roll on Buddy, with a load of coal
How can I roll, when the wheel don't go?

There existed many moments of tension because when a client had a bad day it could be a really bad day, sometimes requiring physical restraint, but mostly the work was rewarding and occasionally memorable. Reward came in the form of both client gains and personal interactions. There was this, for example, from a forty -something year old male schizophrenic. Standing outside my office one afternoon, he beseeched me, "Do you have a cigarette, Pete? Climbing the walls can be treacherous."

In September, the team hired a part-time clinician, a doctoral student who had recently completed her internship at Massachusetts General. Her name was Althea and she was hot. When she showed up for her first interview wearing those delightfully unusual ankle socks, I was intrigued. When she arrived for her second interview, formatted as a pre-planned group activity, in this case a volleyball game involving staff and clients, for which she showed little aptitude and at which she was charmingly terrible, I discovered I was hooked. During the staff's post-game meeting, sitting with my guitar, I found myself strumming the chords to "Heat Wave". After she departed, I admonished my colleagues not to hire her because she would 'cause trouble in my life,' a comment that accurately revealed how I went about things in those days. I doubt, however, that my feelings were that well concealed. Even had I not said anything my colleagues would have sensed my lack of objectivity. In any event, by the time I returned to work early the next week she was at the Xerox machine, quietly vocalizing the lyrics to the Police's "Roxanne."

Gee, You're here quick—nothing like being deprived of a decent interval to prepare myself to deal with the inter-

esting challenge you are bound to present to my current set of circumstances. She told me some months later that while driving her turquoise Camaro to Cambridge after her first interview, she had wondered if she, in reference to me, "would marry that man," to which she immediately added the codicil, *that's the craziest thought you ever had—"marrying a man you don't even know. How crazy is that"?*

To say that I was primed for change was an understatement; in the weeks before Althea's arrival, I had been carrying on a flirtation with a married colleague. Althea's arrival signaled the end of that budding drama. Now in the midst of this new expectancy, I hesitatingly approached the undiscovered country of decisiveness. Having previously filled the niche of the heartbroken wounded, I now chose to behave in a way anyone might choose in such a situation—I delayed telling my present partner. Althea and I were now spending a not inconsiderable amount of time together after work. I returned home to Kira at night, having transitioned by swimming a few laps at the Worcester YMCA in some lame cleansing ritual. I hadn't technically cheated as of yet, but the possibility for that presented itself when Kira announced she was beginning a class on Thursday evenings. On those occasions I drove to Althea's rent-controlled apartment not far from Harvard Square.

She was brown haired blue eyed beautiful, but her mind was the key. She was the mistress of metaphor, self depreciating and refreshingly without sentiment. While participating in a case conference at the area's sheltered workshop not many months into her behavioral consultant position, Althea made her mark. The workshop manager, expressing frustration with the work habits of the client in question, felt the need to remind the assembled professionals that his workshop was, bottom line 'real industry.' By way of reply, Althea pronounced, " Charley, if this is real industry then I'm the Queen of France."

I'd abandoned the notion of a soul mate, and couldn't truthfully reclaim the concept, but that didn't matter. Reasoning tha*t the Tao discussed was not the Tao*-that she and I nonetheless got each other in a way neither of us had up to now. Knowing I would not give her up I eventually faced the music with Kira, moving out during Advent to a room in an upstairs apartment inhabited by a Worcester public media personality. Home also to his Siamese attack cat I ignored the posted warning at my peril, and was soon promptly and predictably terrified. The last straw involved my having been cornered in the bathroom by the ferocious feline. It took thirty minutes to strategize a way through his defensive line into the open field of the living room and into my bedroom where I securely shut the door, awaiting its keeper to appear and calm him down. Althea provided guidance by phone. Trudging up the stairs to face this combative creature on a daily basis proved to be the single most demoralizing aspect of my present circumstances. I perceived it as fair punishment for my abandonment of Kira. My expiation fortunately proved unnecessary, my ex-girlfriend having connected with a man she'd met in her Thursday class, the latter glad for the opportunity to be with her. As Kasia so eloquently had put it, Kira and I both had received "karmic promotions." Kira married him.

At last I rolled out of Worcester into Cambridge to live with Althea the timing catalyzed by the cat confrontations. Around the corner stood the Orson Welles Cinema, the signature movie theatre of the Boston area, where classic films were continusously shown. That spring Clara came to visit. I met her at the airport. Mindful of the little one-on-one time she suspected we would enjoy on this occasion, she chose to discuss vital details regarding her estate as we snaked our way on the T underneath the streets of Boston. My mother, now sixty-seven, had long ago adapted to the on-the-fly nature of our relationship. Herman had not expressed interest in making the trip and was irked with Clara for having done so. His son living in sin constituted yet another unacceptable set of circumstances. It was great to see Clara, knowing that one of my parents was determined to live in the present century.

On the morning of Saturday, Labor Day weekend, I called her but Herman answered. I identified myself and with no hint of recognition, he asked if the caller was Miri's brother-in-law of the same name. I answered, "No, this is Miri's brother," Ascertaining that my mother wasn't home I hung up.

Walking towards Harvard Square together we crossed Bow St, I looked at Althea and said, "Maybe we should get married." Before we reached the sidewalk the decision was made. Her only caveat was that I promise her not to lose my temper while driving, at least not to the level of banging on the steering wheel when irked by traffic conditions or bad driver behavior. The recent shooting down of a Korean jetliner by the Soviet Union may have added a smidgen of urgency to our decision as well. One never knew how the Ragman would respond.

In the middle of October, on a pristine autumn Sunday, we were married by her brother, a justice of the peace, before an assemblage of casually clothed family and friends on a family property facing the Berkshires. During our ceremony I played the last song I've written to date, "Love Does Abound," a song celebrating my love for my life's companion:

Things have changed; I really think so
My love's right here.
And it's not strange, don't even seem so,
That warm is near...

When we met I was so puzzled
At how I was to get to you
But somehow I knew from the outset
That was what I had to do

Things have changed; you'd best believe it
Life does astound
Yes things have changed, live to receive it
Love does abound...

Our relationship has been an inspired one, though not for prolific songwriting, maybe because I eventually forsook the axiom of David Bromberg, who had long ago written the song, 'You've Got to Suffer if You Want to Sing the Blues," or in my case at least, if I want to write them.

We left Cambridge in June of the following spring in a one-year move to Miami where Althea undertook to finish her doctorate. Having heard that she had married, her dissertation committee wondered if she intended to finish, apparently unaware that her husband could hardly be called a meal ticket. Despite my lack of enthusiasm for the environs of South Florida I strongly supported the idea. She was enviably close to completing her degree and that way one of us might achieve income stability sometime in the next decade. We departed the Hub just as the Celtics and Lakers squared off in the renewal of their storied (though up to then one-sided) rivalry in the late spring of '84. The winter nights of the past three and a half years had been made so much warmer by the victories engineered by the likes of Messieurs Bird, Parish, Maxwell and McHale et al. We watched them go down in Game 1 as we packed our last items in Cambridge, thinking they might be overmatched. Hope, however, sprang anew in the Game 2 overtime win when Henderson stole the ball, tying the series, a game I viewed from the comfort of my in-law's den in New Jersey. A second Laker rout ensued while we were visiting Rob and Lina in Morningside Heights, and I was filled with worry. Three days later, though, in the company of Aaron and Artie in D.C., the Celtics pulled out Game 4 in the bruising, thrilling overtime victory in L.A. Game five was a Celtics victory in a Boston Garden so sweltering that some of the Lakers took oxygen.

Then came a close call that harkened back to my wife's recent caveat. Accompanied by Artie, enroute to Aaron's for the purpose of watching game 6, I ill advisedly extended a middle finger to the driver of a vehicle who had cut me off on Route 395. My public defender friend was apoplectic. The vanity plate on the offending vehicle boasted 'ADW1', which translated as 'Assault with a Deadly Weapon'. Overtaking us, the insulted driver then defiantly refused to let us pass, edging us closer to the median. Rolling down his window he insisted I apologize for my offending gesture, a gambit I heard thanks to Artie's reluctant but bold decision to gingerly lower the passenger window. My friend and I were simultaneously amazed and gratified to experience the insulted motorist's capacity for last minute anger management. As these things go, a demand for an apology certainly beat looking down whatever deadly weapon he may have had at his disposal.

As if that weren't enough, the Lakers tied the series, leaving Althea and me to drive to the Smokies to watch the deciding game in a bed and breakfast we'd been told had no televisions. Along Skyline Drive she and I stopped at seemingly every overlook, pondering where we would watch game seven. Sensitive to our plight, the inn's new owners invited us to share popcorn in their unfinished living space where we watched the Celtics claim the title.

Chapter 21

A MUSING FROM SATURN'S REPRISE

The porch had been a good idea. Prior to its construction only a small stoop had occupied the space in the front of our home, but it looked like it had always been there once it was built in 2003. I had lamented its absence the year before when Adele and Fremont, misunderstanding a message about our being out of town, had wasted an hour sharing the small stoop, thinking we'd be back after a short errand during their visit to the area. At least they could have lingered in comfort if they'd been here this year, making me recall a couple of other fallible occasions involving them over the preceding years. Interesting that these had occurred during more stable times, after Althea and I had married. During a visit in '84 to Carrollton, I'd managed to back Fremont's pickup truck into a cement wall off the side of his house, something he took with extremely good humor, wishing only that I would take care of the dents. Nine years later, unable to sleep the night before my dissertation defense, and only days after Herman's death, I made the ill-advised decision to call Fremont in the middle of the night, which he took with much less forbearance. If only Ambien had been available at the time.

Now in 2008, big doings with Rosa's high school graduation and my sixtieth birthday party to follow a week later. The festive quality of Saturn's Reprise, so stark in contrast to its initial return half my life ago, is duly noted, but even without these celebratory events the disparity would have been just as great, as Althea and I have been happy these twenty-six years, blessed many times over with our daughter. Now Daniel and I take out our instruments for another Friday afternoon porch picking session, our long-standing musical association one of life's great gifts. Certainly, neither of us could have anticipated we'd still be at it thirty-three years after sitting down to play in his North Boulder apartment. Although I was gone back east for several years, the connection only deepened once I returned, now married, having chosen to be in proximity to musician friends as I began my dispersed residency doctoral program in psychology. Ushering in our weekends playing music, I think, it really doesn't get much better than that.

Having moved to West Heartland, Colorado in '85, Althea and I had wanted our own time zone, separate from the rest of our families. We chose Mountain, having visited in '83, shortly after our wedding, with Paolo, late of Solar Boogie, and his wife. Like us they had been living in Massachusetts, but Paolo had wanted to move back west. Early into our visit, Althea announced that she "could live here," a surprising but welcome piece of information. First, though, was the matter of her dissertation, waiting to be done or not, which would mean a stint at her Ph.D. program in Florida. Consequently, we moved to Miami from Cambridge for a year where she completed her Ph.D. in Clinical Psychology. About that experience I will say little except to note that the southeastern coastal metropolis of Miami may be unique in having a major expressway named for its iconic professional football coach.

In any event these were the eighties, when the dumbing down of American culture had accelerated with the election of Reagan and the ascendancy of the religious right. Back then, before Fox News, before Rush Limbaugh and Glenn Beck, the inestimable Jerry Falwell and his so-called *Moral Majority* had provided most of the gristle. My attitude could be read on the bumper sticker adorning my Le Car with the logo *The Moral Majority is Neither.* What the eighties had meant for me with respect to my family of origin was the effect of the culture war on the relationship with my siblings, both sisters having become born-again, highly dogmatic, fundamentalist Christians. Miri as mentioned had done so in 1979 after moving to the Pacific Northwest where she had met her eventual husband, and Marta, seven years later. Moreover, two friends from Huzzah Creek had followed suit. On the very first evening Althea and I had arrived in West Heartland, Trent informed us that he, too, had experienced conversion earlier that same day, while doing sound for a Campus Crusade for Christ. He shared his good news as we received the keys, not to the kingdom, but to the apartment that he and Franco had found for us. Trent had lobbied hard for Althea and me to move to West Heartland and I hoped my old friend would not engage in proselytizing, but whether he would elect to or not, I knew our relationship would likely face some unanticipated challenges. Within a few years, Yosha Knifehits also had announced his salvation, an honest-to-goodness Jew for Jesus. Unlike my non-observant sisters, Yosha had been the cat's pajama Jew, president of his synagogue, so his metamorphosis must have been quite a coup for whoever had helped it along.

It wasn't their belief in Jesus per se that felt like nails on a blackboard, but all that went with it. During the first part of my life there had been little evident correlation between those who had considered themselves Christian with right-wing political and social views. Religion was generally considered one's own business, the principle of separation of church and state having mostly been considered a done deal. But with flames fueled by the Supreme Court's 1973 affirmation of a woman's constitutional right to an abortion, social conservatives began pounding away at our nation's pluralistic tradition, something that lamentably continues to this very day. Somewhere someone at any given moment in this country is doing her/his level best to move us closer to a Christian theocracy, some even having gone so far to declare that America as a Christian nation *has gifted* others the privilege to worship as they please, a holier than thou fellow traveler to the smugness of Ayn Rand's objectivism.

Now, in the aftermath of their respective conversions, neither Miri nor Marta tolerated our customary use of profanity, or any joke that smacked of being even slightly off-color. Marta had derided a bluesy version of "Just a Closer Walk with Thee" that I sang for her during her visit to us shortly before her move to Israel, for not being sufficiently 'majestic'. When Althea and I visited Miri and her family in Oregon later that same year, we accompanied them to a Messianic Jewish service, whose sermon expounded on the need to expel all gays from serving in state government-funded jobs, most notably, teaching positions. Covering my face I found myself aghast and speechless. Looking around, I saw my once co-religionists as at best unctious and insufferable, and at worst as collaborators, persecutors of another marginalized social group. Uncharacteristically, I kept my feelings unspoken, except to my like-minded wife. It was Christmas, after all, and my six and three-year-old nephews didn't need to see a reenactment of what my sister and I had so often witnessed in our own childhoods.

I came to regard Miri's mutation as an evolutionary adaptation, (Neither sister no longer subscribed to a biological one.) having moved from their long-held idealization of our earthly father to worship of the Perfect One. Marta's conversion was harder to understand, but it only served to make her more judgmental. Our widening gulf in sensibilities now made for loss, more so for it having included both of them. Fatherless, I had now quite unexpectedly become psychologically estranged from my sisters. Thankfully, in the years since her divorce Miri has moved away from the highly dogmatic fundamentalism that had held her in its grip. Marta, however, is another story. Her rigidity has made interaction between us a no-go, our relationship essentially a dog that won't hunt.

Herman, well, sometime in the mid-eighties he had closed the ironworks. I was not privy to the circumstances and didn't much pursue knowledge thereof. He commenced to set about, of all things, *rambling.* Had we been on speaking terms, I could have asked him where *he* was. The man had outfitted a van and took to the road, traveling the country, Mexico, and Canada. He reminded me of the twilight Lyndon Johnson, who after his presidency grew out his hair, and got back to nature while poking about his ranch on the Pedernales. When Herman needed respite from the road, he'd pull up to either Miri's or Marta's home, insinuating himself for weeks at a time. My sisters hadn't liked the extended stays but wouldn't or couldn't muster the will to remind him that after a decent interval, he should be so kind as to return them their space. Their attempts to convert him to their new- found faith met with mixed results. He believed in Jesus, I was informed, though had been rumored to have determined that *He is never coming back.*

Now I was mercifully spared these extended intrusions. The demarcating event had been the invitation to our wedding. He had indicated his attendance would depend on how he *felt at the time.* My mother had joined his hejira for a time, but the confines of their traveling together eventually proved too demanding, so she got off the bus in Alaska and returned to Allentown by way of Portland and Denver, bringing her children up to speed. Sometime in '86 she informed the three of us that she and Herman had separated, well sort of. She continued to reside in the living unit, more content on her own, while her retro rambling, estranged husband, after the highways, settled in Baja.

* * *

Two days before defending my doctoral dissertation in 1993 Clara called with the news that Herman had died in the VA hospital in San Diego. The cancer had metastisized. I'd been sitting on the family room floor watching Rosa assemble a Barney puzzle. My mother had called, simply saying, "It's all over." I turned my focus towards finding the missing puzzle piece that would complete the face of Baby Bop, but Rosa scooped it up just as I laid my eyes on it. Then I visualized Herman rowing a boat alone on a vast cosmic sea slowly heading for whatever mansion he was destined. The next day my family and I flew to

Massachusetts where on the following day, I defended my dissertation, completing a Ph.D. in Clinical Psychology, a process that had taken nearly eight years.

Truthfully, I didn't think for a minute that I would postpone the defense. The fact that Herman and I remained estranged in this instance, as in others, had eased the way. Perhaps synchronicity had manifested itself, the father dying precisely at the time the son succeeds in a major task completion. My sisters made all the arrangements regarding the funeral, and as far as I know they were the only ones in attendance. I never asked.

All that had passed for communication between us had been the yearly ritual of income taxes, as my sisters (including my half-sister) and I would annually await receipt of the tax form and money that often arrived only days before April 15. I recall having once received a disparaging letter, castigating me for my overall "uselessness" as a son in which he chided himself for having "fathered" someone who had 'contributed' so little. I supposed he thought his charge would motivate me to request removal from this financial arrangement. Correctly anticipating that I would be excluded from his will I had little motivation to also do so from a tax shelter that having constituted little more than an anuual pain in the ass, would eventually bear fruit.

No martyr me, I silently proclaimed. The apple had fallen, taken root, seeded and prospered far from the tree.

As is the custom in my family's tradition, the unveiling of the gravestone occurs one year after death. Clara had lobbied hard for my presence, I think, not because I had not attended the funeral but so that she could be with her children together in one place for the first time since Miri's marriage fourteen years before. That the location for that briefest of renunions occurred instead at Paula's house was due to her having chosen at the last minute to stay behind. Althea and I, Miri, her two sons and Marta schlepped across Manhattan to the burial plot in Queens, and only my sisters, nephews and I stood at the unveiled stone. The unveiling had coincided with Richard Nixon's funeral, so on the car radio, heading toward the cemetary we were, incredibly, treated to Sprio Agnew's 'nagging nabobs of negativism' speech from twenty five years before.

Along with the dates of birth and death was a brief sentence, 'He is redeemed.' My older nephew had brought his trumpet and played 'Taps', as all of us placed small stones on top of the grave. Then we departed, the thought dawning on me that when the plot had been purchased sometime earlier in the century the surrounding area would have embodied a more pastoral, small town quality. Now it sat in a high intensity urban, culturally, and racially diverse environment, something I'm sure that family had never envisioned.

After a fitful night back at the living unit I drove the road to the ironworks for the first time in sixteen years in the hopes of feeling anything akin to grief. Turning off the highway and onto the two-lane that led to the foundry, I welled up for a moment, less from distant and positive paternal associations than from momentarily having stumbled into a memory of Saturn's Return. Arriving, I saw that where the ironworks had been there was now only empty space, with no evidence that an industrial operation had existed on that lot.

* * *

Within a few years of our move to West Heartland, Althea and I were challenged by the *great baby express,* now in full swing among the four couples of our social circle. It was a tough time for us both, resigning ourselves to in vitro, but on Valentine's Day she scuttled the consultation. We didn't need the meeting.

A couple of days after the quiet celebration of the incomprehensible, I recalled a recent Jenna–inspired dream of a distinctly different character, one that hadn't involved my usual astral hovering amidst the Appalachian trees. Instead, I encountered her and Gita standing on a recognizable hillside near Morgan Bridge. Holding her younger daughter's hand, she greeted me, tipping her hat in a gesture of recognition. When in the days following the news that I would be a father, I recalled, *What doors are open for the wanderer and which of us will find his father, and know his face and in what place, and in what time and in what land?**

* * *

The first hint that Clara might have lost a step had been when she under-reacted to 9/11. Customarily, my mother would phone me when a major news story broke, the assassination of Yitzhak Rabin six years earlier likely the most recent example. When I hadn't heard from her that terrible late summer Tuesday morning, I phoned her, thinking she must already know, but she gave no indication. I mentally filed this, recognizing its importance as a cognitive

---

* Of Time and the River Copyright ©1935 Charles Scribner's Sons Copyright renewed 1963 Paul Gifflin, Administrator CTA Estate of Thomas Wolfe

marker, but my sisters were not ready to accept her decline. Miri, having recently relocated to New Jersey after having divorced, was just getting back on her feet, out from a marriage in which she had sustained far too much blame for too many years. Marta, living in Israel, was too far away to be of much direct help. Within the next year she and her husband would move back to the States to help Miri care for Clara, and to live a U.S. style life. My sisters had remained determined that Clara live independently for far longer than I thought appropriate but in 2004, they placed her in an assisted living facility after she had received the Alzheimer's diagnosis. She did well enough there until a series of strokes the following year. At her home, Miri, with Marta's help, cared for Clara during her final months.

Clara was known both in Boonton and at Wasigan to be a great fan of the Hokey Pokey, so when the t-shirt asking the question *What if the Hokey Pokey **Is** Really What it's All About* appeared, I considered the possibility that she'd been on to something, Like the serendipitous connection between his famous nickname and the Zen-like sayings of Yogi Berra, the wisdom inherent in the Hokey Pokey has probably been seriously underestimated.

My mother had loved conversation and being with people. She loved her children passionately and unconditionally, and although she had possessed a Victorian streak, (probably what got to the male Wasigan counselors), she nonetheless possessed a sensitivity to the times. At her memorial service six months after her death, I carefully chose the following words: *Everything that had been good that had happened in my life began with her.* She herself may have anticipated more irony from my comments but the territory wasn't safe enough to risk it, it being more important to consider the attitudes of the living now gathered where her ashes were scattered at the graves of her parents. As events- the sixties the strain between husband and son- exacted their toll on her marriage, she did her best to hold the family together, often at great emotional cost to herself. Upon returning to the cauldron of my Boonton home after my cancelled college commencement, she had given me a hardbound edition of Kenneth Clark's *Civilization* as a graduation gift. I didn't fully appreciate it at the time, but understood her intent. She knew I had to chart my own path, worried though she was for me in the midst of the forces unleashed in the country. My mother was an intelligent, caring, and far-sighted woman.

We thought she would not see in the New Year of 2006, and she lingered near death for several days. Miri was exhausted, and I had returned to Colorado. "When is she going to let go already?" she pleaded in her call. I suggested that she find Beethoven's 4th piano concerto, the second movement, my mother's favorite classical composition, having recalled her visit to West Heartland when she sat in our living room following the rhythm of the piece with her right forefinger aloft, smiling. I like to think that the concerto entering her consciousness was the last thing she experienced before she departed this life in the pre-dawn hours of the next morning.

* * *

A year or so later after the will's execution I received from Miri several boxes of memorabilia. Clara had kept everything. During my visits to the living unit throughout the nineties, she had tried to direct me to those boxes she had stored in that black hole of a closet in the hope I would pick out what I wanted, a task I routinely avoided. The contents turned out to be mostly letters I'd written to her and Herman over the years. There was one from my only summer at the Y camp with Artie and Aaron, noteworthy for having invoked a sudden religious identification brought on from my longing for Wasigan. There were many more—all through college and my twenties, at least from those times when I had my wits sufficiently intact to commit pen to paper. A puzzling folder filled with thirty or so scribbled handwritten notes I eventually identified as goodbye letters from the boys at the technical high school where I had student taught in 1970. There was a jaywalking summons, denoting a $2 fine, issued across from Madison Square Garden in New York City. Now adorning our kitchen bulletin board my younger nephew had suggested I submit it to *Antiques Roadshow.*

My mother had also chosen to save the letter from Herman on the occasion of my twentieth birthday, a bizarre piece of correspondence written from the ironworks in 1968 reflecting his sense of paranoid betrayal over my wish to work in Boonton that summer. "You will need to take me down first before I will recognize you as a man," he wrote. I had no memory of it, but his handwriting, that hard slightly slanted printed scroll brought back recollections of his need for control, his insistence that I *had a lot to live up to* along with his doubts that I would succeed in doing so. Finally, there was a short note I'd composed to Clara providing my address in Morgan Bridge reassuring her she needn't worry about my financial situation, because if things didn't pan out, Artie had indicated I could hire on as his private investigator, aiding him in his career as one of D.C.'s public defenders. The frayed yellow piece of paper, from March of1978, was the only historical record of my interval with Jenna and her children.

When Althea and I had chosen West Heartland back in 1985 one of our criteria was a setting where the quality of the environment could transcend the influence of personalities. That has worked out to some degree. Living so near the majestic Rockies, sometimes just knowing they are there quickly became an ongoing bonus. Althea and I took Hal, Beth, and Artie as part of my sixtieth birthday celebration to the top of Trail Ridge Road. The party the next day that Althea threw for me featured a mighty jam of friends and musical buddies, many of whom I have seen less frequently over the years than I'd wished.

Having also decided to move to West Heartland for the purpose of living in proximity to those musician friends, I cannot escape the ironic fact that most of my regular playing has, for the last couple of years involved jamming weekly at a coffeehouse with bluegrass pickers with whom I have had neither a long-term history, nor in some cases a larger affinity. At times awkward on that account, the experience has also been unexpectedly and oddly liberating. The pickers, all having been professional players during some period in their pasts, have, like me, put that pursuit aside, preferring to show up once a week with only instruments to sing and pick for two and a half hours before a small but devoted audience. I had thought Althea's and my attendance at Barack Obama's inauguration might have raised a few eyebrows, not to mention the one or two left -of -center missives I have episodically sent to the opinion page of our town rag, but happily not. In the midst of this musical fellowship, I have experienced both an unanticipated anonymity and a genuine musical sharing.

And it is just as well that I have, due to *the red shift of affinity*. In my youth my friendships had formed the vital center of life, the thing I held to amidst the slings and arrows of family and romantic drama. They were rich with events, disclosure and anecdote. Then I got lucky with Althea, but that didn't stop my desire to maintain continuity with friends, but interaction between visits has gradually faded, amazingly enough in negative correlation with the availability of free cell phone minutes and e-mail. What remains is memory, now more often experienced as mere memory. Like Hubbell's law, aging has only accelerated this phenomenon, bringing on the inescapable awareness that we each dwell in our respective receding galaxies.

CODA

November, 2010

Dee had driven Althea and I to Boonton that Monday before Thanksgiving. Last year the three of us had gone to Wasigan. A counselor during the mid sixties, she has always been one of my favorite camp people who I found on the Web. She has served as a guide of sorts on these 'closure' missions, first to camp and then to my ancestral home. As it had come into view I was content to view Wasigan from afar, but Dee would have none of that. She turned up the long entrance past the lake and up to the now two houses on what used to be the girls' hill. Confidently she knocked on the door to let the owners know just who we were. Happily, there was no one home so we were able to poke around the land that had once been Wasigan.

There were no remaining original buildings, only a small storage area still covered by its brown, red and white Wasigan painting, the same colors that had once adorned all the other camp buildings. Four white swans swam the lake in greeting prompting us to check our shoes for their leavings on the ground where we stood. There had been forty -four years of overgrowth, but the rusted backstop on the softball field was still in evidence, and the field itself remained recognizable. All that was left of the bunks were their foundation blocks. On the road leading to camp, now named Camp Wasigan Road, there been significant real estate development. Only the steep trestle remained, but grass now covered most of the rocky surface I remembered from when I first scaled the ridge when I was ten. The barns and silos of yesteryear had been replaced by macmansions, the dirt road now macadam. Still, setting foot on this ground now felt totally great.

The weather had turned on our way home so we didn't make it to Boonton, which we decided instead to do this year. This plan had been fortified by Dee's memories of her own childhood visits to my hometown where she had extended family that she often had visited during the years before she came to Wasigan. Althea and I had been back twice before, once in '86 before my twentieth high school reunion, an event I'd only decided to attend at the last moment, having been so inspired by a viewing of "Peggy Sue Got Married", and fortified by some arm twisting from our student body president who, I had discovered, lived not far from us in Colorado. Her political skills had evidently not dulled during the preceding two decades.

During the more recent visit I had, as before, only seen the house from the road. When Rosa was ten years old Althea and I had brought Clara to visit Aunt Rae and her husband in 1998 on which occasion anecdotes of Uncle Duke soon brought sidesplitting laughter to us all. It was especially gratifying for me to see Rosa so entertained in the company of my childhood neighbors. My mother shared both vignettes. First, on a rare visit to the carriage house, the duchess (who was never known to us as Aunt Duchess), thinking that Herman was her husband's employee, once gave him a tip for having moved her car. My mother could never, not laugh whenever she shared that story. On another occasion Clara reported having heard what sounded like a gunshot coming from the mansion. Some months later, after the duchess had passed away from an unknown illness my mother and Rae had become suspicious that foul play might have been involved.

Now we slowed. The house looked beautiful, its three visible yards still verdant this late November. I got out and took a few pictures marveling at the two rooms my father had built, how they'd enhanced the home's aesthetic. A woman opened the door wondering who was photographing her home. The door's opening had swept me down the walk Herman had constructed in 1957. I identified myself indicating that I posed no threat, be it governmental, corporate or mob-based. Early afternoon, Monday of Thanskgiving week, her kids not yet home from school, she let us in. Althea, Dee and I walked my house. The downstairs seemed much the same, the remodeled kitchen and dining room easily recognizable. I laughed in the living room, picturing the long absent Stromberg Carlson stereo playing Tim Buckley, with no accompanying sounds of footsteps coming downstairs. The small upstairs hallway was there, where Miri and Marta's room had converged with our parents' bedroom and had been the locus for our numerous 'sockball' games, where in order for 'baskets' to count, the rolled up folded footwear had to hit the border above the door just right. The longer hallway leading to my room felt so small, but Herman's office and my room had since been consolidated, so there was now no opportunity for that pivot. I peered out the window at the bare forsythia bush. The unusually large transistor radio I'd received as a fifteenth birthday present used to sit in that sill, sometimes serving as foreground to that forsythia which would have been green by June. It was there that I had first heard Peter, Paul and Mary's rendition of "Blowing in the Wind." The WABC disc jockey had said then that this was a very different kind of song, and a significant one that would be sung and heard for a long time. Camp was only two weeks away.

It had been over thirty-eight years since I'd last left this place. It had taken that long to come back inside, but it all felt just fine. It felt all right.

ACKNOWLEDGEMENTS

-Thanks to the following for their contributions: Anne and Fred Richards, Alan Cohen, Norm Gibson, Haven Howell, Louis Krupnick, Meredith LeVine, Jordan Hall,Abe Blitzer, Dee Cohen, Karen Staph-Harris, Dan Ault, Dwayne Epple, Donna Follansbee, and Paul Hebert.

-Thanks to Peter Schwarz for editing/back cover assistance.

-Lyrics from 'Song of the River' Courtesy of Meredith LeVine

-Lyrics from 'Bertha' (Robert Hunter & Jerry Garcia) used with permission from Ice Nine Music

-Passage from 'Flight Before Fury' Of Time and the River Copyright© 1935 Charles Scribner's Sons, Copyright© renewed 1963 Paul Gitlin, Administrator, C.T.A. Estate of Thomas Wolfe

-Pragmatics of Human Communication: A Study of Interactional Patterns, Pathologies and Paradoxes: Paul Watzlawick, Ph.D., Janet Beavin Bavelas, Ph.D., Don D. Jackson, M.D. 1967, New York: W.W. Norton

Cover design/ text formatting by Create Space

-Remember Be Here Now- Ram Dass, (1971)New York: Crown Publishing Group

"Amok Time", written by Theodore Sturgeon, directed by Joseph Pevney; Star Trek the Original Series, Created by Gene Roddenberry.

"Understand Your Man", written by Johnny Cash, melody in part by Bob Dylan: Hal Leonard Publishing.

-Back cover photo by Dee Cohen

AUTHOR'S NOTE

www.ingramcontent.com/pod-product-compliance
Lightning Source LLC
Chambersburg PA
CBHW061424040426
42450CB00007B/898

* 9 7 8 0 6 1 5 4 4 8 6 0 2 *